Becoming
Elizabeth Lawrence

Also by Emily Herring Wilson

Two Gardeners: Katharine S. White & Elizabeth Lawrence—
   A Friendship in Letters
No One Gardens Alone: A Life of Elizabeth Lawrence
North Carolina Women: Making History
   (co-authored with Margaret Supplee Smith)
Hope and Dignity: Older Black Women of the South

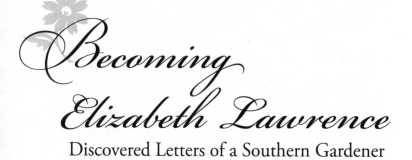

Becoming
Elizabeth Lawrence

Discovered Letters of a Southern Gardener

Edited by Emily Herring Wilson

John F. Blair, Publisher
Winston-Salem, North Carolina

JOHN F. BLAIR
PUBLISHER
1406 Plaza Drive
Winston-Salem, North Carolina 27103
www.blairpub.com

Manufactured in the United States of America

COVER IMAGE

Elizabeth Lawrence and her spaniel, Mr. Cayce, in her Raleigh garden, c. 1942.
PHOTOGRAPH BY BAYARD WOOTTEN.
BY PERMISSION OF NORTH CAROLINA COLLECTION,
UNIVERSITY OF NORTH CAROLINA LIBRARY AT CHAPEL HILL

Library of Congress Cataloging-in-Publication Data

Lawrence, Elizabeth, 1904-1985.
  Becoming Elizabeth Lawrence : discovered letters of a Southern gardener / edited by Emily Herring Wilson.
    p. cm.
  Includes bibliographical references and index.
  ISBN 978-0-89587-375-0 (alk. paper)
 1. Lawrence, Elizabeth, 1904-1985—Correspondence. 2. Bridgers, Ann Preston—Correspondence. 3. Women—North Carolina—History—20th century. 4. Women gardeners—North Carolina—Correspondence. 5. Actors—North Carolina--Correspondence. 6. North Carolina—Social conditions—20th century. 7. North Carolina—Biography. I. Bridgers, Ann Preston. II. Wilson, Emily Herring. III. Title.
  HQ1438.N8 L395 2010
  305.4092'275473—dc22

                                                2010000506

DESIGN BY DEBRA LONG HAMPTON

Contents

Elizabeth Lawrence credited her mother, Elizabeth "Bessie" Lawrence, with introducing her as a young child to the magic and meaning of gardening. This early photograph must have been made when Elizabeth was in her teens.
BY PERMISSION OF WARREN WAY AND ELIZABETH WAY ROGERS

For the little girl who listened with still delight
        to the music of Shakespeare's lyrics
When she stood too small to understand meanings
        of words;
For the little girl who made a wingedy horse of an old bent tree
        and a place of fairy land of Central Park.

For the little girl who loved all breathing things:
            the lambs by the muddy Arno, whom she would be
                    amongst and touch,
            the little runt pig she demanded with passion
                    to be allowed to care for,
        and when no other living thing was near,
                snails, who crawled their silver path
                        about her room;
Who cried when the caged cricket died.

For the little girl who raced over the vast floors
        of the castle of Chillon,
And rode so joyously down the snowy roads at Caux,
        discovering speed.

For the little girl who sat upon the step hushed
        and tranquil
                breathing the mysterious essence of the morning
Before the clothes of day were put upon her.

                        "For Elizabeth,"
                        by Ann Preston Bridgers,
                        c. 1934–1944

Cast of Characters

Alden, Dorothy. Violin teacher. Active in Raleigh music scene. Wife of Edgar H. Alden. During Edgar's wartime service, Dorothy took his place as a teacher at Meredith College for the rest of the year.

Alden, Edgar H. Husband of Dorothy Alden. Assistant professor of music at Meredith College from 1936 to 1946. Active in Raleigh music scene. After his war service, he earned a doctorate from UNC-Chapel Hill, where he taught in the Music Department until his retirement in 1979.

Bradenbaugh, Nannie. "Nana." Maternal grandmother of Elizabeth Lawrence. Lived in Parkersburg, West Virginia. Widowed. When her aged parents died, she came to live with the Lawrences in Raleigh.

Bridgers, Ann Preston, 1891–1967. Smith College graduate. Co-author with George Abbott of *Coquette*, 1927 Broadway hit starring Helen Hayes. Founder of the Raleigh Little Theatre.

Bridgers, Annie Cain. "Tancie," "Mrs. B." Widowed mother of Ann, Emily, and Robert Bridgers, who lived with her. Christian Science Reader.

Bridgers, Emily Norfleet. Sister of Ann Bridgers. Smith College graduate. Crippled by polio as a child. Wrote publications for UNC-Chapel Hill Extension Service. Lived at home with her mother, Ann, and Robert.

Bridgers, Robert Rufus, Jr. Brother of Ann and Emily Bridgers.

Burnaugh, Peter. Kentucky native. Journalist covering horse racing for New York newspapers. Had a romantic friendship with Elizabeth Lawrence during her senior year at Barnard College. Married Betty Stanley. Died young.

Busbee, Louise. "Miss Toose." Kindergarten teacher. Lived in Raleigh with sister Sophie Busbee. Sister Christine lived in New York City. Their brother, Jacques Busbee (a master gardener), and his wife, Julianna Royster Busbee, founded the pottery industry of Jugtown, North Carolina.

Busbee, Sophie. "Sophia." Graduate of the Lowthorpe School of Garden Design. Landscape architect. Lived near the Lawrences in Raleigh with sister Louise Busbee.

Daniels, Adelaide Ann. Daughter of Jonathan and Elizabeth "Bab" Daniels. Her name was changed to Elizabeth after her mother's death in 1929.

Daniels, Adelaide Ann. Daughter of Jonathan Daniels and his second wife, Lucy Croft Daniels.

Daniels, Elizabeth Bridgers. "Bab." Sister of Ann Bridgers and wife of Jonathan Daniels. Died in 1929.

Daniels, Jonathan. Husband of Bab Daniels. His second marriage was to Lucy Croft. Son of Josephus Daniels, secretary of the navy under President Woodrow Wilson and owner of the Raleigh *News & Observer*. Edited the *News & Observer*. Father of Elizabeth (from first marriage) and Adelaide, Lucy, and Cleves (from second marriage).

Daniels, Lucy. Daughter of Jonathan Daniels and Lucy Croft Daniels. Author.

Daniels, Lucy Croft. Second wife of Jonathan Daniels.

Flood, Bracelen. Son of Ellen Bracelen Flood. Author.

Flood, Ellen Bracelen. Friend of Elizabeth Lawrence since they met in New York City in 1924 in a course at Columbia's Extension Division. Mother of Bracelen Flood and Mary Ellen Flood.

Flood, Mary Ellen. Daughter of Ellen Bracelen Flood. Author.

Henderson, Isabelle Bowen. Noted portrait artist who had a historic house and garden near North Carolina State.

Hunt, William Lanier. Distinguished gardener in Chapel Hill. Author of *Southern Gardens, Southern Gardening*.

Huston, Harriet Lawrence Cann. Cousin of Elizabeth Lawrence, with whom she spent summers at their fraternal grandparents' home in Marietta, Georgia.

Lalor, Margaret. "Marge." Biology teacher at St. Mary's School from 1930 to 1945.

Lawrence, Elizabeth. "Libba." 1904–1985. Graduate of St. Mary's School, Barnard College, and North Carolina State College. Taught Sunday school at St. Saviour's Episcopal Mission Church. Author of *A Southern Garden, Gardens in Winter, The Little Bulbs,* and other garden books. Columnist for the *Charlotte Observer* from 1957 to 1971. Lived in Raleigh with her family until 1948, when she and her widowed mother moved to Charlotte to be close to her sister and her sister's family.

Lawrence, Elizabeth Bradenbaugh. "Bessie." Wife of Samuel Lawrence; mother of Elizabeth Lawrence and Ann Lawrence Way. Active member of the Raleigh chapter of the American Red Cross and Christ Episcopal Church.

Lawrence, James Bolon. "Uncle Jim." Episcopal priest and bachelor brother of Sam Lawrence. Longtime rector of Calvary Episcopal Church in Americus, Georgia.

Lawrence, Samuel. "Sammy," "Sam." Husband of Bessie Lawrence; father of Elizabeth Lawrence and Ann Lawrence Way. Engineer. Partner in sand and gravel businesses in North and South Carolina.

Long, Bettie Gray Mason. "Betty," "Gran." The matriarch of the family at Longview, which was built by her grandfather, William Henry Gray.

Long, Caroline Moncure. Wife of Willie Jones Long and mother of Willie Jones Long, Jr., Caroline Moncure Long Tillett, and William Gray Long.

Long, Margaret Ridley. One of five children of Thomas Williams Mason Long and Maria "Minnie" Greenough Burgwyn Long. Lived with the Lawrences when she was a student at St. Mary's. Married John "Jack" Tyler. Lived in Roxobel, North Carolina.

Long, Rosa Arrington Heath. "Miss Rosa." Wife of William Lunsford "Luns" Long.

Long, Ruth Mason. Daughter of Rosa and Luns Long. Married Peter Williams in 1940.

Long, Thomas Williams Mason. "Dr. Tom." Member of the North Carolina Senate and advocate for public health care. Lived in Roanoke Rapids, North Carolina. Husband of Maria "Minnie" Greenough Burgwyn Long. Their five children were Betty Gray Long, Maria Burgwyn Long, Thomas Williams Mason Long, Jr., Margaret Ridley Long, and Nicholas Long.

Long, William Lunsford. "Luns." Fourth child of Bettie Gray Mason "Gran" Long and Lemuel McKinne Long. Business executive who served in the North Carolina General Assembly. A raconteur, he supported progressive causes and was interested in the arts and humanities.

Long, Willie Jones. "Wilie," "Wylie." Husband of Caroline Moncure Long. Their three children were Willie Jones Long, Jr.,

Caroline Moncure Long Tillett, and William Gray Long. The Lawrences had known the Long family of Northampton County since the early 1900s, when Sam Lawrence opened a sand and gravel business in Garysburg and Willie Jones Long lived at the family plantation, Longview.

Pendleton, Sylbert. "Sylie." Member of the St. Mary's School class of 1926. Lived in Raleigh and later in New York City and Washington, D.C. Accompanied Bessie Lawrence to Europe in 1937, after Sam Lawrence's death.

Royster, Wilbur High. Attended the American School of Classical Studies in Athens. Received an M.A. from Harvard in 1911. Taught Greek and Latin at the University of North Carolina while he was a law student there. Returned to Raleigh to run Royster Candy Company.

Sammel, Veronica Gale. "Bill." Married Dr. Athey Ragan Lutz. Lived in Parkersburg, West Virginia, across the street from Elizabeth Lawrence's grandmother and great-grandparents. Before her marriage, she roomed with Ann Way in New York City. Her mother often exchanged gardening letters with Elizabeth Lawrence.

Squire, Elizabeth Daniels. "Liz." Granddaughter of Josephus Daniels and daughter of Jonathan and Bab Daniels. Detective writer. Married journalist C. B. "Chick" Squire. Mother of three sons. In 1979, she moved to the Bridgers family's mountain property near Weaverville, North Carolina.

Thompson, Daisy. Sister of Elizabeth and Lillian Thompson. Worked at North Carolina State College.

Thompson, Elizabeth. Sister of Daisy and Lillian Thompson. Noted interior decorator. Lived with her sisters at 1818 Park Drive in Raleigh.

Thompson, Lillian. Lived with sisters Daisy and Elizabeth. Took care of the household.

Tillett, Caroline Moncure Long. Attended St. Mary's School. Only daughter of Caroline Moncure Long and Willie Jones Long. Married Hugh Tillett and had two sons. Lived in Charlotte until moving to a historic family house in Brunswick County, Virginia, not far from Longview.

Vass, Annie Root. Granddaughter of Albert Smedes, the founder of St. Mary's School. Aunt of Sadie Root, the first president of the Raleigh Little Theatre. Married to William W. Vass, Jr. Lived in Raleigh.

Way, Ann de Treville Lawrence. "Ann," "Annie," "Annette," "Nette." Sister of Elizabeth Lawrence. Wife of Warren Way II and mother of Warren "Chip" Way III and Elizabeth "Fuzz" Way. A graduate of St. Mary's School, she spent her junior year abroad before graduating from UNC-Chapel Hill and then working at Macy's in New York City.

Way, Elizabeth. "Fuzz." Born September 28, 1945. Daughter of Warren Way II and Ann Lawrence Way. Sister of Warren "Chip" Way III.

Way, Louisa. Wife of the Reverend Warren Way and mother of Warren Way II and Evelyn Way.

Way, Warren. The Reverend Way was the head of St. Mary's School in Raleigh from 1918 to 1932, then rector at St. James Episcopal Church in Atlantic City, New Jersey. Husband of Louisa Way and father of Warren Way II and Evelyn Way.

Way, Warren, II. Married Ann de Treville Lawrence Way in 1942. A reservist, Warren was called up for service during World War II and was in Officer Candidate School at Duke in Durham, during which time Ann lived in Raleigh with her family. Father of Warren "Chip" Way III and Elizabeth "Fuzz" Way. Later worked in Charlotte for the Internal Revenue Service.

Way, Warren, III. "Chip." Born October 4, 1943. First child of Warren Way II and Ann de Treville Lawrence Way. Brother of Elizabeth "Fuzz" Way.

Wulf, Fritz. Husband of Irma Wulf. The Reverend Wulf, assistant rector at Christ Episcopal Church, was assigned to its mission, St. Saviour's.

Wulf, Irma. Wife of the Reverend Fritz Wulf.

Elizabeth's 1926 senior picture at Barnard College
By permission of Barnard College Archives

Introduction

Elizabeth Lawrence, gardener and garden writer, would have agreed with Virginia Woolf, who wrote, "Without letters life would split asunder." Letters create a private and parallel world to what goes on around us, holding together what we choose to tell of daily living and reflection and steadying us with a sense of permanence. For Elizabeth, letters, like her gardens, allowed her to give free expression to herself. And for an essentially private woman, letters were the bridge to a world of friends.

Elizabeth described the importance of letters to Ann Preston Bridgers: "Michael [Elizabeth's spaniel] and I have just walked around the corner to post a letter to my sister Ann. Do you always find a special charm in posting letters? A sudden feeling of communication with the person you have written to, as you drop it in the box . . . Much more than in writing it. When you write a letter you are thinking much more of yourself than of the person you are writing to. Sometimes I think up letters to write, just for the fun of walking with Michael to the station to post them. And I have never been able to figure out why it is no fun to walk to the station without a letter to post. And I always prefer to post letters at night. But then everything is heightened after dark."

When Elizabeth, a homebody, wrote to Ann from her garden or the porch steps or her basement study or her upstairs bedroom—and occasionally on the train going somewhere—her letters suggest that she was thinking exactly of the person she was writing. Not only was Ann a friend she had confided in more than anyone else, but she was a playwright who would appreciate the characters and the settings Elizabeth wove for her enjoyment. (Letters Elizabeth wrote to other friends do not compare.) When Ann wrote back, her mind was on her own work; she *answered* letters. In private conversations in each other's houses, Elizabeth and Ann, both by nature reserved, apparently were equally confiding.

In 1934, when their correspondence began, Elizabeth was thirty years old, Ann forty-three. Elizabeth was just starting out on a career as a garden writer, whereas Ann had her greatest success as a playwright behind her. The thirteen-year difference in their ages was significant because Ann, who thrived on independence, seemed older than her age, and Elizabeth, thriving on dependence, always seemed girlish. Elizabeth liked older people; Ann was a great encourager of the young.

In hundreds of letters, Elizabeth, awakening under Ann's tutelage to her powers as a writer, poured forth her feelings. Ann was a seasoned professional writer who saved her words for plays. In her twenties and thirties, she had traveled in Europe and reveled in her freedom as part of the New York theatre crowd.

*Ann Preston Bridgers was a founder of the
Raleigh Little Theatre in 1936 as part of the
Federal Theatre project.*
BY PERMISSION OF THE RALEIGH LITTLE THEATRE,
PUBLISHED IN *CURTAIN UP! RALEIGH LITTLE THEATRE'S
FIRST FIFTY YEARS*

The months that went by without Elizabeth's letters were a sign
that Ann was at home in Raleigh, though now and again when
Ann was in town Elizabeth wrote to her if it seemed especially
urgent to get down on paper what she thought, often following
a conversation.

When Ann was in New York or at her mountain cabin in
western North Carolina, Elizabeth wrote every week. From
Elizabeth's perspective, writing to Ann was the delight of her

life. From a reader's perspective, the correspondence reveals the steps by which Elizabeth became one of America's best-known writers of classical garden literature.

Elizabeth came from a long line of letter writers. The Lawrence family today retains letters written in the late nineteenth century by Elizabeth's maternal grandmother, Nana, on a trip to Europe to recover from the recent loss of her husband (Nana wrote to her daughter, "I must tell you how much pleased I was that you are able to write so good a letter for a little girl. I know of no greater accomplishment than to write a good letter"); courtship letters written at the turn of the twentieth century when Bessie Bradenbaugh, Nana's daughter, was considering marrying Sam Lawrence; letters from Nana and from Sam to Elizabeth at Barnard College in 1921; and letters from Elizabeth's sister studying in Paris in 1926. Letters are often lost, even in the most letter-minded families; the letters Elizabeth and her mother wrote daily to Nana in Parkersburg, West Virginia, have not been found.

When Elizabeth began gardening and keeping records of plants (systematically by 1934), letters became her principal means of learning from other gardeners. In each of her books, letters were essential. *A Southern Garden* (1942) was written contemporaneously with this collection of letters to Ann Preston Bridgers. Elizabeth and Caroline Dormon of Briarwood, Louisiana, exchanged plant information through extensive letters; Elizabeth's 1961 book, *Gardens in Winter*, was illustrated by Dormon. *The Little Bulbs* (1957) was based on Elizabeth's friendship with gardener Carl Krippendorf of Ohio, mostly through letters. And the posthumously published *Gardening for Love* (1987), edited by Allen Lacy, was based on Elizabeth's extensive correspondences. *Gardening for Love* was to be her

Beginning in Raleigh in the 1930s, Elizabeth recorded on thousands of index cards information about plants in her gardens—exact measurements, where they came from, when they bloomed (or didn't bloom). The file cabinets are now housed in the Elizabeth Lawrence House and Garden.
BY PERMISSION OF WING HAVEN GARDENS & BIRD SANCTUARY

magnum opus, based on thousands of letters (handwritten, often on the backs of paper scraps) from her "farm ladies," correspondents who advertised their seeds and slips in state agricultural market bulletins. Indeed, Elizabeth accumulated so many letters from garden correspondents, most of whom she never met in person, that she was too old and frail to write the great book of her life, based on letters.

Although readers may learn a great deal about gardening in Lawrence's books, less is to be learned about her, save that she was a knowledgeable, generous, and witty gardener. She did not reveal much else about herself, though the letters were filled with people and places, family and friends, writers and gardeners, who mattered a great deal to her. Elizabeth is visible half in sun and half in shadow, as through the garden gate.

But for the help and encouragement of Ann Bridgers and her sister, Emily Bridgers, Elizabeth, who was a private poet and a dependent daughter, said she never would have become a garden writer. Nor, I would add, would she have learned to live such a full and satisfying life, still unmarried, still living at home with her mother, Bessie, still devoted to her sister and her sister's children. And thus comes the importance of the letters signed "Your loving Elizabeth" by the woman who would publicly become America's classical garden writer. Readers already familiar with *A Southern Garden* will find *Becoming Elizabeth Lawrence* a companion filled with many of the same plants, people, and places. When Isabelle Henderson and Billy Hunt and Mr. Tong and Jacques Busbee and all the Longs of northeastern North Carolina, as well as irises and colchiums and daylilies, appear in *A Southern Garden*, readers are sure to find them also in Elizabeth's letters to Ann. For Lawrence fans, many of the letters will answer questions about when she began to grow one plant or another and how she learned to write about the garden, as well as what she had to say about herself.

Briefly, let me introduce Elizabeth and then Ann.

Elizabeth was born May 27, 1904, in the house where her father grew up in Marietta, Georgia. She was the first child of Samuel and Elizabeth Bradenbaugh Lawrence of Parkersburg, West Virginia. Four years later, the family welcomed another little girl, Ann. Perhaps the most idyllic years of Elizabeth's life were those of her childhood in Garysburg, a small railroad village in Northampton County in northeastern North Carolina, where her father had a sand and gravel business. In 1916, he moved the family to Raleigh so his daughters could attend St. Mary's School, an Episcopal preparatory school for girls near their home on Park Avenue, just off Hillsboro Street.

They joined Christ Episcopal Church in downtown Raleigh on Capitol Square. In 1922, Elizabeth surprised herself by applying to Barnard College on the recommendation of her English teacher, a Barnard graduate. When she was accepted, she left for four lonely and difficult years. But she made good friends and graduated in 1926. After a winter with her maternal grandmother in Parkersburg and six months of travel in Europe, she returned home to Raleigh to earn a degree in landscape design at North Carolina State College in 1932. Soon afterward, her close friendship—and letters—with Ann Bridgers began.

Ann Preston Bridgers was born May 1, 1891, in Wilmington, North Carolina, the first of four children of Annie Preston Cain Bridgers, originally from Hillsboro, and Robert Rufus Bridgers, of Wilmington. Bridgers men had been prominent since the Confederacy in Wilmington and Edgecombe County; these included elected public officials, jurists, lawyers, doctors, and business leaders, especially in railways. Annie ("Tancie") and the children—Ann, Emily, Elizabeth ("Bab"), and Robert—were living in Alden, Georgia, where Mr. Bridgers was doing railroad work, when he suddenly died. Determined not to run home to the protection of his family but to keep the family independent, Mrs. Bridgers opened a boardinghouse, much against the family's wishes. When insurance and other securities came to her, she saw that Ann and Emily were educated at Mary Baldwin Seminary in Virginia. Ann, Emily, and Bab all graduated from Smith College. Robert, a slow reader who was not successful in school, found a place in the family circle, living at home. Although Emily had been crippled by polio as a child, she was encouraged by her mother, a devout Christian Scientist, to be independent. (Ann and Emily had been brought up in the Episcopal Church but were not active members.) When Bab married Jonathan Daniels, a journalist and son of Josephus Daniels, former United States secretary of the navy under Woodrow Wilson and founder of the Raleigh *News & Observer*, and had a daughter, the family circle was full. Then, after Bab's death in childbirth in 1929, the Bridgers family helped Jonathan raise his three-year-old daughter, Elizabeth.

In 1934, Ann's reputation rested upon the stunning Broadway success of *Coquette*, a play based on a real-life murder in Rockingham, North Carolina. (She had discussed the case with Jonathan Daniels, her brother-in-law, who reported on the trial for the *News & Observer*.) Ann had persuaded George Abbott, an emerging playwright she met on Broadway, to coauthor the play with her, and Abbott had persuaded Jed Harris to produce it. Starring Helen Hayes, *Coquette* opened at the Maxine Elliott Theatre in New York in the fall of 1927 and ran for 366 performances before it was taken on the road (without Hayes in the title role). In 1929, the movie version of *Coquette* won Mary Pickford, appearing in her first "talkie," the Academy Award for Best Actress. Although Ann enjoyed the royalties, which enabled her to live well and to give generous gifts to her family, she had found it emotionally exhausting to work with Harris (as did George Abbott and many others). Perhaps another disturbing reality for Ann was that she had to abandon her original intent to write the play as a comedy about a flirtatious Southern ingenue whose father had murdered her boyfriend (from the other side of the tracks) in defense of her honor. All her life, Ann had laughed at the Southern code of false chivalry that made men powerful and wives and daughters helpless dependents. It was bad enough for the father to have been exonerated in the trial in Rockingham, but when *Coquette*

United Artists publicity for the movie production of Coquette, *starring Mary Pickford, who won an Academy Award for her first "talkie"*
FROM THE COLLECTION OF ED WILSON

premiered as a tragedy before weeping New York audiences, the long, demanding road to success seemed to undermine Ann's confidence in herself, and she fled to Europe. There, she traveled with a Smith College classmate and began writing new plays. Only after Bab's death did she give up her restless travels abroad and return home to help with the family.

In 1936 in Raleigh, Ann helped found the Little Theatre as part of the WPA's Federal Theatre Project. She also served on the board, raised funds, and wrote and directed one-act plays for local emerging actors. Ann noted from her cabin in western North Carolina, where she escaped to write as often as she could, "Even up here halfway up a mountain, midst the lovely rocks and trees, I can't shed the Little Theatre." The Raleigh Little Theatre today is a vibrant part of the city's cultural scene, as detailed in Guy Munger's *Curtain Up! Raleigh Little Theatre's First Fifty Years*.

Ann's emphasis upon her own work was the life she modeled for Elizabeth, who responded to the demands of her family and friends with far less protection for her own time. Indeed, Ann, who was such a public figure, was more of a private person than Elizabeth, who was perceived to be shy but in fact reveled in knowing what was going on in the neighborhood and in the wider gardening world. The friendship was good for each of them, and so it may be for readers, a reminder of their own nurturing by family and friends, and also a timeless testament to how to live a good life in hard times.

Emily Herring Wilson

Part One: 1934–1941

A Life of One's Own

"There is nothing like the revelation of a
reticent person once started."
Elizabeth to Ann

*In the 1930s and 1940s—a period defined by the Great De-
pression and World War II—the old Raleigh, North Carolina,
neighborhood of large, comfortable houses built in the late nineteenth and early twentieth centuries on Hillsboro (now Hillsborough) Street was the setting for a familiar way of life in a changing
time. Porches and parlors echoed with conversations. Books were
read and discussed. Friends shared food and drink—around the
dinner table, in the garden, in front of a coal fire. The State Fair
grounds, Meredith College, the Little Theatre and the Rose Garden,
North Carolina State, St. Mary's School, and shops, offices, and
churches were strung like varied beads leading downtown to formal
government buildings and squares of a capital city that still felt a*

little country, since most people had rural roots. Hillsboro was one of Raleigh's main streets, lined by shade trees, friendly to walkers, accessible by bus. If you were standing on the corner, someone you knew was likely to come along in a car to offer you a ride, especially if you had packages or it was late. Young boys stopped their play to give an assist without being told to. Of course, sorrows beset every household, and one did not have to look far to know that other neighborhoods were less secure. Many shadows (racial inequality was a fact of life) and dark economic clouds (failed banks and businesses, unemployment) marred the landscape, but in this neighborhood and many others like it, families cared for one another as best they could. Churches established missions to serve the poor. One of these missions was St. Saviour's, founded by the wealthy congregation of Christ Episcopal Church, whose members (among them the Lawrences) contributed time and money to both the church and the mission.

In 1933, after years of living in New York City and traveling abroad, Ann Bridgers moved back to the family home at 1306 Hillsboro across from the Lawrence home at 115 Park Avenue. Although Ann would at times leave again for weeks or months to write in a New York hotel or the family's cabin near Weaverville in western North Carolina, she remained close to her family, which included her mother, "Tancie," her sister, Emily, and her brother, Robert. She had a special reason to be with them. In December 1929, the youngest, Elizabeth ("Bab") had died in childbirth, leaving a three-year-old daughter, Elizabeth, and a distraught husband, Jonathan Daniels. Following Bab's death, the family members did what they always did—they pulled together, accompanying Jonathan to Europe to help look after Elizabeth so that he could fulfill his Guggenheim fellowship. They remained close even after Jonathan remarried. For Mrs. Bridgers, Ann, Emily, and Robert, young Elizabeth Daniels was the apple of their eyes.

Across Hillsboro Street, the Lawrence household consisted of Sam, in poor health but still charming and interested in everything, Elizabeth ("Bessie"), a busy bee if there ever was one as a hostess and community volunteer, and their daughter Elizabeth. The other daughter, Ann, younger than Elizabeth by four years, had gone to New York to live and work, finding a job at Macy's. Elizabeth, having graduated from the landscape design program at North Carolina State College, was in charge of the garden and Bessie the house, but they shared both enterprises, as close as hand and glove. They mostly lived on Bessie's inheritance from her family. During the Depression, Sam lost his business and Bessie lost savings. Elizabeth was looking for a life and a means to make money while living at home.

Within the year after Ann Bridgers moved back to Raleigh, Ann and Elizabeth Lawrence became close friends, drawn together by their shared interest in writing. Ann Preston Bridgers (her three names were well known) was the talk of the town because of her success as coauthor with George Abbott of a 1927 Broadway hit, Coquette. *Elizabeth, who wrote poetry, idolized writers. Both were very private women who sought society on their own terms, and they were both close to family and other friends. The differences between Elizabeth and Ann become apparent from the letters.*

On the visit of Elizabeth and Bessie to the Bridgers house that is alluded to in Elizabeth's first letter, emotions must have been high. Young Elizabeth Daniels was visiting, and Elizabeth Lawrence was leaving soon for a trip to New York. Always an anxious traveler, she was willing to make the long trip to a city that had unnerved her as a student because she would be in the hands of another close and protective friend, Ellen Bracelen Flood, whom she had known since college.

1934

[Handwritten, June 22, 1934][1]

Dear Ann:

I think you know how happy Bessie and I were to be with you, and I say it again only for my own pleasure. "Thank you for your loving kindness."

What I thought Bessie was going to say, and asked her please not to, was only about the time we went to see Elizabeth [Daniels] after her mother died. I had been thinking about her little face all day.

Something else is on my mind: I realized—before I had finished saying it—how horrid to say to you that I hadn't any friends, and said hastily, except you. I think you the most considerate person I know, and consideration is like Octagon soap on poison ivy. But please don't carry it too far, and not ever allow me to consider you. I think you can do with it.

[Signed] Elizabeth

[July 5]

At Ellen's you can be alone (sometimes too much) but I don't like to let Ellen get out of my sight, because I hate New

---

[1] The letters were typed or handwritten. Some have neither salutations nor closings; after their first use, I have omitted them except when needed for emphasis or clarity.

York so I am afraid I will hurt it. But I love it on Ellen's account. New York is Ellen's love—so long as you are with her, it is safe. . . .

[On the train to New York City to visit Ellen]

Please don't be mad about the other morning, because I never loved you so much, and Elizabeth [Daniels] was adorable. I wish I had had someone like you when I was little. Nana [Elizabeth Lawrence's maternal grandmother, Nannie Bradenbaugh] was perfect for nightmares and insomnia, but when my voice rose, her voice rose. . . .

[A few days later, 1120 Park Avenue, New York]

I have just had a victory over Ellen. Another such victory and I will be lost. Ellen wanted me to go with her to her tutoring with Wolfe [German tutor], and I didn't want to.

Now that I am sure that no one I know is in New York, [I] have stopped trembling every time the phone rings. Yesterday I was petrified to hear Ellen say "Hello, yes, Libba is here. When did you come up?" but it turned out to be only Mr. Dixon's young daughter [Mary Shirley], whom we had promised to keep an eye on when she came up [from Raleigh] to art school, so we invited her to lunch on the roof, which I don't mind because Mary Shirley was coming anyway so the day was counted out. But I like Mary Shirley. She has red hair to her shoulders and looks like Holbein's portraits of burghers. And now Mr. Bracelen [Ellen's father] is back from his fishing trip, and Bracelen [Ellen's son] is as calm as Bracelen gets; and in spite of a farewell to sleep, I am beginning to feel rested. . . .

[July 22, New York]

Ellen says that Dr. Wolfe hadn't much to say on Sapphics when she first posed my questions, but by the time I went back with her, he had a card catalogue. I asked him about the ones Swinburne[2] wrote, and that I found in your little book, and read to you, do you remember? And he didn't know them, but had them for me the next time, and was perfectly enchanted, and read them beautifully. I am beginning to understand quantity [counting poetic syllables] now, and see its importance, but every time I get my ideas clarified I read something, or Dr. Wolfe says something, or Ellen does, and I am bewildered again.

Yesterday when we were on the roof the little blimp was coming toward us, and two aeroplanes, going in opposite directions, passed over it. That would make a very beautiful dance.

Mary Ellen and Bracelen [Ellen's children] just came in to give me very wet kisses before going out with Rosa [the housekeeper]. Mary Ellen you would love. She is the most aloof baby you ever saw. She is very sparing with her kisses, but I learned that if you tell her she is very beautiful you will get your reward.

I couldn't do without your glasses on the roof. Ellen has a collection of purple, magenta, and terracotta ones that, I think, match her costumes. They are worse than the sun, and she is always trying to get yours away from me.

---

[2] Probably Algernon Swinburne's poems written in homage to Sappho, first published in English in 1866. Elizabeth had read Swinburne as a student at Barnard College in the 1920s.

I think from what Ellen says that *I, Claudius* [1934 Robert Graves novel] would be a good book for us to read aloud. If you see any reviews, check up on it.

The Garden Club follows me to New York, and affords Ellen and me a great deal of amusement. I was told that my subject for the radio talks next winter would be "Putting the Garden to Sleep," and that I could talk about anything I liked. Also a letter from Catherine Taylor, saying "Please, Libba, don't lose the Garden Club records." I can't imagine what she thinks I am going to do with them, and I think she had better have given them to someone else if she is so uneasy. . . .

Ellen and I are planning to go up to see Ann next week [Elizabeth's sister was in Sakonnet, Rhode Island, for part of the summer]. Either driving or on the boat. There is nothing I want to do less, but Ann is very much on my mind, and Ellen is crazy to take a short trip.

Ellen is up on the roof having a German lesson. Her Professor is rather a heavy young man, but Ellen feels it incumbent upon her to have him to lunch when he comes so far in the heat and perspires so freely.

Toward the end of July, Elizabeth left Ellen's apartment in New York and went by train to visit the Ways in Atlantic City, New Jersey. The Reverend Warren Way had been head of St. Mary's School in Raleigh from 1918 to 1932, and he and his wife, Louisa, had moved to Atlantic City for him to become rector at St. James Episcopal Church. Their children—Evelyn and Warren—were near-contemporaries and friends of Elizabeth and her sister, Ann.

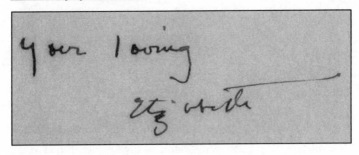

Elizabeth signed her letters to Ann in this way.
By permission of Warren Way and Elizabeth Way Rogers

[August 1]

I am going to the Ways' in Atlantic City Friday, and I shall go home the first of the week. Then I shall be there if you want to come. . . .

I am sorry to go. Ellen and I are having such a peaceful time. It probably won't happen again. . . .

Your loving Elizabeth [first use of the closing that became standard]

[August 10, on the train home to North Carolina]

Truly, this is the last time I will inflict my scrawl upon you but if I wait until I get home to the Corona, I probably won't write—other things are waiting for me.

Yesterday Miss Estelle [perhaps Estelle Depard, a girlhood friend from Parkersburg, West Virginia], who, like you, has always had a notion that I am a down-trodden creature, called me up from Bronxville [New York] and insisted that I stay with Evelyn. I said, "But Miss Estelle, you don't know my mother." She said, "But Elizabeth, I went to school with her, and I think you should stay." I was enjoying myself so much— what with Evelyn allowing me to read her Shakespeare's sonnets and *Golden Treasury* for hours at a time, and what with having gotten over my fear of the sea, and my great delight in swimming beyond the surf with Warren I was tempted to do it. Just as I had made up my mind to send a telegram to Bessie to that effect, one arrived from her and signed, not with the usual affectionate "E. B. L." but with a stern "Elizabeth B. Lawrence," saying "Miss Isabel waiting for you to go to work."[3] Miss Estelle had telegraphed her for my address, and she smelled a rat! . . .

I like staying with the Ways because they are so glad to have me, and because they put me in mind of the Vicar and his family in English novels, and because family prayers lend security. "Almighty and everlasting God, in whom we live and move and have our being; we, thy needy creatures render thee our humble praises." When they go to the beach they take their own umbrella and a hand woven basket brought back from Africa by the missionaries, and the *Atlantic Monthly*, from which Mrs. Way reads aloud.

. . . I like being with Evelyn, because I am as glamorous to her as Harriet [a close Georgia cousin] is to me. Any color is bright against a duller color.

I have been writing a little to you and a little to Ellen. I flipped a page and wrote on Ellen's what I meant for yours. This won't do. Never write on leaving Ellen: I love swimming out to sea with Warren and walking fast on the beach with Evelyn.

---

[3] Elizabeth was doing some garden design work for Isabel Busbee, a graduate of the Lowthorpe School.

Write: the beach is crowded, the water is dirty and cold.

Before I left Ellen, I had a long talk with her, and then wrote Ann that I thought she should stay in New York a month and try to get a job. I think the time has come, and Ellen promises to advertise [advise] me at once if she droops. Suzanne [Ellen's friend] says she [Ann] can't get a job unless she does stick around. I hope she gets one. I don't think it will take her long to get sick of it. In the meantime, I shall have to confess my part of it to Bessie. . . .

Home again

Elizabeth Thompson came to dinner, and said, "How well you look, Libba. Wouldn't Ann Bridgers be pleased if she could see you now."

My first task on getting home was to start again in search of a cook. Bessie was crazy about Fanny, but she won't stay. She says she isn't equal to it. A new one comes in the morning, and I intend to keep her even if she turns out to be a nymphomaniac. . . .

Bessie approves of Ann's getting a job, and has already written her to that effect.

Friday night [later]

I know so well the stages of insomnia that they are like the road to school when you were a little girl, and knew the number of pebbles in every mud puddle and the number of rails in every fence. The worst stage is accompanied by cramps in the toes, and the sound of wind—or a train, you cannot be sure which—in the distance, but never gets any closer.

First, I made an outline of conifers by type—then I made one according to families—then I made one according to uses. Then I made three introductions.

Then I read poetry—an anthology.

Then I reread the famous love scene in French in *The Magic Mountain* [1924 Thomas Mann novel]. It takes place on Walpurgis Night, and is introduced by sly quotations from Goethe's "Walpurgisnacht."[4] All of this I missed in reading it myself, not knowing Goethe. But Ellen read the German and translated it for me—and all of the overtones are apparent. Should I read it to you?

Then I turned out the light again, and listened to the wind—or the train. It whistled like a train, but rattled the windows like the wind—but never got closer—It comes from reading too much Chekhov. Reading his short stories is like being flicked on a raw spot with a fine switch—never read the volume which is almost entirely about cruelty to children and animals.

You read a volume of sordid and poignant love stories, and are unprepared for the children and dogs. You must never read that or [only if] it comes from the excruciating boredom of a garden club tea, which is somewhat relieved by making a funny story of it for Margie [Margaret Lalor, St. Mary's biology teacher] and Bessie but—like everything else—comes back to you with the dark—or from Mischa's saying her little girl [in Elizabeth's Sunday school at St. Saviour's Church] goes to bed at eight, and when you say "Mischa!—at two and a half!—

---

[4] In German folklore, Walpurgis Night is the night of April 30, when witches frolic with their gods. A scene in Goethe's *Faust* is called "Classical Walpurgisnacht."

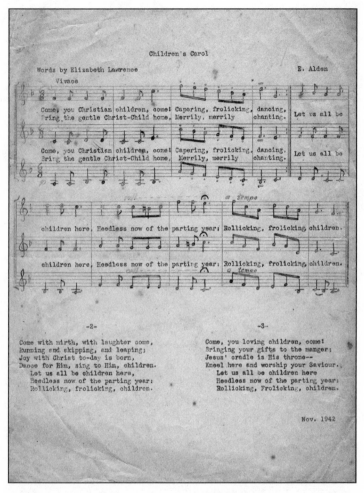

This one-of-a-kind manuscript shows Elizabeth Lawrence as the author of lyrics for a children's Christmas carol and Edgar Alden, a Raleigh musician, as the composer. It was probably prepared on a church mimeograph machine and used at St. Saviour's, an Episcopal mission church where Elizabeth taught Sunday School.

CREDIT BY PERMISSION OF WARREN WAY AND ELIZABETH WAY ROGERS

aren't you dreadful!" she says—almost in tears—"Well, what can I do—she doesn't sleep, and the doctor gives her things, and they don't make her sleep"—and you remember all of the dark nights when you were very little, and the animals on your crib cover all came alive, and you thought that your father's snoring was their snoring.

Then I turned off the light, and listened for the mail plane. Then turned on the light and found it was long overdue. Then it thundered over my head.

Elizabeth came home from New York to the news of a number of guests soon to arrive. One of them, Margaret Long, would be rooming with the Lawrences while she attended St. Mary's School. The Lawrences had been close friends of the Longs since Elizabeth's childhood. When Sam Lawrence was a bachelor working on the railroad, he had so often stayed at Longview, the Longs' home in Northampton County, that the front room was called "Mr. Lawrence's room." In 1912, after he married and had his own family, he moved his wife and daughters to a small house in nearby Garysburg to be close to his sand and gravel business. He continued to see his friend, the senior Willie Long, and Bessie became friends with Willie's wife, Caroline. Several generations of Longs would come to know the Lawrences.

More people in the Lawrence house meant that there was more work to be done, and Bessie and Elizabeth, like others in the neighborhood, employed at least one black woman. Elizabeth also employed a black man named Page to help her in the garden. Segregation, low wages, and the continuing migration of Southern blacks for better jobs in the North help explain the frequent turnover of servants. When the Lawrences moved into the big house on Park Avenue in 1916, they had two black servants living with them for a short time: Sarah Christian, who had worked for Sam's family in Marietta, Georgia, and Dallie P. Harris, whom the Lawrences later helped attend Meharry Medical School. Elizabeth's habit of referring to blacks as "darkies" (she and fellow St. Mary's students had used the word in their senior orations) conformed to the speech of other white Southerners, although it seems unlikely that Ann Preston Bridgers would have used the term. Regrettably, it has not proven possible to trace the surnames of numerous black servants, all called by their first names in these letters.

[August 19]

I am so happy to get back to my rickety Corona; Ellen's elegant new typewriter made anything I had to say unworthy of its attention. . . .

I am glad that you decided to go to New York, because I didn't think you were entirely satisfied. Bessie thinks we would have to give up going to the cabin in October on any account, as Sammy's [Elizabeth's father's] heart is worse again, and she won't leave him. I am very anxious to drive Bessie and Sammy to Maryland when Aunt Elizabeth [Bailey, Bessie's aunt] leaves, if Miss Isabel and I can finish the planting design we are at work on, and if there is time. We have to be back here the tenth, because Margaret Long is coming then. She is to spend the winter with us so she can go to St. Mary's. Miss Estelle's son got appendicitis so she has never gotten here. Aunt Elizabeth came last night, and I think will stay until the first of September.

The Zinnias you raised for us are magnificent. There are lots of those very pale salmon ones that are the loveliest of all, and some very pale yellow ones that Bessie puts in my room.

The red ones are in front of boltonia and astilbe (white). I knew how awful the garden would be. I have come back to it before, and I knew Bessie wasn't going to do anything by herself. But that doesn't mitigate the despair that you feel when you see it. I worked two days and almost got the weeds out of the beds around the summer house. There isn't much left. There has been so much rain that the growth of the weeds was tropical.

Aunt Elizabeth is adorable. When she first comes her middle-western accent is always a shock to me. She remembers every incident of her two visits to us in Raleigh (and all the places we were before we came to Raleigh) and everything every member of the family said, and everything every servant said. At breakfast she said: I see the spot that was made by the hot coffee pot has worn off of the table. She said she remembered it because Bessie jumped on me, and it wasn't my fault. Aunt Elizabeth is my Godmother and takes her position very seriously.

I feel that Sadie [a servant] is made for us. If she doesn't go North or take to drink. Imagine the merits of a darkie that is liked by all of us. (Even Emma [another servant] was sometimes found fault with by Bessie.) . . .

Don't waste any sympathy on me in the heat. I am so thankful to get home and get warm again. The Ways' house was a tomb, and the ocean like ice. I was frozen half the time at Ellen's, and we nearly perished driving up to Sakonnet, and were numb all the time we were there. Even here I sleep under blankets.

How are you off for reading matter? Mrs. [Annie Root] Vass called me up as soon as I got back, and said did you have a nice trip, we are ready to start reading again. I was going to let it slide until you got back. I started on *I, Claudius* Monday night.

We read at Miss Sophie's house, but I was not able to prevent them from deciding on Mrs. Vass's porch for the next time.

Bessie and I took Aunt Elizabeth to Durham to hear the [Duke University] carillon, and when we got back Sammy said that Jonathan and Lucy [Daniels, married in 1932] had been to call. There was a storm, and Sammy said Lucy was very nervous, but he reassured her by explaining that a great many more women were killed by their husbands than by lightning.

Did Bessie tell you that they turned Dave [the name of the car] in for a new Buick? A great grief to Michael [the dog] and me. To Michael because they won't let him ride on the new upholstery, and there is no little shelf, so he doesn't like it any way. It is a light Buick, and much easier for me to handle (and much easier for you to drive), but I don't like those smooth-riding cars, they are so sensitive to every scratch on the road. I feel as if their nerves are all on edge. I would rather be jolted myself. And I didn't see anything the matter with Dave anyway. Sammy and Bessie were very sheepish about the transaction. They did it before I came home because they knew I wouldn't approve. . . .

I am so excited about the last act and eager to read it.[5] I wanted to write you to send it to me as fast as you finished, but I thought you would if you wanted to, so I didn't. . . .

---

[5] Except for *Coquette* and for *Quicksand* and *Carrie Was a Lady* (the latter two produced in the late 1930s for the Raleigh Little Theatre), no other work by Ann Preston Bridgers was produced or published. Yet she continued to write, often working on the same plays (sometimes under new titles) for many years. Ann's plays that Elizabeth alludes to in her letters are not always identified. Quotation marks are used for unpublished plays and italics for published plays. All extant manuscripts are in the Ann Preston Bridgers Papers of the Rare Book, Manuscript, and Special Collections Library at Duke University.

[September 15]

Margaret [Long] has come. A nice child, and fond of dogs.

Mrs. Bridgers is our chief delight in life. She is also in high standing being addicted to two cups of tea.

I started this letter the other night and I was so tired I later couldn't remember what I meant to say. Your letter came this morning, and I would like to always answer letters the minute they come. But that is so discouraging to the writer, so sometimes I answer them, and then keep the answer until a proper time has elapsed. . . .

Bessie says to tell you she misses you, and is going to write to you, but I doubt if she gets round to it. She says to tell you she meant it when she said she couldn't leave Sammy. Dr. Neal is rather upset about him. I am trying to get some action. Bessie says having always lived under the shadow of a strong-minded person like Nana, who not only told you what to do, but made you do it, she finds it hard to realize she has to decide for herself. As for me, I wasn't going to let you and Bessie go off without me, but I can still feel those cold nights that we spent at the roundabout [a cabin in western North Carolina] in October, and your cabin is a thousand or more feet colder.

I don't like the reading group without you. Miss Sophie has moved it up to eight o'clock. (I am writing while we have lunch, and Margaret is telling Sammy about her morning work. She takes French, German, Math, English and biology. She likes all but English, in which the next assignment is a short autobiography, giving the events most influential in shaping your personality. I am sorry the typewriter can't put down her voice saying it. Sammy asked her if her destiny was shaped by love or hate—my idea is both or neither.) [Moving the time of the reading group] vexes me beyond expression though that hour suits me much better. Without you to hold her down Mrs. Vass expatiates endlessly on race inequality and last time we met at her house, and were interrupted every five minutes, and I was wild. We only have one more time on *I, Claudius* (even at that I have had to read ahead and cut it) and then we are going to get a book on Russia, and meet with Mrs. Bridgers. (Sammy wants to know if I think you are going to read all this.)

Turk[6] has attached himself to Sammy, and Sammy is enchanted. Aunt Lucy[7] said he was innocent and proud (Turk I mean). (I can't bear your having missed Aunt Lucy . . . but I think she will be back off and on this winter.)

The other night the dogs were alone in the house, and when I came back Michael knew my step, and got up to meet me, but Turk was startled and ran to the door barking, and then pushed up against Michael for protection; they looked exactly like the picture of the little princes in the tower. . . .

Ann wrote that you wrote that the dress people (I can never remember their names) had an opening in Paris, but she didn't see how she could take it even if given the chance. I wrote back in hot haste that people who got homesick had better stay at home, and she wrote back that of course she had written immediately that she was educated in Paris [during her junior year abroad] and spoke perfect French.

---

[6] In search of a new dog for the family, Sam Lawrence had gone looking in Hamlet, North Carolina, where he had a business; Turk finally was the chosen one, and Sam brought him home.

[7] Elizabeth's trip to Europe in 1928 had included a visit with Uncle Nat and Aunt Lucy Stewart, who lived in the American consulate in Barcelona.

I guess I can't put off getting back to work any longer. I am in Miss Isabel's bad looks at present because I can never copy a thing the way it is, I keep thinking up new things. Checking a blueprint she said "Libba, how did *Laurustinus* get here, I thought we decided on *Ligustrum nepalense*?"

Nana always said she would rather people hadn't come when they went away again.

Margaret wants to know if I am writing a book.

[P.S.] Margaret is just like Miss Minnie [Margaret's mother]— good natured and caustic. She is much too observant to have around comfortably. That is supposed to be a compliment. I meant observant, not curious.

[Fall?]

I mean it when I say that I don't suppose I can write poetry. That isn't being modest; it is true. I know that I can write better verses than most that are published, but that isn't a reason for trying to publish them. There are two reasons for trying to publish things: one is to make money, the other to be read. I can't make any money; and I don't want to be read.

Neither do I need criticism or encouragement. To say so isn't conceit. It's a simple fact: writing poetry is like working out a problem in geometry. You get it right or you don't. There isn't any good or bad, there is only the awareness, and that has an abstract existence. Writing poetry is like remembering—it is as if it had already been written down somewhere, and it doesn't require any concentration. The trick is not to keep your mind on it, but to get your mind off it. I have written many a sonnet, while Margie read aloud to me the properties of herbs, or Bessie berated the Community Chest, or Nana detailed her symptoms. So you need not worry, ever, that garden articles will interfere with poems. It is the poems that interfere with the garden articles.[8]

One of the troubles I had getting the [article on] conifers done was that in looking up a reference to cryptomerias I came across a note that Helen of Troy had her hands full of elecampane where she fled with Paris. I had often read that elecampane was associated with Helen of Troy, and had forgotten it again; but saying her hands were filled with it when she fled, made such a vivid picture of her walking away from the place with Paris, with her yellow hair and the yellow daisies, and the blue Aegean spread out before her that I could not get it out of my mind until I had written a poem about it. The poem wasn't worth writing, but it got Helen of Troy out of my mind so that I could go on with the conifers.

. . . I never write a word of prose—even in a letter—without thinking of the things that you have taught me, and which are as exhilarating to me as a sharp pencil. But when I write a poem, I count the syllables on my fingers just as I did when I was a little girl, and only my fingers can help me. . . . I hope all the studying I did of meters and poetic forms, all the rondos, triolets, rondels, and villanelles I wrote for exercises . . . have

---

[8] In 1936, after a few brief pieces for garden bulletins, Elizabeth would begin writing articles for garden magazines with the encouragement of Ann and Emily Bridgers. Six were published in *House & Garden*. These and others were republished in *A Garden of One's Own: Writings of Elizabeth Lawrence*, edited by Barbara Scott and Bobby J. Ward (University of North Carolina Press, 1997).

done something to me, even if it doesn't show when I want to write a poem about Helen of Troy. . . .

I am tired of writing to you. Come home, I want to talk. There are also things you can say but not write. Last night, half in moonlight, half in shadow, I finished to my satisfaction an argument begun one night at dinner, and carried on to you ever since. When I argue with you in my own mind I find the conclusion is very satisfactory, as you merely listen.

[Enclosed in the letter]

Inula helenium [Elecampane]

Unmindful of all but her beauty,
And careless of blood to be shed,
He led her away from the palace,
Who suffered herself to be led;
Who followed him empty handed
Until, as they entered the lane,
She lingered a moment to gather
A garland of elecampane.

[October 3]

When the telephone rings before seven you know before you are awake that it is to say that Sadie isn't coming. Bessie and I, half asleep and half dressed, gave Margaret a baked apple, and oatmeal in the same bowl, and carried up Sammy's tray, and ate our own breakfast over the stove, and turned to face a kitchen full of dirty pans (I thought: "While greasy Joan doth keel the pot"), and a breadbox full of moldy bread. I thought, if life is going to be like this I don't want to live it.

Then we went to town, and bought a new breadbox and Parmesan cheese, and when we came home the bell rang and Mrs. Hairston with her bright hair and her bright smile had come to stay to lunch. And Bessie made onion soup, and Mrs. Shore brought pink grapes, and we ate in the garden. And that is how you get lured on until the next time.

Margaret has gathered that you are an amazing person, and asks every other day: when is Ann Bridgers coming home? . . .

[October 6]

I came home with the groceries, and found the play ["The Same House"] in the mail and dropped the groceries on the floor and sat down to read it. I think it is grand and I like everything you did to it, and I am so glad no blood was spilled, but I am not sure but what that is a personal reaction: death is so unconvincing to me. But what you did is much worse, and utterly depressing. What a ditzy [?] answer. Just what I had said to myself every morning for mornings. . . .

What is the theme of the play? I am left at loose ends but I am not sure but what that is the best thing about it. Don't you hate smug plays that put a problem and solve it and so they lived happily ever after? But still I think it needs some little touch to emphasize the theme, but I think you have the characters perfectly proportioned now. . . . I love the way you changed Marion. I think her character is consistent now, and all of a piece, only I still don't imagine her saying the things she says in the second act. But, as you said before, if people never said the things I couldn't imagine their saying, you couldn't write a play about them. And anyway there is nothing like the revelation of a reticent person once started.

Please, it isn't a chore to write what I think. But Bessie was putting the clothes away while I was trying to think back through the acts and remember what happened where to lead up to the last, and she kept saying is this your handkerchief, is this Margaret's slip? And Margaret said was there any hot water, and to whom was I writing. So I got very confused, and I would write it over, but then I would have lost my first impression. . . .

Bessie and I spent the afternoon putting out squills and ixias and snowdrops and winter aconite in a chilly drizzle, and planting Italian rye, and going to Mr. Tong's [Raleigh nursery] for plants. We got so mixed up last year on what we had got and hadn't that I thought I would borrow your system, and I made Bessie sit down with Mr. Tong's catalogue before we went and I put down on one of the cards you gave me exactly what we wanted and how much. Alphabetically. And when we got there, Bessie and Mr. Tong wouldn't pay any attention to the alphabet or anything else, and Bessie got everything she saw, and everything Marjorie [Lalor, biology teacher at St. Mary's] saw, and I dashed around madly trying to check the list, and in the end we had no more idea than usual of what we had gotten and hadn't gotten. We had another herb tragedy: I sent a college boy out to weed the chrysanthemums, and he somehow got into the herbs, and pulled up every chive, and the Southernwood from the Bishop's garden, and the thyme. Margie [Marjorie] and I raked the pile, and retrieved some of it, but in a rather lacerated condition. Today we got peppermint and winter savory, and tomorrow Marjorie can come at eleven and we can work all day, if it stops raining. Marjorie says the pennyroyal is thriving.

[October 12]

The rainbow comes and goes, and lovely is the rose. That means that it is a beautiful day, only hot, you wouldn't like it. And I have marketed and got Bessie off somewhere with Miss Rosa [Long], and told Ed [a servant] to paint the kitchen floor any color that strikes his fancy, and told Sadie to let me know when Sammy calls, and not to call me otherwise unless the roof falls in, which she thinks is very funny, but it was not meant that way; and now I shall devote myself to your play which I have just snatched back from Mrs. Bridgers who was preserving in a blue dress.

[Elizabeth here wrote a long critique of Ann's latest play.]

[November 7]

I am despondent over your letter:

About the play: I knew I said too much. I meant not to, but I got wound up. That is what Mr. S [a magazine editor?] did to me last spring. But I knew I was right. Once, when Miss L [another editor?] was ripping me up, I cried so desperately, "but I don't want to lose my idea," that she was impressed, though not an impressionable person.

About Ann [Elizabeth's sister]: I know you meant to be encouraging. But people who are clever about catching on to advantages are just the people I hate—but of course I wouldn't like her not to be.

Rereading what I said above, I see I didn't say what I meant to: if you are writing a play, it is yours. What it is or isn't to anybody else doesn't matter. All that matters in writing is saying what you have to say to your own* satisfaction. . . .

* that means in the Aristotelian sense of "a proper purgation of all the emotions"

[November 19]

. . . The first of the week I picked the last of your red and yellow zinnias, just before the frost finished up everything. But I think gardens are just as pretty in winter. The winter grass is so fresh when you rake the leaves off the beds weeded and covered with compost, and ivy very green, and some sweet alyssum still in the path and that nice raked-up look and the air full of smoke and leaves falling. Nothing is so beautiful and sad as leaves falling. Bessie got two such irresistible bamboo rakes that we have had very good success with the leaf raking. One afternoon Margaret and Ruth and Margie [raked leaves].

Ruth [Long] is the loveliest thing you ever saw. Everybody seems suspicious that a girl could be as sweet and as pretty as Ruth, and she and Margaret [both St. Mary's students] laugh so much and talk such foolishness that I asked Margie if she knew anyone could be so young, and she said "Oh, yes, Ruth and Margaret are much older for their ages than the other girls, because more intelligent."

Uncle Robert [Randolph] raked a great deal and Aunt Lettie [Letitia Lawrence Randolph] some. Today everyone went to the football game and I sat in the sun and read *Troilus and Cressida* until Margie and the college boy came and then we got so much trash out of the rose hedge and made such a grand fire that I wished for Elizabeth [Daniels]. . . . Turk is a delightful dog to walk with, he doesn't ever leave you and you don't have to yell at him every other minute. He is a ludicrous looking pup (though much improved) and such a little clown. The other day I said, Margie what does he remind you of. And she said, Hans Christian Andersen. We had just been reading a biography of him (and were delighted with it), and Turk is really like him: shy and forward, and sad and merry, and pathetic and imposing, and dignified and ridiculous. Walking in the park was never so nice, but we have to love that well which we shall lose ere long, because the C.W.A. [the New Deal's Civil Works Administration] has almost finished enlarging and improving, and then we won't dare take the dogs, there will be so many automobiles. . . .

There are a lot of things in your letters that I don't intend to let go by, but I can't go into all of that, it would be endless, and I shall have to wait until I see you. It is the middle of November.

[December 3]

Yesterday I was so engrossed in writing you a letter that when Margie called and said "Margaret and I are going to *The Count of Monte Cristo*, do you want to go with us?" I put on my hat, and was half way to St. Mary's before I realized what I was doing. Going to the movies was the last thing I wanted to do, and writing to you was the first. I found Margie waiting on the corner with Margaret and Ruth (whose bare heads and arms full of books carried me back to cutting class to go with Jean [a Barnard College classmate] to the Nemo. Do you know the Nemo?—Broadway and 110th). [Margaret and Ruth] are to Margie what Ann and Betty and Bill [Ann Lawrence and her New York City friends] are to Ellen and nobody is to me, but I don't mind, but maybe I will. When we went in to the movie, Margaret said "Heavens the picture has started, Libba will never catch on."

I met a character in search of an author,[9] who was revealed so completely, and with such economy in a few words and gestures, that I couldn't bear not being one. In fact, her asking me with lavish apologies (like the Duchesse de Guermantes [in Proust's *The Guermantes Way*]) if I could possibly meet her downtown, told the whole story. As if that weren't the obvious thing and as if she would have done anything about it if I couldn't. I had to wait some time (although she called and changed the place and hour). She came in at last, very apologetic, but I assured her that it didn't matter as I always carried a book. At that she said intimately "So do I. We have something in common haven't we?" And I said, yes; though I couldn't see that it was significant. She asked how I was connected with the project, and I answered that I wasn't, I only hoped that there would be landscaping. She asked me some questions, and then said that the government would probably use its own landscape architects, to which I replied that I had been told as much. She said if they didn't she would certainly see that I had a chance,

[9] Perhaps a federal employee hiring landscape architects for the grounds of the Raleigh Little Theatre building, a Federal Theatre project.

would take special interest in me in fact, being a woman her-self, and in business. And added (with another intimate smile) "It's fun isn't it?" To my horror I heard myself saying, "No, I hate it." I must be temperamental, she said. No, I said angrily, I was very practical. She said she thought we understood each other (which seemed to me no great feat in so simple a matter) and we left the building together. In the street she said with a short laugh, that she could not fit her stride to my very short steps. I rather thought that it was my quick pace, and not my short steps that bothered her. She asked me what I was reading, and without listening to my answer said that I must read *The Thirteenth: Greatest of Centuries*. I got the impression that it was the only book she had read for some time, and that she hadn't finished it. She said in telling me goodbye, that she hoped she would see me again when she came back, even if she hadn't any work for me.

Mother and Father have at last gotten off on the trip they didn't take last summer, and I had a postal from Beaufort [South Carolina] saying that Father is better already. Margaret and I are very happy. I got out all of my scrapbook clippings and all of my scrapbooks and spread them all over the red room floor, and all of my writing things and spread them all over the front room, and I am perfectly happy. I really have not such a morose nature after all.

I think you were dear not to let Ellen show you the poems [Ann sometimes saw Ellen Flood in New York]. Isn't Ellen a devil? She asked if you had read them, to see if I had told her the truth. It isn't that I mind. I would show you anything I would show Ellen (if not what she discovers by going through my notebooks and bureau drawers) but I can't if I am to read your plays, which I would much rather. . . .

Does Emily's offer to criticize garden articles still hold good? I think I need it. I took great care to write a straightforward radio talk giving the required information, and leaving out the personal equation, and before I could get out of the radio office a woman called me, and said, "Oh, Miss Lawrence, I had to talk to you. I can see that you feel just the way I do about gardens!"

[December 20]

Chills and fever from buying Christmas greens in the rain have allowed me several days in bed with a free conscience. Today is the shortest day. It began being twilight at five. I watched it grow dark, which I love to do, but someone always turns on the lights.

I read *Troilus and Cressida* because of "The moon shines bright.—In such a night as this, where the sweet wind did gently kiss the trees, and they did make no noise; in such a night, Troilus, methinks, mounted the Trojan walls, And sighed his soul toward the Grecian tents, Where Cressida lay that night." But I was cruelly deceived. I had no idea that Cressida would take a Trojan lover. Still I can't think why you call it an unpleasant play. I thought it very funny, especially the part where Pander [Pandarus] praises Troilus to Cressida. I love the way the heroes of *The Iliad* are made over into English gentlemen. The battle scene reminded me of *Journey's End* [1924 R. C. Sherriff play] with them all determined to play cricket. . . .

As for Ellen—the devil—I am sure you can give her points about me, and I only hope she doesn't tell you anything you don't already know.

[December 28]
Monday before tea

The college boy and I have been burning leaves in a snow storm. Turk has never seen snow before. His surprise and delight remind me of the way I used to feel about snow. It is a very pretty snow storm. When I came in there was a silver frost—I just learned the phrase from some person in the country—I have just come back from a wedding in the country.

The letter I tore up was about Ann. But I don't need to write you about things, it seems, as you said just exactly what I wanted you to without. I am as pleased as if I had got absolution without confession. . . .

Sometime in late 1934, Elizabeth's need to write to Ann was not reserved for letters alone. She composed two long, carefully typed manuscripts. One, "Piper, Pipe a Song," was about her childhood. The other, "Love Itself Shall Slumber On," concerned a college romance. Apparently, she had discussed both subjects with Ann in person, and these prose pieces show evidence of her efforts to use the materials of her life for literary essays. Both have fictive qualities—dialogue and anecdote especially—that show up in letters. The essay about childhood, taking its title from a poem by William Blake, was based on Elizabeth's belief that "the pattern of childhood is the pattern of existence." She evoked her early summers visiting her mother's family in Parkersburg, West Virginia. In "Love Itself" (a line from the poet Shelley), she narrated a story about her relationship with a thirty-two-year-old New York journalist, Peter Burnaugh, a romance apparently known only to Ann Bridgers, Ellen Flood, and Elizabeth's sister, Ann. (Peter broke off the relationship after Elizabeth graduated from Barnard and mar-

ried without telling her, then, tragically, died suddenly. All of this was in the story.) It was Elizabeth's most polished piece of writing during this period, with fine literary touches, humor, and sadness. Ann Bridgers saved the two essays along with the letters. They are part of the Ann Preston Bridgers Papers and are closely discussed in "Remembering" and "Peter and Elizabeth" in this author's No One Gardens Alone.

1935

[January 18]

I am going to remind you that it is past the middle of January, when Ellen called me in praise of you and Emily, and said you had no idea of returning to the Provinces. I wish you would come home. I have had dreams about you and Michael. Every time an automobile backfires I dream a policeman has shot Michael because children are more valuable than dogs, and dogs go mad and bite children. I don't know why I dream about you, but I woke up feeling very unhappy. Not that I really count "the bitterness of absence sour" [Shakespeare sonnet 57] if you are better in the city—but I complain on the principle of Ellen's tirades against [her husband] Jack lest you should fail to know how much I miss you.

I have given thought, since last spring, to the question of security. I had never thought of it until you mentioned it, because I always took it for granted that there wasn't any. Now, I have decided that security was in insecurity. That is in moments that take nothing and ask nothing and are complete in themselves. . . .

[Late winter]

Do you know what I think is a nice way to spend the day: Margie and I went to Communion at eight (I set the clock half an hour too early, but Margie was very sweet about it, and said she was awake anyway) and Selina [a servant] gave us our breakfast by the fire, and we sat reading all morning; Margie read me from *A Modern Herbal* that I can get rid of rats by spreading dried mint around (can you imagine anything nicer, even if there were not rats), and I read her from *Sense and Poetry* that there is a fashion in words:

> Ye knowe eek, that in forme of speche is chaunge
> Withinne a thousand yeer, and wordes tho
> That hadden prys, now wonder nyce and straunge
> Us thinketh hem: and yet they spake him so,
> And spedde as wel in love as men now do.

[Chaucer, *Troilus and Criseyde*]

And we sent Selina home and had cocktails and hors d'oeuvres for lunch; and Margie went upstairs to sleep, and I lay on the floor with the dogs and listened to a Mozart concerto. We seem to get the Philharmonic from Durham now. There is some static, but it is so much less objectionable than a family (Sammy and Bessie at Longview, Margaret staying with Ruth [at St. Mary's School]), who spend the afternoon going up and down stairs. . . .

Do you mind my writing to you so often and such silly things (rhetorical question . . . you needn't answer as I don't care anyway). I do, because Ann only wants news, and Ellen only likes my letters when I am amusing. And you like letters from me. Nana is the only other person who liked you to tell her everything. Bessie and I used to write to her every day when she was in Parkersburg [West Virginia]. And when she came to live with us,[10] I missed it dreadfully.

We have had a week of spring and lying in the sun and having lunch out (I have, the rest think it winter). You are going to wait for a blizzard to come home in, I suppose.

[Early spring?]

But I think you are the most detached person from your writing. It is unbelievable to me. I had thought when I was writing to you in the garden the other day that you are as objective as Willa Cather. But I think so many things and it takes so long to write them down that I forget before I am through, or am interrupted. That day Bessie came out with the little curved pruning saw that I had wanted so long, and it is hard to be cross about interruptions like that. . . .

[Summer]

I am excited over the two acts that are ready to be read by somebody—is that somebody me? And are you going to send them to me, or do I have to wait until you come?

Your fig vines seem to be taking hold, and my fig vines are surviving. It is lucky that they arrived in such a rainy summer. I

---

[10] From 1929 until her death in 1933.

went over to see that Clarence [a worker at the Bridgers home] didn't demolish them when he cut the grass, and he had already cut it, but they were unscathed. The cassia and cosmos orange flare are lovely. Everything is growing all too well from the rain, and I do not like to cut them back too much because Mrs. Bridgers cuts flowers for church. The fresh crop of zinnias I planted and the October marigolds seem to have been swamped. Then I planted seeds of a tiny dwarf marigold along the edge because you said last year that you wanted something low and yellow. But they did not come up. . . .

Mrs. Bridgers came over Saturday morning, and she and Page [employee of the Lawrences] and I picked the crab apple for jelly. I was sure Mrs. Bridgers would fall in the pool. Then we sat in the summer house and talked. Mrs. Bridgers is the greatest appreciator of my garden. The grass is always greener when she leaves. Have you noticed how some people sear it?

I borrowed from Emily Elizabeth's *Ten Saints* [by Eleanor Farjeon, popular British author of children's books] to read to my Sunday school children. We loved St. Brigid's hanging her coat on a sunbeam, and the wolf who jumped in to the chariot with her. I had been hard put to it to keep their attention during the summer.

I have been envying you the swimming. Gardening may be good exercise, but it doesn't make up for tennis, riding, and swimming, especially swimming. Especially in lakes. I have been so desperate I almost went to Pullen Park, but couldn't quite make up my mind to it. . . .

You must have read [*House Beautiful* editor] Mr. Beach's mind. Suzanne's [probably another editor's] letter followed close upon the heels of yours. He would certainly have returned that article swiftly. I switched back to the "Night Garden," and rewrote it on the plan you outlined describing the garden, and making a plan. I tried very hard to express personality, but I think you will agree with me that I can never hope to equal— or even approach—Mr. [Richardson] Wright [*House & Garden* editor] in that field—it is too bad that I am so full of material and devoid of personality.

[June 25]

Alas! I discovered immediately after your departure that it was your enthusiasm that made writing gardening articles so simple. And you had no sooner left than the magic vanished, as at midnight in a fairytale, and it got to be the same chore it always was. However, I reminded myself that I am doing you a favor, and went bravely on; and due to your soothing influence I sat down to the typewriter, keeping firmly in mind that it bears me no grudge, and conquered the spacing system in a sitting. In time I hope to be able to strike the right key one time out of ten. Writing is the only thing I don't like about writing. That is what I like about poetry, you can express the most with a minimum of ink. . . .

For writing, I would like a room with a number of tables, on each of which was a typewriter. With only one I am continually being thwarted, because every time I begin to write a letter to you, I remember something I want to tell Ellen, and every time I begin a letter to Ellen, I think Ann would like what I am saying much better, and every time I start to write about the flowers that bloom in the spring, I think of a number of flowers that bloom in the fall, and every time I start a sonnet, I think I would rather write a satire about Sammy and the ice cream. Of course, I can and do take notes in such crises, but then I lose the notes before I get the typewriter free again, so some more typewriters would facilitate matters.

I know why you don't like Turk. It is because he is so much like Uriah Heep?[11] I would even like Uriah Heep if he were a dog.

The peaches off of your peach tree were delicious, much the best we have had.

Dear Ann: I relax all day, and sleep all night (and no dreams come), and I sleep under blankets every night, not that I am cold, just perverse.

[June 30]

That made six gardening articles, so I thought I might go back to "the white dawn." You will allow this to be literal. Now I am going to finish up the others of Maurice Scève that I have worked on, and then I am going to leave him severely alone, and concentrate on Du Bellay.[12] I could easily lose my mind trying to translate obscurities. I could easily lose my mind anyway. . . .

Bessie and I have lapsed into a prehistoric stupor. I have been doing all of the things I have left undone; answering the letter that General Claudon [perhaps a World War I British officer who had once visited in America] wrote me about seven years ago saying he liked to correspond with Americans, and would I send him some pictures of the garden, and his small

---

[11] Character in Charles Dickens's *David Copperfield*, who became a prototype for insincerity.

[12] Both sixteenth-century French poets.

niece some American postal cards. I shall send the snapshots
of the garden, which I have had to reproach me every time I
opened my desk drawer these seven years, but I am afraid the
niece has gotten beyond the postal age; my report that I was
supposed to have typewritten at the meeting in Gastonia for the
secretary, but which I made up as I went along and promised to
send immediately, I hope the Year Book hasn't gone to press; a
letter to Freddie Dorris to admire an article he wrote and sent
me to admire; a letter from Richard Chase [the husband of
Mary Wiatt, a St. Mary's classmate], who wrote me three years
ago (he will be surprised to hear from me so soon); a letter to
Mr. Seaman. I am afraid he had moved from that address, you
have to answer by return mail if you expect him to get it; the
Iris that I dug up weeks ago dipped in potassium permanganate
(I left it on the walk and found Michael sipping it. Several of
our friends cheered up considerably, but it seemed to agree with
him) and set out again; I read in an English magazine that it
was good for Iris to let them dry up before you replanted them:
but much as I would like to think so, it hasn't been proved by
my previous experience. Now if I can just get arsenic of lead
on the basil that Mrs. Steinmetz sent Bessie (and get Bessie to
call her up and thank her) before it is all eaten up by some evil
smelling black bugs, and before Margie comes, my spirits will
be considerably lightened. Oh yes, and the letter to Ruth, and
Margaret Bullett's hat back to her. Ann borrowed it to wear to
Annabel's wedding.

A letter from Ann warning us that she had collected a new
man, and we would probably hear from Ellen that she was
engaged.

Sylie [Sylbert Pendleton, a St. Mary's graduate and close
family friend] is here for ten days. She comes out at bedtime,

and she and Bessie and I repair to the kitchen, and eat fresh bread and apple sauce, and talk about nothing for hours. Bessie has no objection to talking all night if she is doing the talking.

We have had no rain since you left and the trees and shrubs and grass are very limp and brown. I have watered faithfully, and the flowers bloom gaily on.

. . . I am glad you decided to leave the comedy [unidentified] and go to something else. I had a feeling that you couldn't get at something else because of the comedy, and couldn't get at the comedy. You will come back to it. Please don't get in a plutsy over what to do with the garden articles or I will be sorry I was born.

Miss Daisy [Thompson] is back from Canada and has eyed my dried-up garden, and said that in their friend's garden in Nova Scotia the lupines grew to her shoulder, and there were fifty peonies on one bush. I think such display is vulgar, don't you? Miss Lillian [Thompson] is going to stay until fall. I am glad, because I felt bad about not having written to her, and now I have plenty of time to do it.

[July 8]

You are so sweet. Of course I can easily do the rest of the articles by September, especially as I am not going to summer school [offered by the local garden club]. . . . We are not having the reading club this summer for which I am grateful. I do not like it without you.

Sammy [Elizabeth's father, who had suffered a stroke] is ever so much better. Sammy is frightfully interested in the garden articles and even went so far as to read two of them. I think if you had time and strength, you would peddle the articles better than [sister] Ann. And if you go to New York, which I hope you don't. Or is that the wrong thing to say? If not, Ann can do it.

You will be pleased to hear that I went to Dr. Kemp and Dr. West and had a thorough physical examination. They could find nothing the matter with me, so took my tonsils out. I hope that is what made me so yellow, and that you will be pleased when you next see me.

Bessie and I are wild at the thought of the rock terrace [at Ann Bridgers's cabin]. We cannot bear not being there, and I am enchanted with the two boys [who helped lay the terrace?]— and with you.

Margie is reading delightful excerpts from her herb books. She and I have been rereading Maria Edgeworth's enchanting "The Noble Science of Self-Justification" [an essay from *Literary Ladies*]. I cannot imagine why she is so neglected.

Dear Ann: don't copy any more articles. They have to be written over. I didn't realize how awful they were until you sent them back. Why don't you stop me from such effusions? Sammy called my attention to several ridiculous statements. Also I am learning more as I write, and can add. . . .

I knit you a wash cloth but everybody laughed at it, so I am knitting you another.

I have a lot more things to write. But it is not a good idea. I never regret the things I don't say. That doesn't mean anything, only that I am always trying to convey to you a mood that cannot be expressed or to explain something you don't want explained.

Give my love to Emily and tell her, please, that when she comes back I expect her to concentrate on me. She is the most approachable person and you can't get at her at all. You are utterly unapproachable and so easy to get at.

[July 22]

I don't know how long it will last, and I feel as if I were tempting Providence to say so, but we are having a very peaceful time. Sammy is better, and even Bessie is beginning to feel hopeful, and the doctor speaks of two months, which is certainly an improvement on "Indefinitely." Also Sammy has calmed down considerably. I think he is not as worried, and worry is really what has been the matter with him.

The cleaning was $3.58.

. . . Elizabeth Thompson gave us out-of-stock samples to make portfolios, and Margie is reading Jane Austen while we sew. We decided that nothing else is as nice to read aloud, and that we would rather read her over, than something new. So we read *Pride and Prejudice* with much merriment, and have started on *Emma*. Among the samples was a *toile de Jouy* that I divided in two to make me a writing case, and you a folder for dancing pictures. I shall keep it until you come home, as you won't want anything else to pack. . . .

I have some more articles to send you. It would be all right to try the *Christian Science Monitor*, but would they want local things? I judge not from what I read. Whatever you say. Billy Hunt [gardener William Lanier Hunt of Chapel Hill] isn't going to have his summer school (he says on account of infantile paralysis [outbreak], but I imagine he couldn't swing it) and I am very disappointed. But then I feel as if I had been made a present of six weeks, as I had counted those out.

I am reading *Axel's Castle* [1931 book of literary criticism by Edmund Wilson] with great interest. It is just what I wanted, and fills in gaps in what I had been studying this winter on modern poetry. . . .

[July 30]

Your letter came this morning, and I should hastily send you the quotations I copied out of books for you while I was in bed, and a piece about the Russian ballet, which I found in Uncle Jim's[13] *Spectator* and asked him if I might have for you. He said, "Yes, you may have it for her if you tell her it is from me"; and Sammy murmured, "with love." . . .

Sammy came to dinner tonight, clothed and in his right mind. The last is a great improvement. . . .

[August 16]

Bessie and I have just been over to see that the house was locked. Your tenants left things in the most perfect order. Your box was inside the hall door, and looked all right. They had put Emily's stick in the living room window, but I put a nail in, too. I only hope it will come out!

Your commissioning me to see that the house was locked has offered my father much amusement.

---

[13] James Lawrence, Sam's younger brother and an Episcopal priest.

In 1917, the Lawrence family gathered in Marietta, Georgia, for the fiftieth wedding anniversary of Elizabeth's grandparents, seated in front. Elizabeth stands just to the back of her grandmother and to the right of her mother and father. Her sister, Ann, is seated to the right, between two older cousins. Seated on the ground near his parents is James Bolan Lawrence, the beloved "Uncle Jim," Episcopal priest and traveling companion to Elizabeth on a European tour in 1928.
By permission of Robert de Treville Lawrence

[August 29]

I have this afternoon dedicated to taking Sammy to the doctor and putting manure water on the chrysanthemums, so I will start out with a small sheet of paper—faced with a wide expanse I am uncontrollable.

I have finished the thirteen articles, but the one on chrysanthemums is rather sketchy, so I am going to keep it until I get another look at them, and do one on trees.

What shall I do now? Shall I send them to Ann to peddle—or wait until you come home, and do them over? There are so many things I want to discuss with you, and I can't in writing. I should much rather go over them with you, and rewrite them, before sending them off. But then we couldn't possibly get them to Ann before October. Do you think that it is important to start sooner?

[End of summer]

I agree with you that poetry is no longer written, can be no longer written:

> Brightness falls from the air,
> Queens have died young and fair . . .

["A Litany in Time of Plague," Thomas Nashe]

was written, and could be written, only when queens did die young and fair, and not live to have their faces lifted, and write testimonials for beauty creams. . . .

[Late October, Duke Hospital in Durham]

When we [Elizabeth and Bessie] got here we found Father still unconscious and no changes. That makes it right for us to have gone home, and gotten things straight, and looked after our guests. If Father had been worse, or gotten better and wanted us, it would have made it wrong. That's all there is to right and wrong. But I think we should have stayed [at the hospital].

[Elizabeth wrote the following poem in her notebook at the hospital.]

> My father lies dying,
> And all that he has said
> Begins to sprout,
> Begins to grow,
> Is branching overhead.
>
> My father lies dying,
> And all that he has said
> Will bud and blossom and bear fruit
> Long after he is dead.

I have been thinking for some time that I might as well resort to writing to you as I never see you to say anything, and never can say it when I do. Emily is such a satisfactory person to talk to: you can say anything to her at any time, and talk as fast as you like. I think I can say more to Emily in a given time than anyone I ever knew. But then, it is only what I think that I say to Emily.

Why didn't you go to hear Mrs. Shipman?[14] Because it was in the morning? I meant to tell you to be sure to go, but it never occurred to me you wouldn't. I thought the lecture pretty poor—not at all well thought out; she just said whatever came into her head, which is charming but not very helpful at a garden school where you go to learn. She told me with pride, that

---

[14] Ellen Biddle Shipman gave a garden lecture in Raleigh on October 22, 1935. The most famous American woman garden designer, she designed the Sarah P. Duke Gardens of Duke University.

she never read her lectures. "Mrs. Cary,"[15] she said, "reads her lectures; of course it takes much more out of you to speak, but it is the only way." She is right, of course, but a really good lecture has got to have been thought out in detail beforehand and turned in your mind. Then you have to think it all out all over as you say it, and then it sounds spontaneous, but makes sense too. I learned this from what you told me about Helen Hayes—I can't do it.

But you should have heard Mrs. Shipman. Just as you would not miss an opportunity to see a distinguished actress you should hear Mrs. Shipman.

She is old—nearly seventy I think. Once I cut a picture of her out of *House & Garden*. It was from a drawing in profile, and beautiful as Botticelli is beautiful. That beautiful long line of the jaw, wide mouth, and flaring nostrils. A beautifully modeled head, done in a few lines. I said to myself that here was a person I wanted to know. Please, imagine her coming to Raleigh and no one else wanting to entertain her.

. . . Margaret said, "How will you know Mrs. Shipman?" I said, "Oh, I know exactly what she looks like, tall and slender with the same sort of beauty as Miss Rosa.[16]

We sat waiting in the station, the train was not in, and I said, "There is Mrs. Shipman." Bessie said, "But the train isn't in." But I ran after her, and said, "Are you looking for someone?" and she said, "Yes, Mrs. Lawrence, are you Mrs. Lawrence?" And I said, "No, I am Elizabeth."

She had flown to New Orleans to see about a garden that

[15] Mrs. William Cary, another of the speakers at the Raleigh garden seminar with Mrs. Shipman.

[16] Rosa Heath Long, voted "handsomest" in the class of 1907 at St. Mary's School.

wasn't getting along as she liked, straightened it out, and came all the way here which takes over twenty-four hours, and it was 9:30 P.M. when we got home. And she is nearly seventy. I said, when we got home, "Wouldn't you like to go right to bed?" and she said, "No, if you are not tired, I would like to sit down and talk to you."

I said, "Mrs. Shipman, I think it is 'extraordinary' (I was mimicking her—she calls everything 'extraordinary'—I don't know whether from reading Henry James or being born in Philadelphia) that you can do gardens all over the whole United States. Aren't you the only landscape architect who does?" She said, "I really do not know. I really don't know anything about what other landscape architects do. I have three children and five grandchildren so I don't have much time."

I said, "But you must be extraordinarily versatile to do gardens in such different places as New York, Los Angeles, New Orleans, Winston-Salem, the middle-west."

She said, "But the principles are always the same."

"But how do you get the individual character of each place?"

"Because I am architecturally minded."

"And what about plant materials? Surely you can't know the plant materials for all those places." (It takes a lifetime to learn it for one.)

This, of course, is the whole thing. She was very much annoyed. And at once on the defensive. She said you didn't need to know the plant material. She said, "I ask my clients what they like and I use that. A garden should be a portrait of the person for whom it is designed."

To make up, I said, "That is the secret. It is because you do not try to express your personality, but your client's—so you can never become stereotyped."

Then to prove her great interest in plant material, she got out a little notebook, asked the name, height, blooming period, and characteristics of the milk-and-wine lilies, saying "You see, this is how I pick up information wherever I go"—whereupon Bessie got out her blooming date books and began to reel off bulbs for the South. Poor Mrs. Shipman never having heard of any of them before, and being a worse speller than I, tried to take down *Lycoris squamigera; Hymenocallis occidentalis; Amaryllis belladonna; Chimonanthus fragrans; Sternbergia lutea*—looking utterly bewildered. Finally, she said, "Frankly, I am no botanist, you know. I think gardens are best when they are planted with a few things, that you know will do well and give the right effect. And I am not interested in horticulture."

I said, "Mrs. Shipman, you are not a gardener, you are a landscape architect." She was indignant at that. She said, "But I am a gardener." (Her own garden is famous; that is how she got started—her own garden was so perfect, that an architect asked her to design gardens for his houses. She never had any training as far as I know, but she is nevertheless, a thorough workman—like you, and in the same way—and has learned a technique, I feel sure. I tried to find out how, and I think it is by eliminating nonessentials. My weakness is caring so much about everything, and not emphasizing the essentials. I feel pretty discouraged at this point.) [Mrs. Shipman said,] "I work in my own garden with my own hands—I *am* a gardener."

I said, "But no, you are not, you don't love plants for themselves. You only think of them as part of the design." (I was thinking of you.)

Mrs. Shipman looks right at you when she talks and her pupils get very small and sharp and bright.

I hope I wasn't as rude as this sounds. I don't think I was. And I don't think she thought me so. And all of the conversation was impersonal, and not at all heated; intense but not heated. I think if she had thought me rude she would have stopped talking. I was criticizing her, but not as a person. I wanted to find out from the best landscape architect in the country, what is essential in designing a garden. I thought I did when she said, "A garden must be a portrait of a person."

Bessie kissed her goodnight. She left her door open while she undressed, and kept talking to us.

In the morning I took her her hot milk and orange juice. When I went back in, she was sitting up in bed with the tray in her lap, and in a blue dressing gown, and her eyes are blue when she wears blue, and gray otherwise. I never saw anyone so beautiful. Michael and Turk were sitting on the rug staring at her. They will never believe there is no bacon, just because they can't smell bacon.

When I told Sammy how beautiful Mrs. Shipman is, he could not bear not having seen her. I told Mrs. Shipman this, and she laughed, and said he would have been disappointed when he saw a wrinkled old woman. She said it the way Nana said she was a wrinkled old woman, knowing she was, and knowing it didn't matter.

When I told Sammy about Mrs. Shipman, he said wistfully, "I wish you could have seen more of her while she is here." He seemed to forget that the garden school is what she came for. I said, "Oh, but I saw her a lot; last night, and taking her to the Woman's Club, and this morning before she got up." It isn't the amount of time you see a person, it is how responsive they are in that time. Mrs. Shipman doesn't waste a second. Sammy said, "Did you tell her you are a landscape architect?" I said, "No, she isn't interested in what I am." He said, "You were afraid to." He said, "Why didn't you ask her where to study?"[17]

I said, "I did not want her to think I asked her to my house for what I could get out of her."

Sammy said, "Isn't that what you asked her for?" . . .

Mrs. Shipman said in her lecture, "If anyone asks you 'who landscaped your place?' the landscape architect is a failure." Her slides were ravishing—all of little gardens, and more of very little ones. She likes doing little gardens—some were adorable.

1 9 3 6

The absence of letters during the first six months of 1936 may mean that Ann was in town, but other explanations are possible as well. First of all, Mr. Lawrence's health worsened, and although the household continued to function in normal ways—familiar friends for supper, work in the garden and in her study—Elizabeth perhaps was even more alarmed than her mother by the impending loss of her father. (After accompanying Elizabeth on the train for her first year at Barnard College and delivering her to Brooks Hall, Mr. Lawrence had left an affectionate note that said, "You know I am a believer in some kind of telepathy, so get your mind tuned up with mine and we will keep in close touch by this means of communication.") Elizabeth admired the philosophic essays her

---

[17] On September 11, 1934, Elizabeth had requested that her transcript from North Carolina State College be sent to the Lowthorpe School in Groton, Massachusetts, where Isabel Busbee had studied earlier. Mrs. Shipman lectured at the Lowthorpe School and employed some of its graduates in her New York office. No other mention of Elizabeth's interest in the school has been found.

father wrote for a men's club; he and Elizabeth often sat quietly together, working on their manuscripts. By contrast, her mother communicated with direct instructions. After Nana's death, Bessie had learned to make her own decisions and to handle things with dispatch. So Bessie took charge and Elizabeth followed, leaving her ample opportunity to think about losing her charming father and soul mate.

[Handwritten, July 16]

Father died tonight.[18] Don't worry about Bessie and me. We are all right. Miss Ray [perhaps Mr. Lawrence's home nurse] is slightly hysterical.

[July 20]

Bessie came into my room with this clipping[19] this morning and said she knew you would be dreadfully upset. I know you will, and I am upset for you and terribly distressed. I don't see how you can expect me to have a cheerful nature. I really cannot bear these things.

Would you like to have me come to stay with you? Ann has persuaded Bessie to go to Europe with Sylie [Sylbert Pendleton] for six weeks, sailing August 8th if Sylie can get back her

---

[18] Samuel Lawrence was sixty-two years old.

[19] Perhaps a story about a New York college student who was murdered in an Asheville hotel on July 16, 1936.

*Sam Lawrence, father of Elizabeth and Ann Lawrence
and husband of Elizabeth "Bessie" Bradenbaugh
Lawrence, in an early 1930s photograph thought to have
been made by Bayard Wootten*
By permission of Warren Way and
Elizabeth Way Rogers

just-cancelled reservations. I would drive up when I could get somebody to drive me. Bessie will not let me drive alone. I would like to stay here for awhile and recuperate from getting Bessie off, and get my garden in order, and yours. Bessie doesn't like that idea, but I feel perfectly desperate: I can't seem to get the rock garden article done, and I can't even start on the conifers until I get to the [North Carolina] Arboretum [in Chapel Hill] again, and see Dr. [W. C.] Coker; and we have millions of thank you letters to write, and Bessie has to get vaccinated and passported, and all of those things. . . . Ann went back to New York this morning in very low health and spirits. . . .

The Longs are driving up sometime, and if I can go then, one will go with me; if not, there will be someone else. Can one telegraph you in any way that you will get with any quickness? I feel as if you were on Mars, or some remoter star.

[July 25]

You need not be so stern. I have no idea of doing anything other than coming to you, and it was only just thought when Nette [Ann Lawrence] suggested that Bessie go with Sylbert. Miss Toose [Louise Busbee] will drive up to Linville with me. Bessie is going to leave on Wednesday (August 5) if Sylie can get her passage back, and stay with Ann and Ellen a few days, so Miss Toose and I will probably drive up Monday (August l0). I am not at all insulted and very grateful for all advice and I shall bring the wool dresses and underwear. I will bring my things if you say so, but will there be room for me to write? Don't you think I had better concentrate on my private affairs, which need only a pencil and a notebook and a flat stone in the brook? . . .

[August 5]

Miss Betsy and Mrs. Montgomery [daughter of North Carolina Supreme Court justice Walter Alexander Montgomery and his wife, Mrs. Lizzie Wilson Montgomery, author of *Sketches of Old Warrenton, N.C.*] came to tell Bessie goodbye. Miss Betsy wanted to know where I was going, and when I told her to stay with you, she said, "I'm glad of that. I don't know Miss Bridgers, but I can tell from looking at her that she is a nice person who leaves you alone and lets you do as you like."

Miss Sarah [Cheshire, daughter of Episcopal bishop Joseph Blount Cheshire, Jr.] came to tea and stayed until other people had left, and she and Bessie and I had a grand time talking about your play [*Quicksand*].[20] . . . Miss Sarah said what she liked was the construction and the way it all moved to the climax with no loose ends. . . . Bessie said she was so absorbed in it that she didn't want to talk to anybody about it. . . .

Bessie was to have gone in the morning. Dr. Penn made her get vaccinated, and it took, and she is in bed. She hopes to get off by night.

My suitcase has been packed for two weeks.

Finally, Bessie and Sylbert departed for Europe, and Elizabeth joined Mrs. Bridgers, Ann, and Emily in the mountains. Of course, Bessie wrote letters to them. And Ann wrote to Bessie about what a fine time they were having with Elizabeth, a letter discovered in the Lawrence family papers. Emily once described Mrs. Bridgers to Elizabeth Daniels Squire as "a great solid tree you could hold onto." Elizabeth found comfort with the Bridgers family in this critical period.

---

[20] The second production of the Raleigh Little Theatre, which was still using the stage of a local school. The *News & Observer* reviewer, E. Clifton Daniel, Jr., said *Quicksand* was "the most substantial thing ever presented by amateurs in Raleigh."

[Ann Bridgers to Bessie Lawrence]
August 25

Dearest Bessie,

We were so happy to get some letters from you. First to arrive was the one to me and then the one to Ann and Elizabeth with the picture of you and Sylbert, which was, if anything, better than the letters. I love it almost as much as the one of you sitting laughing on the post some thirty years ago.

Elizabeth is looking splendidly. The scar from the boil on her nose is healed up and she has a splendid color. Because you were having an uneventful crossing, she thought at first you were not enjoying your trip. Evidently she is incapable of the kind of relaxation I enjoy—and you, I take it—on a boat. It must be uneventful to be enjoyed.

I imagine Elizabeth has written you about the cake. We shared it (gingerly) with the community, and it aroused a storm of appreciation out of all proportion to the size of the sharing, but not to the quality of the cake. We have enjoyed our lion's share ourselves daily. And we are overcome that you would take the trouble to make it for us when you were so miserable with your vaccination. Mine always take hard and feverishly, so I can appreciate how you felt.

Elizabeth finished the rock garden article some time ago and is working on the narcissus one.[21] The rock garden one is excellent, I think—and arouses even my enthusiasm to build a rock garden. We are so happy to have her here with us.

[21] Elizabeth's articles on rock gardens and this one on narcissi have been reprinted in *A Garden of One's Own: Writings of Elizabeth Lawrence*, edited by Barbara Scott and Bobby J. Ward (University of North Carolina Press, 1997).

We are planning to drive down to Raleigh on the 11th [of September]. Mama is anxious to get home and that will give Elizabeth time to get things in order and be in New York to meet you. That will be a joyous time for the three of you I know. We talk constantly of you and Ann.

Give my love to Sylbert. I like to think you are being so well taken care of as Sylbert is capable of doing. And I know she enjoys having you with her.

A heartful of love,

[Signed] Ann

[November 19]

It is very late and very chilly, but I think I shall treat you to a typewritten communication instead of writing to you in bed as I have been doing of late. I always have the feeling that you are not very thorough about my handwriting, and I do want to be read. So I went down, and put some lightwood on the coals, and smoked a cigarette which I didn't want but will smoke when Bessie leaves them around, and ate an apple, and thus fortified shall tell you what is on my mind, which isn't anything at all, but that is none-the-less important.

I think Mr. Hayward[22] is going to prove one of my chief delights in life. I wrote him a long letter, and sent him an order and got back one twice as long and twice as ingratiating. He says he had no idea Mr. Wright [editor] would send his letter on to

---

[22] Wyndham Hayward, who supplied Elizabeth with crinums and lycoris.

me, or he would have written it entirely differently! That he did think I was writing from Florida, and that I needn't mind about the little matter of calling the hyacinth an amaryllis since it was Mr. Wright's job to catch those slips. I'd like Mr. Wright to hear that! I think the trouble was that I recommended California growers for tender bulbs, and you can scarcely blame him. He also gave me much valuable information and I feel there is more to be had for the asking. He is certainly fond of committing himself to paper, as his first letter was followed by a second telling me what to do with the things I ordered, and telling me that most of them would not be hardy here. I can't bear it if he is right about the hybrid crinum, the Empress of India.

I have been taking advantage of the glorious weather and a new college boy that I have acquired (Mr. Baker) to make up to my garden for some of my past neglect. It is really cold but the mornings are warm and sunny, and Bessie and I spent this one putting out the new things from Wayside [in Greenwood, South Carolina]. Bessie is so responsive and gets speechless as another and another root comes out of the box. I can never remember when the things come, what I ordered and why, so I take the catalogue to the garden and look them up, and find that *Coronilla cappadocia* is a vetch that is especially good for the South, blooms all summer, loves dry hot weather, and settles down in a warm, sunny border. But I struck a snag: can you remember the darling *Achillea sibirica* that we took a (not very good) picture of at the college? I searched eagerly for its little silvery scalloped leaves and finally realized that the plant that had its name was a coarse furry thing. And now I don't know how to check on it as Mr. X at the college is less than a moron, and I don't trust Wayside either, and Mr. Rehder[23] says don't send

---

[23] Alfred Rehder (1905–1940), Arnold Arboretum taxonomist.

anything but shrubs for the Arnold Arboretum to identify.

Bessie says she doesn't know where I am going to put the rest of the things I ordered as every time we dug, I dug up something I had planted last week. And I have dug up all of the seeds that I planted and I am afraid yours, too, when I planted the pansies from Miss Toose (they were magnificent plants, the pansies, I mean). We had our soufflé in the sun and wished for you. Bessie says this is the most beautiful fall we ever had, but I remember a more beautiful one. We had a killing frost night before last, but it didn't kill everything. In your garden are some late yellow chrysanthemums, and some ageratum and some alyssum still in bloom. In mine the same, and a Louis Philippe rose. Mr. Baker and I untangled it from the hedge, and found it full of the most gorgeous hips, fat orange globes. Mr. Baker is a good worker, but a great talker. He gave me a long lecture today on the evils of tobacco, and wound up with "and now I guess you won't ever want to smoke again." I felt discouraged at first because every time I asked him to do anything he said, "I can't make any promises, but I'll try," even if it was no more than to dig a hole. Today he said "Miss Lawrence, we sure are going to have a beautiful garden next spring."

I love the way you always begin a letter by saying you wish you could talk instead. I consider the written word vastly (here I had to stop and wind the typewriter ribbon onto the other spool) superior. For one thing you can say what you mean better, and for another you don't get interrupted by your audience. Every time I sit down to talk, I think I wish I were writing this in a letter. And you are the perfect person to write to (as you may have suspected) but don't suppose that that is a compliment. Contrariwise. I am sorry this got so pale. I forgot to notice. And if you don't like this thin paper, I don't have to use it.

And I am utterly depressed by the poverty in this world. I thought I should investigate why my new Sunday school class had two of its eight members present on a bright Sunday morning, and went with one of the faithful (the two said they never missed). "You love Sunday school, don't you?" One did. The other said her Mother would beat her if she came home and said she had played in the street instead of going to St. Saviour's. I was much impressed that it never seemed to occur to her that one could lie in such a situation, when she added, "and it wouldn't do no good to tell her a story 'nuther, she'd ask me what the lesson was." Which discourages me about her imagination to look up the rest. I had forgotten those places under the railroad, and I couldn't bear for those very little children who came to Sunday school and begged to sing "All Things Bright and Beautiful" to have come out of them. I went home to Bessie in a funk, and she had no patience with my maudlin tale, and said people always had lived like that, and always would, and they liked it.

Don't send me the primary colors and white and black. You know I would do nothing without you. . . . Did I tell you about Isabelle Bowen Henderson's[24] lecture on color at the garden club? She says we can't discount the psychologists, and that tints and shades are made only by adding white and black. She discussed all this at length with me later on the street corner. She is here for the winter and her husband is at Meredith. I shall have her to tea and give her cinnamon buns. I think she is a delightful ass.

My fingers are now icicles. I wish Ann's room wasn't so

---

[24] Henderson (1899–1969) was a well-known portrait artist and gardener who kept a beautiful house and garden. Her former home on Oberlin Road in Raleigh is on the National Register of Historic Places.

cold. I don't see how Margaret studied back here in the really cold weather. I shall have to give it up, and I have come to think two rooms of one's own a sine qua non.

Ellen admires you extravagantly. (I hadn't a chance to tell you when she was here.) She wrote that you had come to tea radiant, and in a stunning "outfit" (Ellen's word) making her feel worn and faded, and proving her theory that New York is a tonic for strong spirits although weaklings (me) might sicken, away from their native heaths. I replied that I was perfectly willing to subscribe to all of that. Ellen gives me great satisfaction as to you and Nette [Elizabeth's sister Ann], not to my other enthusiasms, alas, alas.

When noise is past enduring I think of the perfect quiet of our house. It is nowhere near a landing field or railroad or thoroughfare, and no neighbors are within radio distance. . . .

1937

[January 23]

Having collected my plants from the nursery (the car looked like Birnam Wood on its way to Dunsinane) and driven 300 miles, and dressed and gone to Miss Rosa's to dinner, and got the dogs back from Mr. Wright [the veterinarian], and met Becky's Aunt's train and conducted her to the hotel, and it being near midnight, I still feel that I must go into the color situation before I go to bed.

But, my dear Ann, do you suppose that after all of your training I would still abandon a manuscript to the United States mail, without keeping a carbon of it?

I am utterly discouraged about the color article. You are right, of course, and I knew in my heart that you would say it. And especially, as the Daffodils came back from *House Beautiful*, with a very nice letter from Mr. Beach saying of course people ought to be interested in daffodil classifications, but they weren't, and he felt the article was too technical for his readers. And after I had simplified them until there was nothing left. I knew what you would say, and I wrote the color article first without explaining the color theory, but it was nothing. The whole point is that all of the articles you read are about color schemes, and what flowers to plant together, and that no one can ever plan a garden that way. You have to get at the fundamentals. . . . And here I am in the mood you hate. . . . But I really try . . . but I have relapses. Any way you are right. But anyway I shall try once more to say something without seeming to say anything. And after some more articles come back, I will give in, and not say anything and not seem to say anything.

You say "leave out the undigested part." I guess that is the truth of the matter. It is undigested. If I ever get unstrung from driving so fast, and so far, and seeing so many people, and from the excitement of all of the new plants I saw, and meeting men who could tell me things, I will take a deep breath and try to digest it. I will send you back your letter with this as you may have forgotten what you said.

Bessie and I did not get back in time to see *Coquette*.[25] Margie did, and was deeply impressed. She had not seen it before.

---

[25] The Raleigh Little Theatre hosted the North Carolina premiere of Ann's Broadway hit, coauthored with George Abbott. Some local theatregoers may have seen *Coquette* when it opened in New York in 1927 or later when it was taken on the road. Ann apparently stayed at the mountain cabin instead of coming home for the Raleigh premiere, perhaps recalling how overwhelmed she felt by the attention following the New York opening.

She said that it was a remarkably good performance, and very moving. Both those who had seen it, and those who had not, thought it was a good performance. Miss Minnie Baker asked Margie if she cried. Margaret [Long] said "Miss Minnie, you

A 1937 playbill for the Raleigh Little Theatre announced the first local performance of the 1927 Broadway hit Coquette.
BY PERMISSION OF SPECIAL COLLECTIONS AND ARCHIVES, GEORGE MASON UNIVERSITY LIBRARIES

know nothing could drag a tear out of hard-hearted Marjorie." . . . I noticed that Margie didn't deny having shed tears, however.

I expected to find Raleigh very bleak and wintry after the Azaleas and Camellias in Augusta, but my garden is full of flowers: paper white narcissus, little white Roman hyacinths, winter aconite and the Christmas rose just coming out, violets, enough pansies to make a splash of color, and tomorrow there will be daffodils . . . (or frost). Marjorie brought a friend, and had lunch in the garden today. Tomorrow . . . if it doesn't rain . . . I shall spend the day putting out the plants that I bought in Florida and Georgia, and collected off of friends and relatives. And tomorrow if it does rain I shall spend the day putting the plants out. The seeds have come from England. I shall plant a lot of them as soon as the ground is dry enough, and shall save some for you.

[January 31]

I think one of the most delightful things about you is the way you say "write to me" when I light one letter on the tail of another as if they were cigarettes, and I were out of matches. It makes me feel as Father said he did, when after five helpings of chicken, his hostess said: "Have some chicken, Mr. Lawrence."

I am accumulating things for you in two piles—one is things to read to you, a very exciting translation of the *Alcestis* which I borrowed for you from Uncle Jim (a present from his friend at Hartford, and I think it was enchanting for a scholarly old gentleman to be sending him an almost impressionistic translation), and some letters of George Moore about the writing of his last book, to a young man who is reading the manuscript for him. I thought you would be charmed with his querulous "Would an evening be possible? Must our meeting be always over teacups?" The other pile is things to discuss, such as counterpoint in poetry, and my sister Ann. The second pile is even more easily mislaid.

It is so nice to be home. I do not ever want to go away again.

Emily looked very skeptical when I told her that I would like to look for something in your desk drawer. I was delighted to be able to tell her that I found it at once, right on top. It is a pleasure to open your desk. It puts you in a class with Mrs. Sammel [an old family friend in Parkersburg, West Virginia]. Your room has the odor of your presence, and reminds me of

> And if the spirit be not there,
> Why is fragrance in the hair?

["Doubts," Rupert Brooke]

It is turning colder rapidly, and everything will be killed, probably including the plants from S. Georgia which I would bring because I was so eager to have them, although they told me to wait until spring. I couldn't believe it wasn't spring.

I hope the postmen didn't sit on the flowers before delivering them [to New York]. I thought it was useless to try to send you daffodils. The ones Bessie sent me at Brooks Hall always came in such a wilted and forlorn state and distressed me so. But I thought the shrubs might do better. . . .

Don't think you would be sitting in the sun in a flower-scented garden if you were at home. The weather has been very oppressive, not at all like those balmy winter days we had the first winter you were here, and it has poured rain practically every day for nearly two months. As much rain as there was snow last year. On the other hand it is very lucky for you to have a mild winter in New York, and has probably saved you from being sick. . . .

[February 15]

. . . One day there is ice on the pool, and the next it is so warm that we can lunch out. But the flowers do not seem to be hurt, and everything blooms along as if it were March—Miss Ellen's starry magnolia, and the purple leafed plum, and the silver bells. Today when I heard the children playing games in the street, and the whir of the lawnmower and smelled freshly cut grass, I was convinced that it was mid-summer. . . .

It is interesting to see in the English magazines that they have had an unusually warm winter too, with all sorts of expected and unexpected things in bloom. Elaine Lady Bellew writes from Kilkenny, "I picked today (January 11) 24 varieties and made a delightful little spring garden in an open bowl of moss. . . . The mild weather here in Ireland is also responsible for the rambler roses all bursting into leaf which is sad, as the cold winds and frosts will check these later." She is a little ahead of me, I think I had 20 varieties on that day. It is interesting, too, that both lists include violets, snow drops, violas, winter aconite, *Jasminum nudiflorum*, polyanthus, narcissus, the Christmas rose; and that she had *Iris stylosa* which we usually have at this time.

[March 2]

You were very sweet, dear Ann, to take so much trouble with the outline. I went to work with the scissors and a box of pins and moved the paragraphs around as you suggested. I had three left over. These I rolled into one and neatly inserted between the two halves. I don't think they interrupt. I am sorry to be so muddled. It wasn't carelessness. I really did struggle. I will never learn not to try to say everything all at once. You were right about its being too much material for one article. I see that now. . . . You are so satisfactory. . . .

[March 8]

Here, it is the time of year I hate most. Dull, cold, rainy weather, and not really spring when everything is in bloom and you feel it should be spring. Bessie and I went out to Mr. Tong's yesterday, and he said, "Elizabeth, do you know what Mrs. Moor [unidentified] calls me? She calls me the groundhog. She says every morning I go out to see what the weather is like, and if I don't like it I go back in, and stay in." He was disgusted with me for not getting to a very wonderful lecture in Henderson [North Carolina], an English woman who lives in California, and is one of the best lecturers on rock garden material. "But Elizabeth, there wasn't a person there who knows what she was talking about. It went right over their heads," he chuckled and made a sweeping gesture. "They couldn't even understand the names of things."

I hope you were listening to the concert Sunday. I went to the Busbees', thereby incurring the displeasure of Margie and

Bessie, who had settled down to spend the afternoon reading. I thought I had never heard anything lovelier. And it was so peaceful, just me and the Busbees, Miss Isabel cutting flower pictures from catalogues, and Miss Toose sorting, and Miss Sophie and me sewing. The way to listen to such music. We cut off the second half of the program, and had tea. . . .

I have three new friends this winter, all of them very old and very young. One is Margie's "Auntie" who is staying in Chapel Hill with Mrs. [Jennie] Toy,[26] and doing work in the library. She is a New England spinster minus all of the sharp qualities, and plus all of the gracious qualities that we like to think of as southern. Another is Miss Hall . . . who spends the winters with Mrs. Hunter, and is very distressed that the spring is so early as she has many visits to make on her way North, and must get back to "greet her blossoming cherry tree." I thought she liked me, as I had put myself out to be charming to her, but discovered it is the dogs she comes to see. She said: "But even I, dog lover that I am, had to remonstrate when I saw a very dirty little dog on the street kissing a nice clean baby. I think that is going too far." I am sure that you will agree with her.

The third is very, very old. It is he who told me about the plant geography, "but it is in German." I said, "But I have a friend who will read it to me." "But it is very technical, some of the words aren't in the dictionary." "But my friend knows a German professor." "You are very fortunate," he said wistfully. "Here, there is no one who knows more than I do." Still, it is a consolation to find a person who knows less. He said he would always be glad to talk to me. "I don't like," he said, "to talk to people who want to tell me, but I am glad to talk to you."

---

[26] The widow of University of North Carolina German professor Walter Toy; she lived on West Franklin Street.

Sunday

I went to take Elizabeth [Ann Bridgers's niece] her book. She seemed delighted to get it, and very glad to see me which pleased me no end. She is in the pink, and was adorable.

I went to the Bridgers to borrow the garden hose and Mrs. Bridgers said: "Did you know Ann is coming home?" And I said, "Is she really?" And Mrs. B. said, with surprise, "Why of course; she said she was." I haven't many hopes, but pray that it is true (if you are ready to come)

> . . . that I may forget
> These matters that with myself I too much discuss
> Too much explain

["Ash Wednesday," T. S. Eliot]

I sat in [sister] Ann's room at the open window and heard a weak croak and a splash which was the first appearance of the bullfrog and the first of spring. Also there is beginning to be a pale green, or a red haze about some trees. And a purple shadow on the hills.

My garden is denuded and uprooted. Denuded because the hedge man persuaded me to let him cut the hedge down to a few sticks the way the colored man cut yours, and uprooted because there is always something to be changed. I don't know why people always say they do not like a garden that is finished. I should love a garden that is finished, and not always under construction like the streets of New York.

You have hyacinths in two colors. I hope they last to greet you. I am afraid the wallflower was one of my worst ideas. We must discuss that. My ideas about color are changing rapidly. Everything about me changes rapidly. I wish it wouldn't.

Margie was able to get the out-of-print color chart [Robert Ridgway's *Color Standards*] for me. I had not thought of its being beautiful. The colors are on gray mats. Bessie and I match flowers by the hour. We are enchanted. Bessie is wonderful. She has a very good eye. As good as Ann's ear. I wish I had an eye and an ear.

[July 20]
Saturday

I have been soaking up this magnificent heat which has penetrated my marrow, and baked out the rheumatism. I think I have been previously a salamander. I only feel myself when I get really warmed up. Emily has fallen back upon my company since the majority have fled from, or been prostrated by the heat. She and Mrs. Bridgers sit in the garden and water, and one night Jonathan [Daniels, young Elizabeth's father] came. I had never seen Jonathan with the Bridgerses before and it was as delightful as you said. I particularly relished the [story of a] man whose death gave universal satisfaction. It is at those moments that I wish for Nana. Did they write you about the way they made him sit on a stool, and he said he couldn't do it with a lap full of stomach, and he kept groaning and begging Emily and Mrs. Bridgers to give him their chairs? And the plumber he routed by answering the door in his shorts. Can't you see Jonathan in shorts and those glasses? This was brought on by Emily's criticizing Paul Green [North Carolina playwright and family friend] for having his picture taken in shorts, and Jonathan said he had just had his taken in his bathing suit, which couldn't be seen as it was under the table. Emily said I suppose in the next picture you were under the table.

Do you remember Norf [Norfleet Webb], the wistful boy who is in charge of the Duke gardens (I think he is your cousin), the day we took the daffodil pictures? I wrote to ask him about a vine at Duke, and he wrote back the saddest little note saying that the garden is all to be torn up and done over by Mrs. Shipman. It is to be planted in trees and shrubs, and a formal garden back of it with "stone walks walls and terraces." He adds, "It is awfully hard to have to tear up something that you have worked on for three years just when you are beginning to see the fruits of your labors."

We had a sad little note from Madame[27] today, too: "*La vie est en France difficile et très chère, on se fatigue plus qu'autrefois parce qu'il faut faire plus de choses*" ["Life in France is difficult and very expensive; we get tired more than we used to because we have more things to do"].

I had an awful moment the other day. I was snooping in your flower bed pulling up cleomes that were pink, and Mrs. Bridgers caught me. Mrs. Bridgers said she didn't know why it was, but the colors of the flowers at the church were so awful, and the ones she took were so beautiful. She said, "You know, anything you pick out of that bed and put together is pretty." Emily laughed and said it wasn't funny at all when Ann and Elizabeth spent hours working on the colors. I said, "Well, Emily, I know you hate to admit that any of our activities have proved anything but futile." She laughed and said, yes, she hated to admit it but it was so.

---

[27] Perhaps a woman in Paris Ann Lawrence had boarded with during her junior year abroad at the Sorbonne.

Monday

Michael and I have just walked around the corner to post a letter to my sister Ann. Do you always find a special charm in posting letters? A sudden feeling of communication with the person you have written to, as you drop it in the box. A physical feeling. (Ellen would say what other kinds of feelings are there? But there are other kinds.) Much more than in writing it. When you write a letter you are thinking much more of yourself than of the person you are writing to. Sometimes I think up letters to write, just for the fun of walking with Michael to the station to post them. And I have never been able to figure out why it is no fun to walk to the station without a letter to post. And I always prefer to post letters at night. But then everything is heightened after dark.

Bessie has fallen down the steps in the dark, and fractured her toe. And covered herself with bruises. I knew something was going to happen. Two peaceful weeks was too much. But I got a lot done in the garden, and my files in order, and magazines caught up with, and material organized, and an article written. I never had two uninterrupted weeks before. There is nothing I love like the summer. In winter my fingers are always so cold that typing is misery. In summer I only get called to the phone on an average of twice a day. And fewer people about. Almost none. And with Aunt Elizabeth to go to market with Bessie I could get to work by nine. I hadn't meant to bother you with the article. I have read very scathing remarks lately about the people who use small letters for all specific names, and Billy [Hunt, Chapel Hill gardener] is against it as a slovenly practice (Billy is a stickler for form), and I have decided to abandon it as you will see. But the system doesn't make sense. Rosa bracteata for a rose having bracts, and Rosa Banksiae for a rose named for Lady Banks, is all right, but wouldn't you think it would be a capital *C* for Rosa cathayensis, a rose from Cathay? But no geographical names get capitals, only those named for people. I think all small letters is really better. I didn't realize how much material I had collected this year, and I sat down and wrote without thinking how long it was, and before I came to, I had nearer 6,000 words than the less than 3,000, which Mr. [Robert] Lemmon[28] wants. Then it was a mess to rewrite it leaving out over half of it. So tell me if it sounds as if that has been done.

Billy and his henchman and a professional camera arrived this afternoon to take pictures of the plant that I have been calling Amaryllis belladonna all this time, and had begun this spring to suspect. I telegraphed Billy that it was in bloom and he came over and pronounced it *Lycoris squamigera* var. *purpurea*. He had never seen it before and had a fit. Any one would: six iridescent pale lilac lilies in a circle on top of a tapering applegreen stem. He picked it (it has no foliage) and stuck it back in the ground where there was sun and picked the silver foliage of the artemisia for a background with some deeper pink phlox showing through. He said a deeper color made a better composition, when the picture is black and white. They took both black and white and color pictures. I asked the photographer if he thought they would turn out, and he said yes, he and Billy went all over the state together taking flower pictures and they never failed. He worked with Mrs. [Bayard] Wootten[29] for

---

[28] Editor of *Real Gardener* and other gardening magazines.

[29] Well-known North Carolina portrait photographer who had moved her studio from New Bern to Chapel Hill.

six years. He has hazel eyes and a nice voice. He says he does not ordinarily do developing and printing, but would do it for me. But of course I never argue with Billy. In fact I try not to argue with anyone who doesn't listen, and that leaves me only you to argue with.

[July 23]

I was practically sitting at my desk wishing for a fig vine when it came. It is not supposed to be hardy here, but I wanted to try it anyway, though everyone says there is no chance of its living through the winter. I tried to get someone to give me one when I was in South Georgia last winter, and everyone said she would, but no one did, and I came back without it. I put it on the wall of your house by the window that we are to have the seed bed in; that is frightfully dry, but the warmest and sunniest exposure either of us has. Then I put it at the foot of the wall to your rose garden. Because that is damper, and protected, but it is shady. Then, I put it in my new stone steps and by the pool, and by the summerhouse (not having any bricks) and against our house foundation, but that is both dry and shady. I don't see why it shouldn't climb on wood, but I can't ever remember having seen it do so; anyway we will find out what it does. Mabel [Mrs. Bridgers's worker] was very much excited when I told her that Miss Ann had sent it from Charleston. She promised to cover and uncover it and some small zinnias that I stuck in the bed, and to see that they didn't dry up. Mrs. Bridgers promised, too. I think she is a more faithful gardener than you are.

Bessie is still in bed and very sore, but takes it very cheerfully. This in marked contrast to Michael, who has mashed his paw, and preys on the sympathies of Bessie, Page, and me. He comes and leans against us and holds up his paw, and looks pitiful. Then he sees a cat and pounds off on all fours.

[September 2]

You are very sweet to take so much trouble with me. It mortifies me to continue to be so disorganized in spite of your help. The article is supposed to be about night-blooming flowers, but that sounded prosaic so I changed it to "Gardens at Night," and added white flowers. The part about a night garden just got in somehow, but is now out. I also cut out all of the tender bulbs. I didn't realize until I had got it written how much of the material will do for the Mid-South. So I will save the tender bulbs and use them in an article for Mr. Lemmon, writing it from the point of view of a night garden for hot summer weather, as you suggest. I cut the weather out of this too, and I am struggling to be more expansive about what is left. But you know it bores me to be expansive, and I do not like to be bored while writing. . . .

Bessie and I went to Chapel Hill to spend the night with Luce, who is holding the fort while Paul and Elizabeth [Green] are away.[30] . . . You turn off of the highway onto a straight mile and a quarter of road through thick woods that brush the sides of the car. At the end is the house, in a clearing, with two enormous trees, and a drop behind, and chickens, guineas

---

[30] "Luce" was Lucy Lay Zuber, sister of Elizabeth Lay Green. Both attended St. Mary's School, where their father was rector. Elizabeth Lay married Paul Green, a North Carolina playwright who won the 1927 Pulitzer Prize in drama for *In Abraham's Bosom*, which depicted the plight of the American Negro in the South.

and ducks meandering. The house is white outside, pine inside, with wrought iron candlesticks and lots of flowers in pottery, and the *Red Fairy Book* on the telephone table, and disorder, but plenty of cleared spaces to read in. Elizabeth raises flowers and vegetables in addition to the children, arranges the flowers and children, does the first draft of all of Paul's work from a Dictaphone, entertains frequently, and keeps her temper. Besides jumping when Paul says jump. . . .

I have been sitting on the steps listening to the crickets, and staring at the moon, and smoking cigarettes which I didn't want, because Aunt Elizabeth left me a carton as a parting gift, and thinking on sorrow. It isn't that I enjoy taking a gloomy view (as you accuse me of doing) but that I think. Most of the things that matter are sad. Then you have either got to not let them matter, or be sad. Nette [sister Ann], if an important thing makes her sad, puts it out of her mind, and replaces it with something less important which doesn't make her sad. But she isn't really any happier. You let the sad things stay, but pretend they are outnumbered. You aren't any happier either.

[September 7]

I took advantage of a change of lodgers[31] to slip in to the red room to get the volume of Greek plays. And met Uncle Jim at 5:45 A.M. full of the *Antigone*.[32] He had sat up all night on

---

[31] The Lawrences usually rented out several rooms in the basement of their house.

[32] Uncle Jim read *Antigone* aloud to Bracelen Flood, Ellen's son, who was spending the summer with him in Americus, Georgia, while clearing brush for the local REA power lines. Uncle Jim was rector at St. James' Episcopal Church in Americus.

the day coach as he could save almost enough to buy the French Academy's new dictionary, and looked somewhat worn, but a cup of coffee reinforced with Scotch restored him completely, and he started in to repeat choruses from the *Antigone*, which was an extremely fortunate enthusiasm on my part (I am not usually apt with Uncle Jim) as he has recently been memorizing it while he shaves: "Blest are they whose days have not tasted of evil. For when a house hath once been shaken from heaven there the curse falls evermore, passing from life to life of the race" which, he said, is the same as "the sins of the fathers are visited upon the children unto the third and fourth generation." And did the Greek have any meaning to me? It did. What looks so alien on the page sounds like Latin. The poetry is as clear as English, and it is as beautiful to listen to as the Bible, which it is so like, and that is why this translation that sounds like the Bible is so in accord with the words. . . .

I said that I couldn't understand why the *Antigone* seems such a modern play, with superstition for a subject. He said the subject was the struggle between church and state, which seems to me no more vital. But Ismene and Antigone are the first real characters I have found in a Greek play;—even Alcestis when she is most touching is not a real person. But Ismene and Antigone are any two sisters who have everything in common except their temperaments. Then I asked why the Greeks ignored love as a theme for plays. He sputtered, "ignored love!" and quoted the chorus: "Love unconquered in the fight, Love, who makest havoc of wealth, who keepest thy vigil on the soft cheek of a maiden; . . . no immortal can escape thee, nor any among men whose life is for a day; and he to whom thou hast come is mad."

And I laughed and said that isn't love, not the love that says

"Believe me, love, it was the nightingale." . . .

Mrs. Thompson[33] died on Thursday which makes me very sad as she is my last friend of her generation, and we had so much in common, as how Bessie and Cora would put paper bags in the refrigerator, and how Bessie and Elizabeth would not let us prune properly, and as how difficult it is to find fine needles with big eyes, and how no one else really appreciated fine needles and small stitches. There is still Mrs. Hunter, but that makes me sadder still, because she looks like Nana, and is so weak that when I go to see her she can only cry although she tries hard not to and tells me gaily about how she fell in love with Dr. Hunter without meaning to at all, because she was years older, and thought of herself as his Mother.

[Late October]

I went to the Busbees' this afternoon for the first Philharmonic. It is so peaceful lying on the couch with my eyes closed, with Miss Toose and Miss Isabel and Miss Sophie sitting in a row with their sewing, and knowing that they are not going to speak. I think I might as well move around, with operas on Saturday afternoon, and Toscanini Saturday night, and the Philharmonic Sunday night. I always hope you are listening if it is what I like, and especially this afternoon as I wanted to know if the second movement of the Seventh Symphony is a saraband. I think next to the Ninth it is my favorite. Then they said they would make me tea, and I said no, I must go, and then stood for an hour in the door talking on sympathetic subjects,

---

[33] Sallie J. Ellington Thompson, age eighty-two, the mother of Lillian, Elizabeth, and Daisy Thompson.

such as the best place to get manure and what operas we want Mr. Johnson to give this winter.

I have a new friend. She is Elizabeth Rawlinson who edits *Garden Gossip* and who is the best garden writer to my way of thinking. I brought her home with me from the garden school at Winston-Salem [North Carolina] to spend the night, and wondered when I got her here why I had thought she would want to come. She is very homely and shy and difficult and just when you are getting along she suddenly gets difficult, and just when you are about to give up she is responsive again. We have the same ideas and problems about everything and make fun of the same people. Violet [Walker, garden correspondent and member of the Virginia Garden Club of America] was at the school too, and gave a grand talk on lilies, but we hadn't any chance to talk. But she promises to come to see us.

I have a feeling that you are going to come home about the time I take off for New York. Bessie and I are going to spend Christmas there, and I am going sooner to see Ellen and look up [information about] Lily Turfs [ground cover]. Ann says the other girls will be gone and she can have Bessie, and I will stay with Ellen. Ellen couldn't come this fall. We expected her daily, but she wrote that there were complications about the children and Jack. Ann says that she is so happy in her new apartment, and that she is the only happy person she knows.

This is a terrible letter, but it is so late, and the house is so cold and I am numb. I could not write to you because I write only of myself and I am sick of myself. I have been feeling the way I tell you not to mind feeling as it will not last, but of course you don't believe that when you tell it to yourself and this time it seems to be going on indefinitely, only lifting a moment when I suddenly stopped planting and sat down in the sun to read an article in one of the English magazines about [Dante's] Paolo and Francesca. And was gone before I could get it on paper.

[October 26]

Turk and I went to call on Emily and Mrs. Bridgers this afternoon, but they were not at home so we went out to look at your garden, and found a pet rabbit. I am pleased with your garden. The cassia has been in bloom for a month, and is still lovely. The orange flare cosmos is still gay but spent, the blue of the ageratum and salvia is lovely with the orange. The plant that someone gave you and we didn't know, seems to be a summer chrysanthemum. It is just beginning to bloom, and has white daisies. The second crop of sweet alyssum is coming, but the other seeds I planted never appeared. And the October marigolds seem to have been crowded out. That is my chief disappointment. They make such pretty fresh foliage. The crotalaria definitely does not do if the beds are covered with peat moss. These last two years have proved it. I planted it all over the back border, and it only grew where I hadn't put any peat moss. This is a problem. The crotalaria won't germinate until after the time to put peat moss on, and won't grow in peat moss, and I must have peat moss. Both of your fig vines are taking hold. Only one of the five I planted out is left, and it is barely left. The Autumn Glory is in its glory.

[Fall]

. . . I was trying to decide this morning while I pulled chickweed, why you love flowers more than I do—more than anyone I ever knew, and why I feel that you should have all of the flowers that are to be had. I decided that flowers appeal to me intellectually. I always think of them as plant material—a good early narcissus, or a yellow rose with nice foliage—and aesthetically—color—marking or form; while you like them for themselves because they are flowers, because they grow out of the earth, because they are fragile, because they are beautiful. And that is what I meant when I said you are a mystic. It is a spiritual quality. By spiritual I mean not intellectual, but not emotional (Santayana's definition is delightful but it is not what I mean by spiritual). You love people for themselves. That is spiritual. I love people for what they are to me. That is emotional, and inferior. Maybe mystic is the wrong word, but what I mean by a mystic is a person who enters into what he worships. A person who is not a mystic makes what he worships a part of himself. You can see how inferior that is.

[October 28]

I would like you to know how well I appreciate you. I never file a card without a grateful feeling. When I think of my confusion, and the notes in old mountains of paper that mostly got lost, I shudder to think what I would have done without you—and I would never have thought out a system for myself—and I couldn't do anything in the way of organizing plant material without one. The psychologists who said you are what you want to be, are all wrong, because no one hates being stupid and confused more than I do, or gets more satisfaction out of order.

Ann was at work on a play based on the life of John C. Calhoun, traveling to his home in Clemson, South Carolina, for research and sending drafts to Emily and Elizabeth. She spent many years researching and writing the play but never found a publisher for it, though apparently it was given a reading in Chapel Hill. She also went to New York for the theatre season and wrote about what she was seeing for the Raleigh Times *and the* News & Observer. *She was there for three weeks, returning to Raleigh for the Christmas holiday. Meanwhile, Elizabeth was going to New York to visit Ellen Flood.*

[December 1]

I dreamt that I was dancing in a room filled with music, and the dance was a cradle song. I could feel that the positions of my body were right and a perfect expression of the music, and I thought: I shall never be able to explain this to Ann, and I shall never be able to do it again. Then one of the dogs barked and shifted me to another sphere of consciousness, and I thought that it was not a cradle song, but a new born child feeling all of the possible positions of the body. (By breakfast time I remembered that that was something that you had told me.) . . .

It worries me not to be able to tell you how deeply I feel that Calhoun lives again. I have never felt it before about an historical character which is why I have never been very deeply moved by historical plays or novels. St. Joan is a perfect example. She is an exciting and living character, but she is Shaw's creation. I never think of her as Joan of Arc, even though the words are all words that she said. I don't think of Calhoun as your Calhoun, but as Calhoun. I was thinking as I cut back the herbs, and burned their fragrant tops how nice that you are interested in gardens too. You might so easily not be. And if you were any less interested you could never make time for it at all.

When we were decorating the church for Thanksgiving Miss Kate Moore turned to me suddenly when we were tying up sheaves of wheat, and said: "Elizabeth, you remind me so much of your grandmother." When I looked surprised, she said "not in looks, in manner" which I thought even less likely. But the sudden warm picture of Nana which her tone of voice created made me glow for days.

[December 5]

I think I shall come to New York the end of next week, if I can get Bessie settled, and if nothing else turns up about the house—The boys have been back at us with fresh propositions, and have us both suicidal, but I hope we are through with them now. I sat in my window watching the snow melt from the trees, and thought that nothing in our new house will be as nice as that window to work in.[34]

[Well-known Raleigh gardener] Isabelle Henderson came up to me at the garden club tea and commented upon my

---

[34] "The boys" may be tenants or North Carolina State students, but it is unclear what "new house" Elizabeth alludes to. Perhaps she already is thinking of the design for the house built in Charlotte in 1949.

appearance (than which nothing can be more annoying when one's dress is torn, faded, and inappropriate) and mentioned for the second time that she read my articles in *House & Garden*, and was charmed with my whimsies.

Nevertheless I prefer warm hands to a warm heart.

[December 14, on the train to New York City]

A whole day on the train is as long and as hurried as night. I think it is because you can only sit that it is elastic. When there is a possibility of doing more than one thing time shrinks.

The sun just up lights the frost fronds on the windowpanes, but people scratch them with their finger nails to see the names on the stations.

At Ellen's

When I got out of the elevator this morning to go to church, a smart and lovely young person sitting on the bench in the lobby rose to meet me: my sister Ann. We went to the Church of the Heavenly Rest. The Psalm for today was so beautiful. It said: "They were afraid where no fear was."

I always feel as you do, even if I don't know it. Last night we went straight to a cocktail party from the train, and when I got here, and the children came running to throw themselves on me, I could not bear smelling of gin. Did you ever see anything like the change that has come over the children? They are so darling, and so good. . . .

Ann de Treville Lawrence was Elizabeth's younger sister. After spending her junior year in Paris and graduating from the University of North Carolina, Ann lived in New York City and worked as a personal shopper at Macy's.
BY PERMISSION OF WARREN WAY AND ELIZABETH WAY ROGERS

1938

[January 1, at Ellen's]

At dinner Mr. Bracelen held forth as usual on the subject of the blunders of the administration. When he had finished, Ann turned to Ellen, and said that her beau who was coming from California for Christmas had been stopped by the arm of the law just as he was boarding a plane—something political that I couldn't follow—but I said, "All Mr. Roosevelt's fault, no doubt." Mr. Bracelen looked up in surprise, and then threw back his head, and laughed and laughed and laughed. Then he said, "I've been waiting over a week now to see what Libba would say and when."

This morning Ellen spent at the hairdresser, and I spent

with the children. First I helped Mary Ellen with her Christmas cards. . . . Saturday morning, the children, Ellen, Mr. Bracelen and I went to the children's concert at Carnegie Hall. . . . This morning I searched Ellen's dance records, and found one minuet, a darling one, and taught it to the children to do for Bessie for Christmas. . . . We had fun, and interested children are angelic. But I can never play with children unless I have them all alone.

. . . You had better use the house. You should appreciate a whole house—not even dogs—and I shall have to stay here an extra week, if not two. Bessie will not go home. I am so anxious to get back to my garden. Did the Christmas rose bloom? the new flowering apricot? pansies? violets? Will you make a list? It is so temperate here that I think Raleigh must be spring-like. And I am so anxious to get to work on more articles. I did not mean to sound horrid about Bessie. She has not had as long here as I have. And she has no reason to go home. . . .

Later

The New York Botanical Garden Library surpasses my wildest expectations. You can go right into the books, even the ones in offices where the Botanic Garden people are working. The librarians go to no end of trouble to find things, and to make you comfortable. . . . I haven't yet to ask for a book without having it handed over to me. Only I get so excited I can hardly read there, only it doesn't open until ten, and I have to leave by two to get back to engagements, and so far have only been able to go twice. It takes an hour to get there, but once there I don't have to waste one second.

Bessie is having such a good time that it is a pleasure to look at her.

[January 7, at Ellen's]

What a great relief to Bessie and me to know that you are in the house, and I had been resistant at the thought of sending the dogs to Mr. Wright [the vet]. They cannot bear to be shut up. Nevertheless I laugh whenever I think of you and the dogs—and then I cannot bear not to be there with you. It is too ironic, and then I am so glad for you to be there. Bessie takes great pleasure in it. She said, "I like to think that my house is open to my friends even if I am not there." Nothing you ever said delighted her so much as your telephone [call].

We are having such a happy time. One of Bessie's old friends came up from Baltimore to spend today with her, and her daughter, who is my friend, and is married and lives in New Jersey, and Ellen and I. We had lunch at Ann's apartment, and Bessie took both her friend's hands and said, "Oh, Catherine, I feel as if I had found something I had lost." It wasn't just seeing her friend again. It was Parkersburg [West Virginia] and before she was married and all of her friends and picnics on the [Ohio] River. . . .

[April 30, Raleigh]
Friday night

I cannot bear for you to be away on your birthday [May 1]. You never have. I love May Day, and I always lacked an excuse to rise early and pick flowers in the dew. I have always dreaded my birthday due to some long since forgotten but still strongly felt episode of childhood. I love yours. . . .

I am hoping to get down to Jugtown this week to see Mr. Busbee's wonderful collection of Delta iris, which should be in bloom. When I was there before Mrs. Busbee gave him the afternoon off (she minded the shop)[35] to talk about them, and we crawled in ecstasy among three-inch shoots that all looked like the same kind of grass, and he said, gloating, "This is *alba spiritus* [unidentified] and this is *astrosanguinea*." But it would be nice to see them in bloom. But it is like playing with explosives to get Bessie and Mr. Jacques Busbee together. I was in misery all day. . . .

I wish I were going with you [to Washington, D.C.], not that I would with buds of *Talinum calycinum*. I am aching to get at a library. And I would love to go with you to the Phillips Gallery, which is my favorite one anywhere, and the Freer, and to see my old friend at the Park Book Shop. . . .

[May 2]
Sunday

I hope that your birthday has been as unbearably beautiful there as here and that you have been sitting in the sun at the

---

[35] Jacques Busbee, brother of Elizabeth's friends in Raleigh, and Julianna Busbee had gone to Seagrove in the North Carolina Piedmont in 1917 to focus regional and national attention on the old pottery industry, which was languishing. After getting things going again, the Busbees marketed North Carolina pots in a tearoom Julianna opened in New York's Washington Square. They moved permanently to Seagrove, established Jugtown Pottery in 1921, and supervised the building of a shop and then a log cabin for themselves. The community of many potters thrives today.

Lincoln Memorial, as I have been thinking of you as doing, and with the expression in your eyes that I hope is there.

This morning I said, "Margaret, don't be so cross," "Billy [a servant], what is the matter with you today?" "Willa Bell [a servant], you must have got out of the wrong side of the bed," until Billy sadly said, "Miss Lawrence, there is something wrong with everyone but you this morning." I looked at her sharply, and when I saw there was no sarcasm, I said, guiltily, "I am afraid it's wrong only with me, Billy." . . .

You can tell what to expect from the paper (and the time of day). Ten cents store paper means that I have nothing to say, and am consumed with the need to write to you. This is the 1,000 page novel mood of which you should be wary. But needn't be too wary as I cannot have these moods long, having inherited it [the paper] from my father's office supplies, and it is nearly gone. Margie and Bessie are sleeping away this beautiful afternoon that will not come again. Isn't one of the things that amuse you most the superiority people who don't sleep assume over those who do? I have often come down to breakfast in a stupor and looked at the rest of the family who were rested and alert, and thought, "You clods, you stones, you worse than senseless things."

. . . Last night I put on my bathrobe, and lit the fire and stretched out an automobile rug, and sat waiting for ten to turn on the radio; and it was going by daylight saving and the Beethoven was over, and a wretched something begun. Nine is a horrid hour.

Heath [Long][36] and Jimmie [Beckwith] appeared while we were having tea on the steps. Have you seen the plans for the

---

[36] Active board member and second president of the Raleigh Little Theatre, who worked closely with Ann Bridgers and Cantey Sutton to found the theatre. She married James Payne Beckwith in 1939.

theatre? Heath says she likes them, and that Mr. Dietrick calls them "Egyptian" for the sake of the people who are put off by anything modern, which is what it really is.[37] You will like Mr. Deitrick. I begin to feel very much excited.

[May]

We had a grand day at Jugtown. Mr. Busbee and I went out into his blazing garden under Japanese umbrellas and picked the Iris and brought them into the cool twilight of the cabin to discuss. Mrs. Busbee had gray stone jars full of mountain laurel, and cool things to drink. I don't know how she gets ice out there. Mr. Busbee was in a mellow mood and so was Bessie— and the exchange of easy, sparkling and timely wit that goes on between the two Busbees at meals is something rare and delightful. I tried to remember some of the conversation to tell you but it is the kind that melts like snow. It is drinking from a deep well to be with two people who are so perfectly matched and utterly content with their lives and their work. . . .

I am [part] of a committee to wait upon Mrs. [Cantey] Sutton in the running to decide whether the Garden Club is to take over the formal garden (if any) for the Little Theatre. . . . If I have to see much more of Mrs. Sutton I shall be in Dix Hill.[38]

---

[37] After two years of performances in other places and protracted discussions between Federal Theatre bureaucrats and Raleigh Little Theatre volunteers, plans for the new building were designed by architect William Henry Deitrick. A WPA grant paid the major portion of the $139,056 cost. Mrs. Cantey Sutton was credited with raising more than $40,000 in local gifts. The building and amphitheatre, located on Pogue Street on the old fairground site provided by the city of Raleigh, were dedicated September 12, 1940.

[38] The state mental hospital in Raleigh, named for Dorothea Dix. Elizabeth, a poor speller and a better wit, wrote, "Dick's Hill."

[June 7]

It has troubled me for a long time that once, when I started to tell you about something you wanted to read, you said, very bitterly, "Don't tell me, you will try to make me like it."

I never mean—ever—to try to make you (or anyone) like anything that is unsympathetic to you. I have too much respect for your integrity. Things I think you won't like, I don't mention. They aren't many! But sometimes, I make mistakes, which seems a pity. Things I think you would like I never read of, see, feel, or even taste without wanting to share them. But I never mean, or even want, to force my taste upon you, only to share my pleasures. . . . But I cannot believe that loving "when I love thee not, chaos comes again" [Shakespeare's *Othello*]; you would not love "so are you to my thoughts, as food to life/or as sweet-seasoned showers to the ground,/and for the peace of you I hold such strife/as 'twixt a miser and his wealth is found" [Shakespeare sonnet 75].

[July 25]

I went over to snip back the phlox, petunias, and cosmos the day after you left, and had a conversation with Pearl [the Bridgers family's housekeeper] through the kitchen window. I asked her if she weren't lonesome, and she said, no, she was too busy. "But you miss Miss Ann, don't you?"

I have been reading Horace, Calhoun, and American history. Calhoun has sent me back to the history, which never seemed real before. And having read enough to follow the development of the ideas of the play somewhat, I can better appreciate the skill with which they are balanced by the emotional sweep of the play. And I realize more and more how vital the issues are today, more even than then, don't you think? I shiver to think how many people must be as unaware as I am of American history and the ideals of democracy, and how much our future depends upon their being foremost in our minds and hearts. . . .

August 21

Epistle to Ann
(upon her retiring to the mountains, leaving me with a copy of Calhoun)

Haec tibi dictabam post fanum putre Vacunae,
Excepto, quod non simul esses, caetera laetus.[39]

[Horace epistle 1.10]

Dear Ann, I long have wanted to
Attempt this form addressed to you:
For models having drawn upon
The works of Horace, Keats, and Donne,
And those of Burns which Nana knew
By heart, and introduced me to.
I find them all affectionate,
Simple, sincere, and intimate.
Unwittingly the poet paints
His own self-portrait, and acquaints
The reader with the character
Of him to whom he would refer

---

[39] "I am dictating this for you beyond the crumbling shrine of Vacuna [a Sabine goddess],/Except for the fact that you are not with me, otherwise happy."

His problems, his philosophy,
Ambition and adversity.
Epistles in this form occur
In ancient poetry, and were
(It has been pointed out to us)
Adopted by Theocritus;
While sullen Sappho was another
To use them to berate her brother.
However, Horace was the first
To write his letters out in verse.
He crystallized the form, and found
The perfect blend of the profound
And grave, the playful and ironic:
A Style both lively and laconic.
He liked to slight the town, and praise
The excellence of country ways.
Donne, like Horace, would exhort
His friends not only to resort
To some untroubled country scene,
But in themselves to be serene.
And Keats would lessen his despair
By writing verse as light as air,
And to his reverie commend
His brother George, or George his friend.

The letter writer's common vice
Appears to be to give advice:
Herein I offer none, but do
Repeat what I have learned from you,
Commanding you, as Burns was use,
His "daintie davie," to the Muse.
And thank you, now that you have gone,
But having left me not alone.

[October 12]

I went over and planted some golden asters in your garden this afternoon. I have been looking for the low yellow plant for fall that you said you wanted, and I think this is it. It is about a foot high, covered with small yellow composite flowers in September and October. I think it will be permanent, and will spread. My friend, Mr. King, got it for me in the fields, is still in bloom and is a lovely bright splash in the edge, but the gold aster should be something that you won't have to remember to sow. The lilies I planted have made bright green rosettes. I did a little trimming and weeding, and was overcome by the effect. The Autumn Glory is tall and sturdy and full of bloom. There is some bloom on the cassia still, and a couple of those same daylilies that have been in bloom all summer. That is one of the most remarkable things I ever heard of—alyssum. The alyssum that we sowed before you left is very fresh and pretty. That border is really, really remarkable for having something always in bloom.

Mr. Luns[40] says I can relax now, and needn't read the papers, as there won't be a war until spring. Did you know that there is a season for wars? It seems they only start them in spring and fall.

---

[40] William Lunsford "Luns" Long, married to the handsome Rosa Arrington Heath Long, known as "Miss Rosa." He was the fourth child of Bettie Gray Mason Long (known as "Gran") and Lemuel McKinne Long, who died young. Luns Long served as a young man in the North Carolina General Assembly and was known as a progressive interested in the arts and humanities.

1939

[April 5]

Your May pole is still in the chest wrapped in tissue paper. I am sorry it is not to come out for May Day, and that Bessie and I will not be with you. We will think of you and be grateful to the day [May 1, Ann's forty-eighth birthday]. And picture you on that mountainside where we sat one afternoon under the apple trees.

I went to St. Mary's to see the play so I could tell you about it. Even with those badly trained girls in all that cheese cloth on that tiny stage, and speaking in Miss Davis's best elocutionary manner,[41] they caught an unbelievable amount of the quality of Hanya Holm's dances.[42] The poetry was as lovely as some of Yeats, and their voices rose and fell like wind in the pines and the sound of the sea, and had the same quick and slow, and pulsing rhythm of Hanya Holm's percussion instrument. . . .

I am very much ashamed of having spoken to you so unthinkingly of Mrs. Roosevelt's Peace Message. When Mr. Luns explained what it had already accomplished, I saw that I had been stupid. When people talk against Roosevelt you should go to Mr. Luns to have your heart warmed. I got him all to myself, and had a chance to ask him all of the questions that were assailing me from undigested magazine and newspaper reading. And when he had cleared them all up, he gave me two

---

[41] Florence C. Davis taught elocution and drama at St. Mary's from 1911 to 1957 and in 1939 directed the choric drama *Culbin Sands*.

[42] Holm (1903–1992) was a founder and teacher of American modern dance. She stressed feelings and ideas over technique.

copies of *Foreign Affairs*, and after reading them all night I am all muddled again.

Richard Urquhart came in with a clean shirt and his face shining with soap, and Mr. Luns said "Going out on the turf tonight, Richard?" Richard said he was. I said "Turf?" Mr. Luns said, "The race, you know. When I say 'the turf' Richard knows I mean Olivia Root."[43] Which is exactly like [Roman poet] Horace, who never mentions that love is over, but that the battle is won, or that having been shipwrecked he will go to sea no more. Do you know in New York two people who can answer questions better, or be more entertaining than Mr. Royster and Mr. Luns[44] in the provinces?

When Dr. Holt said that people seen once only may be most in your mind, I thought of your sister Elizabeth, who is often in my mind—not from talking to you, but from the night I went to return the vases and she came to the door. It was one of those wet spring nights when everything is sweet-smelling. I always think of her on wet spring nights, standing in the door, saying "You write poetry." I said, "No, you must be thinking of someone else!" And she said, "I am thinking of you." When I try to define the quality that made her unforgettable, standing there in the doorway, "outline" is the only word that I find in my mind. I have known only one other person whose outline was impressed upon me. Do you believe there are people who

---

[43] Mr. Luns liked to tease, as here when he alluded to young Richard's efforts to compete for Olivia's attention. Both young people belonged to Raleigh families well known to Mr. Luns and the Lawrences.

[44] Wilbur High Royster studied classics in Athens, Greece, at Harvard, and at UNC-Chapel Hill, where he taught Greek and Latin before retiring to run Royster Candy Company on Fayetteville Street in Raleigh. Luns Long studied Latin and Greek at Longview and at UNC-Chapel Hill, where he taught Greek to undergraduates while he was a law student.

have auras? When I heard that she was coming to live near us, I was delighted, and began to think of the things I would like to talk to her about, so that when she died I had a sense of loss as for a person I already knew well. And you came to live in the house instead.

[May 1]

If you are sure that it is a good idea, I will come up on the bus the first of the week, and come back with [a Raleigh acquaintance]. I don't feel altogether happy about it, because I think you ought to be left alone where you go away to yourself to write. And just the idea that a person's coming makes you unsettled—don't say it doesn't, because I know.

[May 1, Longview]
Tuesday

If you don't hear from me ever again you will know it is because I took it in to my head to ride horseback after not having been on a horse for over 10 years—and of course rode all afternoon. It is how the movements of childhood stay with you. Little Caroline [Long], the children's governess, Miss Jolly, a thin dark young thing, Mr. Mac and I started off on the four Longview horses, with Bill leading on his bicycle, his dog Dot, a black and white setter. Miss Jolly and I were going to ride again before breakfast if I can manage, my last time, to climb on the horse.

[May 3]

. . . This morning when Page [an employee] called me in to the phone before I had finished my breakfast, I came up to my room, and stood in the middle of the floor trying to unpack my bag so Lily [another employee] could have my soiled clothes. . . . Bessie was saying, "Minnie and Margaret [Long are coming] to supper, and if we have the Thompsons, too, it had better be just supper"; and I could feel my book lying in the next room with great holes in it that I have been trying to fill up all spring, and as fast as I begin to fill up one I see ahead, and have to go on, and that makes another hole; and I kept feeling that something was hacking at the back of my head, and I realized that William [an employee] instead of digging kudzu (which he hates to do) had taken the weed chopper and gone down to the wild flower garden, and the sound of it was cutting me [along] with the flowers; and I made several ineffectual movements toward extracting my half unpacked things from those Miss Minnie left strewn all over my room; and then I felt as if I were sitting on the terrace in the sun looking deep into the woods (which gives me much, much more feeling of distance than looking at far away mountain ranges), and that if I wanted to speak to you I could; and I felt time opening and shutting like a fan. Do you remember when we read that beautiful thing, you knew what it meant, and I didn't? I do now.

So I stopped William, and gave Lily the things, and settled Bessie, and the Thompsons (for the time being), and left all of my and Miss Minnie's things, and sat down to write to you. I tried to write last night after I went to bed, but I was too tired. I got off of the bus at the corner and two Boy Scouts carried my things. They appeared out of the darkness just as I was looking for someone. . . . There was a little one who carried the plants and a bigger one who carried the bag. They said they weren't at all heavy. Bessie and the Herberts had gone to the bus station to meet me. . . . By the time I . . . got to bed it was 1:30 A.M.

How would you like a red hat with your dress, dark red, a sort of wine? Maybe you could find one to match it? I think cream was wrong. Your first idea of something darker was right. It is too dark a shade to use anything lighter with. Or white. And be sure to have Blanche [Penland][45] get the hem straight. . . . It hasn't two even inches, and don't get any thinner. You are just right. And don't forget that you promised to rest. You were a different person after those afternoons.

Later

Don't worry about my room. I think it is going to be all right. Miss Minnie has worked out a way to make a passage through the cedar closet. She says Bessie is to sign a paper promising never to go through my room. Bessie is not amused.

I think you are going to love having me in the cellar. And I don't think I will be visited as much there. I am thinking a little of a key (two keys), but I don't think I could think behind a locked door.

Anyway, privacy is like time. It is inside. I never have those exaggerated ideas of my own powers except when I am with you, but it is a comfort the rest of the time, that at least I can imagine endless time and utter privacy as in my possession, even if I can't keep it up.

---

[45] Probably a local friend from among the Penland families well known in western North Carolina.

Half way down Black Mountain I remembered that I have a garden. It came to me as a shock. Like money in a pocketbook that has been put away for a long time.

June 5

By the time I got to the Little Theatre meeting the business part was over, so I did not see Betty Rose preside, which was what I went for. Three people pounced on me. . . . Heath [Long] said, "Is Ann very mad with me?" and Christine [Coffey],[46] "Did she get the books?" I felt as I used to when I came home to Nana, and she said, "What did they eat, who was there, what did they have on?" And I couldn't answer a question. Later, when I had gone by the station to tell Margaret good-bye, I at last got to your house, and Emily and Mrs. Bridgers wanted to know where the new spring is, in what beds and in what places you, Blanche [perhaps Blanche Botherton, a Smith College classmate, or Blanche Penland, a Weaverville neighbor], and I slept, and how much cover each had; and if any was left over, what we ate for every meal (I could answer that), how often we bathed and how. Emily said it was sheer affectation to bathe every day. I felt the strain of giving a full account and giving the impression you would want me to—not being exactly sure what that impression is. Emily was at her darlingest. There are times when I think she loves you as much as I do.

Elizabeth had been over here to get tadpoles out of the pool,[47] with the idea of raising them into frogs whose legs

---

[46] Christine Coffey worked at the North Carolina State College library and sometimes boarded with the Bridgers family.

would be sold for 75¢ per pr. Margie discouraged the undertaking by saying that it would be three years before the legs could be eaten.

[June 5]
Sunday

I find that [British essayist Charles] Lamb's letters are not letters that you can dip into at your own convenience, you have to wait for them to cast their spell. I was put off by a critic who said that Lamb was like a pointer who pointed everything he came to, and much of it was worthless. This is not true if you read him in the right way. You can easily see why the only people who read him at all are his enthusiasts. One letter that I thought you would like was the description of his lodgings. "I prefer the attic story for the air. . . . I have neither maid nor laundress, not caring to be troubled with them. . . . When you come to see me, mount up to the top of the stairs . . . and bring your glass, and I will show you the Surrey Hills. My bed faces the window, and supporting my carcass with my elbows, without much wrying of my neck, I can see the white sails glide by the bottom of the King's Bench Walks as I lie in my bed."[48]

Boots passed the card with the mountain view that you gave me for her around the Sunday school, and this morning the children were waiting with questions about mountains. Buster said, "What color are mountains?" A funny little boy

---

[47] A half-century later, Elizabeth Daniels Squire still remembered fishing for tadpoles in Elizabeth Lawrence's pool, as related to this book's editor.

[48] Charles Lamb to Thomas Manning, April 1801.

next to him, who is soft and brown-eyed like an animal, said, "Mountains are purple." Faye Marie (my favorite) said, "Miss Lawrence, is it true that you can touch the clouds when you get up in the mountains?" (I told her you could gather great armfuls), and Mary Stewart (I always thought her such a dull little creature) said, "Is it true that you can wash your face in the clouds?" And another boy asked if the mountains were really hard or what they felt like; and another wanted to know how high. Was 6,000 feet a good height for a nice sized mountain? I wanted to sit down and cry to think that one post card could start so much imagination among the comparatively unimaginative. But I had to get back to the Trinity (today being that Feast) and it was exceedingly difficult to make three persons in one God compete with touching clouds. Besides I had to go back and gather up Pentecost (last Sunday) as that had been skipped in my absence . . . and hastily picture the Holy Ghost descending in tongues of fire . . . but it was all an anticlimax to present day mountains.

[Summer]

I have won out and we are going to Maine for [sister] Ann's vacation. This cuts out the mountains, of course, which is hard on Bessie as going to the cabin is the only thing she really wants to do. However, I think it is much the best for you not to be interrupted (I had thought that I would get a chance to read what you do on the play, but probably that is best too, because I would get cross if Bessie said it was time to get lunch—it is bad enough when you do it). It seems a little senseless for Bessie and me to do exactly the last thing that neither of us wants to do. . . . We are both definitely against Maine at this point. . . . But I cannot allow Ann to come to Raleigh in August when I know what three weeks in Maine will do for her after Mr. Macy, New York, and the World's Fair . . . and when I remember the way she looked last Christmas. I am to stay with Ellen (who has a house this summer) and Ann and Bessie to stay with Margie. This means that I won't have Ann to myself at all. But it seems to be the best that can be done. Tomorrow Bessie and I are starting out on our trip, beginning with Elizabeth Rawlinson,[49] and ending up with the Lily show in Fredericksburg [Virginia].

The back garden has never been so lovely. I have two new herbaceous spires (some oriental kinds) that have creamy spikes of flowers misted with very fine very pale pink stamens just the shade of the pink eye of Miss Lingard [phlox], which is magnificent for once, and with the red violet and lavender-grey Japanese iris they are exquisite. The combination being an accident (of course) due to all liking having moist soil. In the upper bed the day lilies are at their best, ranging from pale yellow to deep orange, with yellow marguerites, the little white aster, and great spikes of white and dark blue larkspur.

I sent you the papers of Sammy's. I thought they were adorable, and did you ever have a clearer picture of any group of people than the men in the Sandwich Club as Father characterizes them by their opinions and prejudices.[50]

---

[49] Elizabeth Lawrence's friend and frequent correspondent and the editor of *Garden Gossip* in Richmond, Virginia.

[50] Elizabeth's father, Sam Lawrence, founded the Sandwich Club for men in Raleigh in 1924. The members met once a month in one another's homes to read their original philosophic papers.

[June 10]
Winchester, Virginia

Elizabeth Rawlinson says that garden lilies-of-the-valley are the same as the wild, and you cannot tell them apart. It seems they grow in the mountains of Europe and also in our mountains. I think the big columbine on the hill above the cabin must be one that has crossed with Mrs. Penland's cultivated ones. E. says they will if there are any near and one-half mile is not too far. There is no other wild one than *Aquilegia canadensis* (under your chestnut tree) and A. *coccinea*, which you and I could not tell apart—and which some botanists cannot tell apart—the main difference being the blooming season.

We took our lunch, and spent yesterday collecting endemics (plants that grow in one place only, and nowhere else in the world—e.g., the Venus' Fly Trap, only around Wilmington and a little in S.C.) from off the shale barrens—and when I had dug them out of the shale I wished for you to pack them for me. Elizabeth—who has learned these from Dr. Wherry[51] who discovered them—can tell you that this is *Oenothera arguillicola* [primrose] and that *Arabis ramosissima*, but when I asked the name of the little veronica at the cabin, said—"oh, that is one of the veronicas"—then, when I began grueling over the thalictrums (meadow rue to you) she said, "There is no use in your trying to tell them, Elizabeth, the botanists can't"—and the moral of this is (and the reason I am writing this letter) that I wish I had never mentioned scientific names to you—and you must not go about the mountains with that worried look trying to identify everything on the mountainside. . . .

---

[51] Dr. Edgar T. Wherry, botanist and author of books on native plants.

This afternoon we came to the experiment station at Boyce.[52] Dr. White was not there, but a young Canadian who is getting his Ph.D. (student of the University of Virginia) by studying hardiness from the point of view of cytology (which means to try to see if there is any relation between the arrangement of chromosomes and the plants' resistance to cold) showed us all over the place (a number of miles and two stiles and several thousand plants). . . . He is working on Eucalyptus and Jacaranda—and when I told him about my Jacarandas was very much excited. And I saw *Magnolia tripetala,* and you can see the hairs without a magnifying glass.

[June 23]

I have copied out every shred of action in the *Vita Nuova.*[53] I do not see what you can do with it, or that it could be fitted into any of your ideas, but I can't even tell it as I told you. Anyway I loved doing it because it made me understand Dante so much better. I don't know whether I am intellectually lazy or just dumb, but I never much begin to understand poems until I try to translate them or do something like this that requires putting the idea in your own words. . . .

I have weeded my garden and yours, and cleared out the closets, and got the blankets washed and put away, and the winter things to the cleaners . . . and all of my possessions moved

---

[52] The state arboretum of Virginia, part of the Blandy Experimental Farm, established in 1927 and named for its first director, Dr. Orland E. White.

[53] Elizabeth's copying of the "action" in Dante's *Vita Nuova* required her to read his text of verse and prose, including forty-two commentaries linking his poetry to his life.

to the cellar and put in order, and now, if I can just get the rest of it cleared out, I shall be able to look time in the face. . . .

The opera [Verdi's *Il Trovatore*] was darling. It was very clever to choose *Martha* to do out-of-doors.[54] The scenery was awful. I thought they weren't going to attempt realistic scenery? And the costumes out-Lillianed Lillian [Thompson]. Christine [Coffey] told Emily that they had all learned a great deal from the production. I think it was remarkable that they did it so well when they had never done anything out-of-doors before. I can't imagine anything nicer than sitting out in the summer night hearing a gay opera sung by charming-looking young people with sweet, fresh voices.

I thought it was a great mistake for them not to have a formal opening of the outdoor theatre . . . that wasn't featured at all. And it would have meant so much publicity in the paper if they had had the governor or someone to open it the way the garden club does at the flower show. There was nothing at all, just the opera, and no one but me dressed.

Yesterday morning Mr. Haskell was ordained at St. Saviour's. It is a very beautiful thing to see a good man ordained into the priesthood. It is very beautiful to hear the Bishop ask, "Will you maintain and set forward, as much as lieth in you, quietness, peace, and love, among all Christian people, and especially among them that are committed to your charge?" and hear the young priest answer, "I will do so, the Lord being my helper." The quaintly worded form for the Ordering of Priests is enchanting. At one point the Bishop inquires whether the

---

[54] *Martha*, a popular nineteenth-century opera by Friedrich von Flotow, was the first performance in Raleigh's new amphitheatre. A *News & Observer* reporter praised the "almost indescribable beauty" of the voices, the costumes, and the setting, noting, "Nowhere else in the United States has a Little Theatre built such a drama center to serve its own and a community's needs."

candidate is "apt and meet for his godly conversation."

Ann had spent most of the summer at the cabin, where Emily joined her for the last two weeks in August. Ann would return to the cabin in October.

[September 13]

. . . Don't you envy people who do what their fathers and grandfathers did? I am a great believer in inheriting acquired characteristics, even if it has been practically disproved. . . . I would like to live in the same soil as my ancestors, and walk under their trees, and do what they did, and think their thoughts. I don't want progress—except for hot water. . . .

[November 1]

This summer, having had much to endure from ages beyond my control, I found to my horror that I was taking pleasure in saying to the children, "No, you can not have an ice cream cone!" There is the same danger in criticism. I learned this from poems sent to Ellen for an opinion, and which we slashed with great glee. Later, when I told Peter Burnaugh[55] he looked at me without smiling, and said "You will never read anything I write." The poems were undoubtedly improved by our shears, and the remnants were published. But I could never again have so little regard for the writer. It is so easy to destroy

[55] The man Elizabeth had loved while a student at Barnard College, about whom she wrote a story for Ann entitled "Love Itself Shall Slumber On."

without understanding what is being destroyed.

I don't think that you need destructive criticism from me.[56] You have it from Emily. It tears you up, but it stimulates you and makes you more sure of yourself. When you ask me to read a play I try to analyze it as dispassionately as I can, and to tell you in what way I think that you have accomplished what you set out to, and in what way I think you have failed. I cannot remember ever having left unmentioned anything that I felt was wrong, or to have said that anything was right without believing it, but I shall never say of anything that you write, "Ann, this is no good." You need not ask it of me. Besides, what is the use. You and I have the same set of values.

I feel as responsible to you as to the children at St. Saviour's to tell you the truth as I see it. I consider it a matter of prayer . . . which I cannot put much faith in as a means of ending war, or holding off death. How well I like what you write (or fail to like it) has nothing to do with criticizing it. No one who writes as you do needs encouragement. You do need appreciation. But it is for my own sake that I try to communicate to you my pleasure in your work, because sharing it is a delight that I hold above all others. . . .

[November 16]

Since the little children don't come when it rains I took over a teacherless class of eight boys this morning. I think they were about twelve years old. When we had been through their lesson twice there was still time to pass so I asked them who

---

[56] Elizabeth was reading drafts of Ann's new play.

they thought planted the bomb.[57] The smartest, to my great distress, answered glibly ("the British" before any of the others had even understood the question, the sudden change from Abraham being very startling). The most thoughtful said, "The Russians." And then to my delight someone contributed, "The Nazis." Then I asked if it was a good idea. All were agreed that it was. So then I tried to sell them the idea that violence never solves any problem. This was a flop. They were sure that the only possible solution was to extinguish Hitler. The littlest thought he would like to go do it himself. They were all against our going into the war. One said, President Roosevelt has fixed that. I said, but suppose Hitler comes over here. He can't do that, they all laughed. We have our Coast Guard. But suppose he takes South America and comes up through Mexico. They said it would take him a long time to take South America.

[Christmas season]

. . . I awoke this morning to a profound melancholy which proved to be very ill humor at being hounded into promising to take a Christmas decoration to the Woman's Club, and wear an evening dress and pass cake. . . .

---

[57] Perhaps Elizabeth alludes to the November 8, 1939, failed assassination attempt in Munich on Hitler's life.

1940

[January]

. . . I have something perfectly awful to tell you: it doesn't matter whether my book ever gets published or not. I have had the fun of doing it, and I have learned what I need to know. Now I can write another book. It is going to be about the amaryllis family, but it will take a very long time, because it will have to be done in libraries and in catalogues and in gardens. . . .

The brief January 2 letter about Elizabeth's sister's visit home included family dialogue that is irrelevant and difficult to follow. At the end of it came a mysterious note, with no further explanation.

[January 2]

. . . Ann said, "Ann Bridgers looks well, and young and beautiful." I did not tell her why.

[July 14]
Thursday morning

In the morning mail I had a letter from a Miss Johnson [at the University of North Carolina Press] who said that she (and not the one I talked with) now had my manuscript [of what would become *A Southern Garden*], and would I come over to talk to her, that "It really is in excellent shape and I believe two hours talk would clear up my questions." I took the work out of my typewriter immediately to tell you about it, but I shall try not to call Emily before she gets home this evening, though I dislike, in this sad world, keeping any one from a hearty laugh any longer than absolutely necessary. What do you suppose she gets? It reminds me of Nana's idea saying that she had never worked in a house where they were so sweet to their grandmother. I wondered what most people did to their grandmothers, as Nana, Ann and I quarreled with animation from morning to night. . . .

[July 18]

. . . This has been a chilly day of mist and rain when you would like to get out tweeds and walk on the moors with the dogs, if there were any dogs. But [my day] was spent over the fire in a sweater. Except I took advantage of wet and clouds to put out three crotalarias in your garden. I plant seeds in vain every year. Now I have got a kind that transplants. But I haven't much hope. And I took a hammer and two stakes for the tithonias, and when I got there had forgot the raffia. Then I started to take flowers to Christ Church, and get the [laundered] clothes from Miss Carrie. When I had got as far as the church I realized I had no money. So I stopped and borrowed two dollars from Dr. Penn. When I got to Miss Carrie's I had forgot the basket. Miss Carrie said, "Miss Elizabeth . . . of all times for you to forget the basket this was the worst." I said I would try to be careful, but dropped a dozen embroidered napkins in the mud on the way to the car. Fortunately Carrie did not see. I shall wash them myself. She would be furious.

Friday night

Your garden has half of the heavens, and mine the other half. The Dipper is yours. The swan and the Milky Way are mine.

[August 10]

I am sorry that the chestnut tree is gone—for the sound of falling bark, and on general principle. I do not like change, even for the better, or even the removal of dead wood. Especially in the church. Mr. Haskell [at Christ Church] was telling me this morning that the communion service must be simplified. It was one of the perfect pieces of dramatic writing in the world, having been evolved during fifteen hundred years to meet the needs of the human spirit, and having been translated into English in the great period of the English language, the time of Shakespeare. He says people cannot be expected to put their minds on anything so long (twenty minutes). I said: "You are an egg." He laughed and said, "If I am, so is the dean of the theological seminary at Sewanee, who is the authority on church liturgy." I said, "The dean is an egg."

. . . I woke up in the night as much shaken as if I had had a nightmare. I had been dreaming that it was late fall, and I had gone to a place where I had once planted some bulbs. They had spread into a wide patch, and were in full bloom. They were all white, but in every conceivable form, and they smelled of vanilla. I started to pick them for you, but before I had enough the whole patch had vanished, and the ones in my hands too.

[August 11]
Friday night

. . . I would love for the play to end with Myrtle's saying, "a man has to be blood kin before he sees him as his brother." It is one of Myrtle's best lines, and sums up, don't you think, Myrtle's method of finding a way? I am amazed at the work you have done—but where did you do it? In New York? But you couldn't possibly have done all of that in a winter. You have knit it together, clarified and strengthened it without losing any of the intensity. I cannot see how you got time to do all that work—or where you found the energy. You *scare* me. It is a very beautiful play. And a wise one . . .

[August 20]

I have finished [the chapter on] Summer, and have only [the chapter on] Fall to do—which is short. I hope I can get it done quickly, and have time to rewrite after your reading.

If you get back before I do [from a trip with Bessie and sister Ann], and can find time to look into my garden, will you see if *Nerine undulata* is in bloom, and if it is, pick it when all of the flowers are out, and put it in your refrigerator until I get back. It bloomed last year while I was gone, and I have never seen it, and it is the most exciting bulb I have. I enclose a map of where it is, and of other things that might bloom. Don't bother about any of them—don't look for Ridgway [color chart]. I am taking it with me in case we get to any nurseries. . . .

[August 22]

Do you remember giving me leave (one Sunday morning) to present the other side? Will you listen? The reason that I feel so passionately concerned about the Germans is because my viewpoint is new to me, and easily disturbed. I only recently acquired from you your belief in people, and I cannot believe that it is only in America, England, and France that the people are fundamentally right. I cannot believe that a just peace can come to one nation before it comes to all nations. (I said, "Emily, so you hate the Italians, too?" "No," she said, "I can't really hate the Italians.")

Ruth was reading the other night a book of my father's that Mr. Luns has (much underlined, as was my father's habit). It was written right after the world war by a man who had been in Europe for all of it, and with the German troops part of the time. He predicted that the Germans would do as they have done, that they would always do as they have done to the end of the world, if they were not held down by force. It is very hard, when you see them doing it from Attila to Hitler, not to believe him. But to believe him is to believe in the end of civilization. It is the sort of reasoning that holds that democracy will be a failure always because it is its nature to be open to attack. Must you say (quote) that I talk as if I wanted Germany to win because I cling to the belief that there are still Germans who do not want war, and are just as eager for a just peace as are fair-minded people of all nations.

You are not very sympathetic when I said we think alike. I did not mean that you think as I do, but that I think as you do. I know that there is no use entering a discussion with Bessie, or Al [unidentified], or the Thompsons (or almost anybody) because they will always think as their kind. But you think as a human being. And I try to.

I finally went to Emily with the outline of my book. It is too late to do much about it, but I could not do it before, because I kept changing it. I did not like to ask her to read what I have written, but she said she would like to, so I am going to leave it with her.

[August]

. . . Bessie used Mary Wiatt [Elizabeth's St. Mary's classmate] as an excuse to stay away from the luncheon and we were sitting under the trees reading Saki [the pen name of Scottish writer H. H. Munro] when Mrs. Padgett (she we took out of the street when Miss Lily had her fire,[58] and she has never understood that our sympathy was momentary) appeared, and said: I rang, and no one answered so I just came on out . . . don't let me interrupt your reading, and sat down to tell us about her leaking heart, and I got sick, and had to go. Perhaps in another three years she can spend another day with us. Our garden has a stone wall with broken glass on top all the way around it, and one iron gate with two keys which we wear around our necks in the day, and keep under our pillows at night.

The Evening Primroses (your lack of appreciation of which I cannot understand) have begun to bloom. This year I have a big white one that is like moonlight on the desert.

---

[58] Apparently, Mrs. Padgett had been rooming at Miss Lily's when tenants had to leave because of a house fire.

1941

After Doubleday rejected Elizabeth's outline and sample chapters of A Southern Garden, *she turned elsewhere. On June 6, 1941, she signed a book contract with the University of North Carolina Press, after years of working on the manuscript. It had been necessary, first of all, to grow many of the plants she wrote about; to correspond with other gardeners to check her information; to write articles that would enable her to learn how to present her material; and, finally, to go through many drafts, read by Ann and her sister, Emily. Despite the demands upon her as a gardener and writer, Elizabeth continued to be fully engaged as a daughter at home with Bessie, with her Sunday-school class at St. Saviour's, and with her many friends, Ann foremost among them.*

[July 17]

Mr. and Mrs. [the Reverend Charles F. "Fritz" and Irma] Wulf—the present incumbents of St. Saviour's—came to dinner with us last night, and Mrs. Wulf having heard about my pipe and wanting someone to play duets with her, brought her shepherd's pipe. It is the kind that I told you about, that the group of pipers at Little Switzerland [North Carolina] plays. You cannot buy them, but you buy the bamboo (for four cents) and make them, and I have the book telling how. I cannot wait to make one for Elizabeth [Daniels] . . . or better still you and she can make one. . . .

We tried to play together, but the pipes were out of tune, so we were in despair and Mr. Wulf, who is a musician, stepped out of conversation with Bessie, and elongated Paula's flute by pulling out the mouthpiece a little, and lo, they were in tune, and we did play a little until I laughed too much to go on. Mrs. Wulf cannot count either, which annoys Mr. Wulf, so he counts for us and that is what makes me laugh. . . . Mr. Wulf is an odd and gentle little man who is, I think, only partly present. When I was talking to him about some of our St. Saviour's problems, we got on the subject of clerical collars. He said he felt naked without his. I said I did not like a minister to be a man among men. "No," he said. "It is not possible. My wife complains that I am a priest first, a priest before a friend or a father or a husband. And she is right. You must expect that when you make your choice. It is a lonely calling."

[July 18]

Mr. [William T.] Couch [director of the University of North Carolina Press] says that when he comes upon a book he likes, he does not read it through, but lays it aside to save for a time of despair. I said that I would not dare read any words that I had not already read (and read often) in that mood, and that I turned on such occasions to Barrie or Kipling. He said he had never read Barrie. Thinking it over later, I thought, but I wouldn't read anything. I would weed.

When I am too tired to sleep, I read the *Oxford Book of Greek Verse*. I guess there is no book in the world that covers so much variation of mood and intellect in its pages—and twice over—for there is the feeling of the original Greek mind seeping through somewhat, as well as the interpretation of it by the English translator. I have been comparing the translations of

Sappho with the literal ones in your *Lyra Graeca*, and thinking how much more the poetry of all ages is founded on homosexuality than on normal sex. Shakespeare, Baudelaire, Verlaine, Sappho, Catullus, Aurelius—"do you hope to take my love," "the very fairest youth in all the world . . . your tricks are vain: The lad is mine, and mine he will remain" and Housman and Edna Millay ("Evening on Lesbos": "Twice having seen your shingled heads adorable/Side by side, the onyx and the gold,/I know that I have had what I could not hold"). Well, maybe not more, but quite as much. I love the modern version with shingled heads. . . .

Mr. Couch seems to spend much of his time in despair. He cannot speak long on any subject without some reference to it. On the surface one would think he had the pleasantest and most satisfying of lives, with the least to despair of. Which all goes to prove that despair has no connection with what happens.

Sunday morning

Mary Wiatt spent three days with us and gave us great pleasure. She is in no way different from the direct, frank, and eager little girl who came to me at fourteen and said, "Libba, I am not very popular in this school, and you not at all, and I think we should make friends of each other."

She says that she thinks she and Richard will come East. She thinks the only essential for a writer is to live in the country he knows. She said, "Why, how can you get to know people in California enough to write about them? Why, they even resent it if you ask where they were born. Now, in Louisburg

[North Carolina], I don't have to ask. I know everybody, and my grandmother knew everybody's grandmother. Whatever a person does or says I see or hear in relation to what this person has done or said as long as I have known him." (This wasn't meant to be a boast, and wasn't one. She has that kind of memory.) "Why, I could get material for ten novels by just sitting on our front porch, and enough for ten more by listening to my mother's telephone conversations with my aunt."

[July 26]

. . . I am going to get the manuscript back before it goes to the printers. Mr. Couch suggested it himself. So I feel better. I am still thinking of things I left out. So I write them down and take them to the editor.

[Late summer]

Emily came to dinner last night, and was very much charmed with Mr. Luns, who came in with Miss Rosa. They were only here for the night, and had driven all day, and were very tired. But Emily does not miss an inflection, and Mr. Luns provides plenty even in his dullest moments. . . .

Sunday

I had supper with Emily and Christine, and we went to the movies. Last night they came to dinner. I think the party was a success so far as Emily and I were concerned, as we both felt guilty of having done all of the talking. I don't know about Christine and Bessie. Christine said that she hoped when you went home she would be spoiled. Emily said: "That was what Ann did for me. She thought of everything before I could think of it myself. And I have written to her since I got back [from the cabin]." I said, "I guess you don't need to write to Ann. I guess you and Ann are like Boots and her granny [at St. Saviour's]." Granny was so complaining of how Boots never thought of her while she did so much for Boots, so I said: "Boots, can't you try to be more appreciative to Granny? You can pick her some violets." And Boots looked at me in a way she has, clear and intense and simple, and said, "Granny knows what I think of her." I have seldom felt so foolish. Christine was very sympathetic with my chagrin, but Emily thought that the moral of the tale was that Boots should take the violets to Granny.

[August 30, Weir's Cove, Tennessee]
Thursday afternoon

Bessie and Ann are taking their naps and I have been sitting on a rock in the stream playing nursery rhymes on my pipe. We found an adorable book at the 5 and 10 in Knoxville with English, French, and German ones. They are perfectly enchanting, especially the singing games.

Annette [sister Ann] and I swim every day, and walk in the woods. Annette is superior to you in the woods, in that she never thinks of snakes, and doesn't much mind wading through streams with her shoes on; but she is inferior to you in the woods, in that she flatly refuses to take an interest in nature.

She really does not care whether an hepatica leaf is pointed or rounded. Today I saw, across a ravine, an almost perpendicular slope covered with high branched small pine trees all the same size and with the brush cut out so that there was only pine straw and a small saxifrage to cover the ground beneath them. And among these trees a tall white hunting dog was leaping in regular arcs. It was so like those beautiful Italian murals on the walls of the Palace of the Popes at Avignon. And then I realized that seeing the white dog among the symmetrical pine trees, and remembering the pattern of the walls of the red building was so much more beautiful to me than any of the views of the mountains that I have seen in the 609 miles between Front Royal, Virginia, and here.

I am always amazed, and somewhat discouraged, to find out how much better the body remembers than the mind. It seems strange that you can ride or swim as well when you have not done it for years as when you have done it every day, while not having played the pipe for two weeks, every note is forgotten.

We are going to Marietta [Georgia] in the morning to see my Uncle Donald [Sam Lawrence's brother]. Home Tuesday night.

[September 13]

I have been trying to find time to sit down and write to you on the typewriter, but there is never time to write letters on a typewriter, because at those times you could be pulling weeds or making notes or carrying St. Saviour's children sweaters and skirts collected for them to wear to school, or pressing socks for

British refugees or polishing silver. The only time to write letters is when you have gone to bed and cannot sleep. I have been lying in the dark thinking how life grows more complicated every year: new interests are added, and old ones never cease.

I have been thinking of how simple my life used to be: taking Bessie to market, taking Father to his office, cutting flowers for the house, talking to people who came and went away again, and in between reading and writing. There was added gardening and keeping records to absorb all the minutes of the day and night without wanting to give up any minutes of reading and writing. Now is added searching out 17th century melodies and copying them and learning to play them; that takes every minute of the day and night, and still without wanting to give up any minutes of reading or writing or gardening or keeping records.

If I live to be as old as my grandfather (94), how do you think I will manage?

Do you get very tired of my writing so much and so trivially? It makes you feel closer to write of trivial things. And I always feel closer to you when you are away. In the same way I feel closer to the dead.

I wish all days could be like today: that I could feel full of energy and know what I want to write and think I can write it. But there is only one day like this out of a year, and it is not enough. If I could ever remember on the other days that I once felt like this. But I always think that I have never felt anything but despondent. It doesn't seem reasonable that you should look at a garden one minute and see only dead plants, and at another and see bud and bloom in the same garden, or that you should look into yourself and see no thought, and again a quickening.

The other night I had been playing my pipe, and when I put it down and came out I heard a pipe still, and looked and saw Mrs. Crowson sitting on the swing in the dusk piping very softly.

[September 23]

The Aldens [Dorothy and Edgar, Raleigh musicians] came in at tea time on Saturday. Did you ever hear of anything so darling as their thinking they must pay a party call? They were very pleased over the festival and the way it turned out. I said what were they going to play this winter and they said they did not know yet. Then they talked along and he said, "Dorothy, how about doing so and so?" and in a little while, "Let's do an all-Mozart concert for the 150th anniversary of his death." They said they could not get the first program ready before Christmas, and Mrs. Alden said, "Besides, I don't want Ann Bridgers to have to work so hard, but I want to wait until she gets back." And Mrs. Alden had on a dark blue dress and a little hat and looked so sweet.

[October 7]
Sunday night

I spent most of the afternoon dismantling my room. Bessie and Annette [sister Ann] have finally worn me down, and it's being done over. It was very dirty, but I will never like it so well. Having told Elizabeth [Thompson] that I must have yellow or I would get depressed, that I could not bear anything but plain white spreads on my beds, and that I require monotony, I ended up with pink walls, red furniture, and chintz counterpanes. Bessie and I had to make the counterpanes, redrape the dressing tables (with crinoline covered borders) and upholster the chair. I do not know where the time is coming from.

By the time I had moved all of my books into the hall, I wondered what I wanted with them. There are so few books you can really live with—almost as few as people. And I thought again of Peter Burnaugh's story about the man who never let his library be above a hundred volumes. I said, "But, Peter, I have more than a hundred books just at college with me." And Pete said, "You would need only one volume of poetry. One you made yourself." He said, "If you liked a poem well enough to want to read it again, you would be willing to go to the trouble of typing it, wouldn't you?" . . .

Thursday afternoon

I have been writing an article on herbs for Miss Isabel [Busbee] for the garden club bulletin. I have got so interested I have decided to start all over. Isabelle Bowen Henderson grows herbs under an oak tree. I don't think it is the tree. And I must have skirret. I must have shallots.

I am very much excited over making a talk to the garden school at Rocky Mount [North Carolina]. It is at night, and I am to use my slides for the first time. I have more than enough for a lecture.

I am so glad you are out of this heat. It is grim. This is the only heat that I really mind. In the fall you haven't time to be hot.

[October 13]

Twelve people came to Mr. Williams' [director of play reading] meeting number one and were much interested, and out from under Bessie's stony stare he is not so foolish, and conducted it very well. They decided to meet the last Monday night in each month, and were eager to meet more often, but I know how hard it is to get the people and books together, said we had better begin with one per month, and work up to more. All new people. Not one (but me) from last year. But some I liked, and all were sweet. . . .

I got an unexpected $2.78 from the Commercial Bank, and collected $1.22 off of Bessie, and I am going to give it to Mrs. Wulf so she can belong to the Little Theatre. She said when I first came home that she had five dollars for her birthday, and which

The Raleigh Little Theatre opened the 1940–41 season in a new building, helped by funds from the Federal Theatre project. Shown here near completion, it continues today as part of the artistic life of Raleigh.
BY PERMISSION OF THE RALEIGH LITTLE THEATRE, PUBLISHED IN
CURTAIN UP! RALEIGH LITTLE THEATRE'S FIRST FIFTY YEARS

should she do: join the Little Theatre or go to the Civic Music. She said she loved the Little Theatre and was used to working in it. I said, "Oh, the Little Theatre. Those concerts are a bore." And she said, "Yes, maybe for you, but you know, I have never heard any good music. I never even heard a symphony orchestra until I heard the State Orchestra last year. And it was so wonderful I have not gotten over it." Later, I said which did she do, and she said, "Now I can't do either, I took Fritz to the Circus, and I spent all my money. I didn't know the circus costs so much." (Fritz is her little boy.) She is very creative and will be a wonderful worker. Besides, she has time, not a great deal, as she has many demands on her, but I think she does not have any social life as Christ Church does not take up the vicar's wife after the first polite calls. Not that she would want them to, but I think she needs things to do.

I am so excited about your working on Calhoun. It colors all my days.

[October 14]

I was asking Margaret to help me fathom the meaning of a poem in the *Yale Review* by Robert Frost, "I could give all to Time" (of which I like one sentence: "I could give all to Time except what I myself have thought") and I said, "What did he mean, 'For I am There'? Where is There?" And Margaret said, "The only 'there' that I know is the place where Uncle Luns used to play poker when he was at the University."

The Thompsons arrived before I had had a chance to retire to the basement last night, and I had to explain over again that I had not been [to see them] because I had spent practically all waking hours working on galleys for the last ten days. Margaret said, "That's what she says, but she spends them playing her pipe."

[October 25]

My book [*A Southern Garden*] will not come out until January. On account of the paper they say, but it won't be ready before that anyway. I could have done so much to it if I could have had it a little of the time that it was lying around the press offices. I wish I had not been brought up to do what I say I will do. People do not expect or desire it, and it is much better if you do not expect it of them.

Mrs. Wulf and I have been making a cast (out of plaster) of my Madonna (in my studio) for the children's altar at St. Saviour's. When I saw the charming altar at Christ Church, and thought of our broken-legged table with a moth-eaten cover and a worm-eaten cross, I felt conscience-stricken. Even so, the children love the candles and flowers so much that they inch their chairs up the way they did at the marionettes (remember?) and when the times come to kneel, I haven't room to do it. The superintendent is going to have a new altar made for me. A real one, not a table. And I am so happy. It is the first time I have ever got any help since I have been working at St. Saviour's.

I made the bread bowl full of turkey salad this morning, and took it down to the Parish House for lunch for Bessie's [Red Cross] workers. This is the big day. They are packing the finished product, the fifty "toddlers' packs." They all said it was the best chicken salad they ever ate.

What I started out to do was to tell you about the weekend

I spent with the Couches and the ridiculous English woman who called me the next morning to say she was so afraid I would think she was not loyal to England because she said Churchill did not understand Labor, and about the Mozart Clarinet Concerto, and the hill that got in the way of the view, and children and the intelligentsia. But even I am beginning to feel a little embarrassed at the length of my letter.

Do my foolish letters bother you? I always have a feeling that you do not like to have me write to you when you are working. But it is hard not to when I think about you so much, and like everything else, there are only two ways to write: a lot or not at all.

I try never to say that I miss you. But this time it is not bearable.

Mr. Couch said, "You mean they told you in the office that your book would come out in January? But that wouldn't do. No one would pay any attention to it right after Christmas. We will have to wait until March."[59]

[November]
Thursday night

We went to St. Mary's Chapel after dinner tonight to see Sarah Thompson (Joey's sister) confirmed. It was the first time that I had been to a confirmation since I was confirmed myself, when I was twelve years old. Being a very literal little girl, I had thought that when the Bishop laid his hands on my head (the office is called "the laying on of hands") I would feel the Holy

---

[59] *A Southern Garden* was published March 7, 1942.

Spirit enter. When I did not, I thought I probably hadn't any soul after all, and I was very sad. I still am.

Tonight, Bishop Penick raised his exquisitely beautiful hands above each of the shining heads of the girls that knelt before him, and said in his beautiful vibrant voice, "Defend, O Lord, this thy Child with thy heavenly grace; that she may continue thine forever." It was as if the spirit that Christ created in

The chapel at St. Mary's School in Raleigh. Elizabeth enrolled at St. Mary's in 1916 when the family moved to Raleigh. She graduated in 1922. She regarded her education at the Episcopal St. Mary's as superior to the one she received at Barnard College in New York City.
BY PERMISSION OF ST. MARY'S SCHOOL

the Apostles and which they in turn laid upon the first bishops, and which succeeded from bishop to bishop for two thousand years was visible in his finger tips. . . . And I realized what I had felt, but never analyzed before, that Bishop Penick is a great actor. And I thought that the reason that Shakespeare's plays and the *Book of Common Prayer* have been the means of crystallizing and preserving the English language is that they were not only the written word, but the spoken and acted word.

Saturday night Emily came to dinner and had a good time and was in grand spirits. I was very much relieved. She had been so frayed when I was there, the way she gets when her work is too much for her. Now that I have got her to let me come for her and take her [to and from her office job in state government], she doesn't go home more tired than when she came. I always know this when she says, "Elizabeth, come in while I order a Coca-Cola."

I took the galleys over to Chapel Hill this morning, and the page proof will probably come in three or four weeks.

[November 1]

While the reading group was holding forth in one of the dressing rooms, scenery was being painted in the department, the workshop plays were being rehearsed on the new stage, and Sam [Leager] was holding tryouts in the auditorium. . . . The tryouts are my favorite phase of the Little Theatre. There is far more drama in them than in the finished product. . . .

Uncle Jim came up on Monday to marry his little friend (the one who, last year, was entering upon a brilliant career of playwriting, remember?), and as Bessie was in bed with flu we were left to our own devices, and spent the time from 5:30 A.M. in alternate flattering and fighting. When we are together, we have family prayers. Uncle Jim always begins with a psalm, because Grandpapa always did (being a South Carolinian, he pronounced ["psalm"] like "Sam," and Uncle Jim, when he was a little boy, said, "Papa, when are you going to read some "Jims"?) and he took the prayer book and said, first let me tell you a joke. The joke was his favorite one about the optimistic old maid who looked under her bed even when it was a Murphy bed.

The Family Prayers begin: "Almighty and everlasting God, in whom we live and move and have our being; we thy needy creatures, render thee our humble praises, for thy preservation of us from the beginning of our lives to this day." I sometimes think that my grandfather's voice saying those words is the most beautiful thing I have ever known. . . .

[November 4]

You know my letters do not look to any answer. That is my theory in general as regards the pastime, but when practiced on you, it is mere self-indulgence. Correspondence is of another order. It has no connection with letter-writing, its purpose being an exchange of ideas, usually on some special subject. I have many correspondents. If they did not write to me I would not write to them. But letter-writing is an end in itself. It is the simplest, most natural, and (to the writer) the most delightful form of self-expression. He has something to say and says it (as you once so perfectly phrased it) to the most receptive person. In letters all questions are rhetorical, but they are necessary to impart the conversational tone that is inherent in the genre.

And you know that if I thought you would feel called upon (or even prompted) to reply, I would not write to you. You have no need for that form of expression, and it is essential to you, when you are writing, to have no demands of any sort on your energy or even your interest. That is why I hesitate to write at all at the times when you are doing concentrated work. I have learned from you that what matters in life is that all gifts are brought to their fullest development. Yours are very rare.

I say this from the bottom of my heart. From the top of it I cannot answer, but must say with Julie de Lespinasse:

> Write to me often, seldom, not at all,
> But do not think me equally content.

At the end of 1941, Ann stopped writing "Who Treads the Boards," a column in which she reviewed New York plays for the News & Observer, *citing her desire to give herself full time to defense work, explaining, "I am one of the women who is free to do so." Although she continued to advise the Raleigh Little Theatre, she decided about this time to begin work on a play set in the Filter Center, in which she and other volunteers helped relay reports of planes. In the play, she made an impassioned statement about Americans' need to stand together in defense of liberty and freedom.*

Although references to war and to matters of race are too limited in Elizabeth's letters to say clearly what consistent attitudes she held, she thought about those issues a great deal. A daughter of the South who had lived abroad and in New York for many years, Ann clearly was more experienced, progressive, and liberal, but without her letters, it is also hard to say what her political attitudes were.

On the subject of race, one of Ann's plays gave the Raleigh Little Theatre its first opportunity to use black actors and actresses. Later, she wrote an opera about a black woman. Elizabeth knew blacks only as servants, and her difficulties in hiring them in her home as the black migration north continued led to a prescient observation in one letter to Emily: "I cannot see how the community can be so oblivious to the volcano they are sitting on, and worry about war in Europe."

Meanwhile, the family was changing. On December 30, 1941, Ann Lawrence and Warren Way, Jr., married in the chapel of St. Mary's. Dr. Way, Warren's father, and the Reverend James B. "Uncle Jim" Lawrence officiated at the ceremony. Ellen Flood's young daughter Mary Ellen was the maid of honor, and Bessie Lawrence entertained the wedding party and out-of-town guests at a luncheon at home on Park Avenue. Although that passed unmentioned in letters to Ann Bridgers, Elizabeth's interest was as intense as a mother's after Ann and Warren had children.

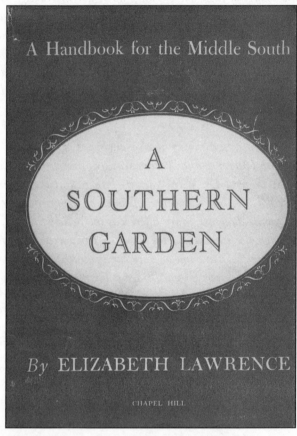

A Handbook for the Middle South

A
SOUTHERN
GARDEN

By ELIZABETH LAWRENCE

CHAPEL HILL

A Southern Garden *was published in 1942 by the University of North Carolina Press and has remained in print. In 1991, on the occasion of the fiftieth anniversary of its publication, the press released a special edition, adding original watercolors of Elizabeth's house in Charlotte and some of her favorite plants.*
BY PERMISSION OF UNC PRESS

PART TWO: 1942–1948

A Book of One's Own

"One thing about the war suits me
perfectly. Staying at home."
ELIZABETH TO ANN

The publication of Elizabeth's first book, A Southern Garden, *was almost lost in the news of America's entry into World War II, but with the help of local newspaper coverage and garden clubs, word got out to dedicated gardeners, who wrote to thank her for a book about Southern gardening they felt had been a long time coming. Sales were slow, but nothing was modest about the flow of enthusiastic letters that continued until the end of Elizabeth's life. Of course, Elizabeth wrote back. With her first book, she began acquiring a reputation as the quintessential Southern gardener, read (and read aloud) and quoted. Elizabeth was invited to give lectures and workshops. Although tire and gas rationing made travel difficult, she went—sometimes with Bessie, sometimes alone by bus—to*

Asheville, Tarboro, Rocky Mount, Durham, Chapel Hill, Winston-Salem, Wilmington, and Warrenton.

Her garden was mature, her book was finished, and she had found magazine editors who would publish her articles. Now, Elizabeth turned her attention to the war. She and her mother were active participants in a number of volunteer efforts, which helped Elizabeth—and others—feel they had a part to play. Bessie, a stalwart, long-serving Red Cross volunteer, led a group of women who knitted socks and other articles of clothing (Bessie made a pair of socks for Ann Bridgers), and she and Elizabeth worked at the USO reception center and provided meals and lodging for soldiers coming to Raleigh from nearby military bases for weekend entertainment and rest. Elizabeth volunteered at the Raleigh Filter Center and helped Ann with details for the play she was writing about it, called "Possess These Shores." It was an exciting time for Elizabeth. Although she sometimes struggled with periods of melancholy and insomnia, her letters are lively with anecdotes and reflections.

1942

[June 27]

Does it seem to you sometimes that the loneliness of people weighs down upon you like the air before a summer storm. And without being lonely yourself. You aren't lonely, are you? I do not think I ever am.

There came in the morning's mail a letter from Mr. Starker[1] which began "Dear Friend" (the extent of our friendship being

---

[1] Carl Starker, Elizabeth's correspondent from Oregon, who would come to see her Charlotte garden in 1977.

Elizabeth working in her Raleigh garden on Park Avenue near Hillsborough Street. This photograph accompanied a review of A Southern Garden *that ran May 3, 1942, in the* News & Observer.
BY PERMISSION OF THE RALEIGH *NEWS & OBSERVER*

that I have ordered plants from him for several years, and once wrote to tell him my special interest in alliums and please let me know of any rare ones he had that were not listed in his catalogue) and went on for pages with a clinical report of his wife's illness. . . . He goes on to tell me of his plant troubles. *Convolvulus mauritanicus* [Ground Morning Glory] simply "went." And also the *Veronica satureioides* and *gentianoides.* "It was too wet and too cold all at once, I guess." Also he can get no help in the nursery. A man is out of the question, but at last he has found a seventy-year-old woman. He ends with "I sigh for some good sunny weather," and says he is sending some plants that he thinks got left off my fall list, and an iris that is a present. Can't you see him going into his office late at night, too tired to work and too tired to sleep, finding my order and worrying about whether it was filled properly, sitting down to ask about it, and writing about his wife instead, and the state of the garden—it is weedier than he has ever seen it. . . .

Elizabeth's trip to Louisiana to speak to garden clubs included a visit to Evelyn Way, a friend from St. Mary's, now a professor at the University of Mississippi in Oxford. Evelyn drove her by William Faulkner's home, and they had an unexpected meeting with Mrs. Faulkner. Elizabeth wrote Emily Bridgers about her impressions.

[Elizabeth to Emily, July 16]
Wednesday night, Oxford, Mississippi

Dear Emily,

The landmarks of Oxford are the town hall and Mr. William Faulkner's house. It is a square white house set far back in a dark, abandoned grove of cedars and magnolias. The drive goes in at an angle so that you cannot see it from the street. Evelyn said she would like to take us in, but Mr. Faulkner does not like callers. Mrs. Faulkner is very friendly. Mrs. Bondurant, driving me over the town in the morning while Evelyn was having her classes, spoke in the same tone. She said, "Estelle is not like my other friends. I never feel I can just go in, and I did not think to phone her we would come." And then, to my utter mortification she added, "But I believe I will just go in and speak to her anyway."

She left me in the car while she went into the house. I

sat looking at it, trying to decide why such a pleasant looking house should impress me as sinister. When Mrs. Bondurant reappeared she had with her a person I took at a distance to be a young girl. A thin figure in a blue cotton dress and a white apron made like a child's pinafore. She wore red shoes. They came down the long avenue of mournful cedars that leads to the doorway, and when they were close I saw that she was not young, and that her painted face showed all that had happened to her, and a great deal had happened. I was as startled as if a young person had grown suddenly old before my eyes, as they do in fairy tales, and it did not help me to have Mrs. Bondurant say, "Would you believe she is a grandmother—she always said she was going to be a grandmother at forty—and she was."

Mrs. Faulkner was, as Evelyn said she would be, almost pathetically cordial, so much so that I did not realize until we had gone on that she never asked us in. Mrs. Bondurant told her I was interested in gardens, and said to me that Mrs. Faulkner had a lovely one, but she did not offer to show us that either. Much to my relief, for I had thought I saw a man disappearing into it as we came up the drive. I had been looking at the old brick wall that surrounds the garden on three sides, the house on the fourth, and the top of an old summer house, and the tangle of magnolias and cedars and crepe myrtle that showed above the wall. . . .

[July 30]
Raleigh

I learned something at the cabin [with Ann in the mountains]—that the style of letter-writing acquired (after long years of trial and error) in order to please you (it does please you, doesn't it?), is not the preference of everyone. In my excitement about Oxford I put down everything I could remember, and then reduced it one third (I should probably have subtracted another third if Miss Daisy [Thompson] and Bessie had not been in a hurry to get to the village). When I got to the cabin Emily said: But what was the house like? What did she say etc., until I had recalled all of the details that I had been at such pains to leave out.

The difficulty is that in letters you are supposed to be spontaneous (which of course you cannot be and be anything else too) and if you inquire: How did you like my description of the sunset? Could you see the colors that I did not mention? you would destroy forever the illusion of careless intimacy. Writing to you is especially difficult because, if you mention a letter at all it is years afterward and indirectly, and by that time, though I know at last that I chose the right word, I don't remember what it was. However, a word to the wise is sufficient, and goes a long way: as when, after talking to you for years about Anna Braun[2] without arousing the least interest, I said I could not think why I loved the little shop in Stalls Alley [in Charleston, South Carolina], except that I once went in and found Anna Braun sitting in front of an open fire. You wrote back at once: "Who is Anna Braun. Why haven't I met her?"

[August 2]

I had a letter from my charming cousin Alex Cann [her cousin Harriet's son] in Savannah, with a review of my book

---

[2] Illustrator of children's books, whom Elizabeth visited in Chapel Hill.

which he says "seems to be quite favorable." He adds "I told the Little House [bookstore] to order a few copies which I am sure can be disposed of." The review says "Miss Lawrence gets her information across in an informal manner. Quite a bit of her book sounds as though it were taken from a woman's garden club meeting." Quite a blow . . .

Miss Wilson [at the Little Theatre box office] says they took $540.00 in spite of the lowering clouds. Miss [Robertine] McClendon had thought they weren't going to have any crowd because the tickets did not sell in advance. She kept saying: "Oh, those beautiful people!" Miss W. did not know how much the expenses were, but she thought they were paid and the "debts" paid (whatever they were, she was vague) and some left in the treasury.

Mrs. Bullock, one of my favorite characters, and my friend, Mrs. Bowling, came to see me yesterday, each with a little box of wilted herbs to be identified. And one wanted hers named. Mrs. Bullock said, "Elizabeth, do you get a royalty on your book?" I said I did, and she said: "Then I am going to buy it. I have read it, so I wasn't going to bother to buy it if you had sold it outright, but if you get anything out of it I am going to buy it."

Mrs. Bullock was telling me about her grandfather's house, still standing on the old Rocky Mount Road. It is an old inn. In her grandmother's day the garden was full of rosemary and lavender and dill and sage and hyssop and comfrey and basil and more herbs than she can name. They have all disappeared now, but the exquisite fan light is still over the door and I am to look for it next time I go that way. She congratulated Bessie on Ann's marrying in the church. She said to her sons: "The main thing is to marry church people. I would rather you would do that, even if it is somebody I don't like." Sometimes I think the Mrs. Bullocks in the church are like the exquisite little fan light, all that is left.

Mrs. Bullock says she certainly is glad that the W.P.A. is through with her, for she was through with it. And now she can re-collect the herbs her grandmother once grew in the garden. Especially rosemary. And she wishes she had the old house.

[August 29]
Saturday

I sent your wings[3] this morning. I asked Lt. Kaiser if I might have them to send to you and he said, with pleasure, and he wished you had been there to receive them, and he hoped you would be back soon. Be very careful. The catch is no good, and I lost mine on the way home, remembered hearing something chink, and went back and found it. The ceremony was very nice. I feared the worst, but it was short simple and to the point. The Major emphasized the fact that volunteer work is not at an end, and that it will be a very long time before the paid workers can take over the Filter Center entirely. . . .

Treasure Island [in the Little Theatre's amphitheatre] was delightful. Especially Mr. Fletcher and your little Sennay [unidentified]. She was excellent. She looked just like a little boy, and talked like one and her eyes shone like a little boy's eyes, and she was perfectly unselfconscious. The audience was small in number and stature, but highly enthusiastic. Three little boys crept up and sat on the stone wall of the fountain, right against

---

[3] Awarded to volunteers at the Filter Center.

This formal photograph of Elizabeth, perhaps in her late thirties, may have been made for publicity reasons following the publication of A Southern Garden *in 1942.*
BY PERMISSION OF WARREN WAY AND
ELIZABETH WAY ROGERS

the footlights, and when the play was over the children all surged up on the stage like an ocean wave. The pirates were the very best. I have never seen such record-breaking spitting since "Mammy" used to spit on the back of the fireplace to make animal pictures for us.[4] All the audience joined in the spitting. A little dog who sat on the front row and said "Woof!" every time

---

[4] Elizabeth's childhood memory of Garysburg, North Carolina.

a sword was drawn added to the hilarity, and Ben Gunn was a child's delight, or anyone's; he really is superb. I haven't seen such excitement in an audience since the little French children at the puppet shows in the Tuileries.

Irma's sister Jane is here. She is a darling person like Irma, perfectly simple and natural. She stopped at Fort Benning [Georgia] on her way, to see a friend stationed there. She had called ahead to make reservations at the hotel, and they said there was not room. So she put on her Red Cross uniform (Motor Corps), and presented herself and asked for a room, and they said but certainly they had a room, and did she think she would be doing duty overseas.

She has taken over her father's business (coal and ice) and is running it and sending her young sister to college, and for that reason cannot fly bombers to war zones, which is what she wants to do. She seems to have a flair for flying, and thinks of nothing else and cares for nothing else. It seems so awful, when so many are being sent with no enthusiasm for the game, for any one who wants to go not to be able to.

Elizabeth enjoyed friends she made at Meredith College (the Aldens), North Carolina State (B. W. Wells, Frank Lyell), and St. Mary's School (Margaret Lalor, Florence Davis). The schools and the Raleigh Little Theatre provided her the kind of stimulation that Ann Bridgers had in New York, but on a small scale, and close to home. In the 1930s, Eudora Welty had come to Raleigh to visit Frank Lyell, a friend from Jackson, Mississippi. She was entertained in the Bridgers home (Mrs. Bridgers was an excellent cook). Although Elizabeth may not have been at that gathering, Ann later introduced her to Welty, and she began reading Welty's stories as they were published. Perhaps Elizabeth was more taken with the idea of knowing a published Southern writer than she was with Welty's stories, which she often found obscure. Welty introduced Elizabeth to reading the market bulletins, and they exchanged information about country plants and people. For over a half-century, the two women occasionally saw and wrote to each other.

[August]

When I sat down to write Eudora what an appreciative reader she has in me for "The Winds,"[5] I said that it is perfect, and I almost added: "You will never write anything any better."

And then I thought, with the fierce sort of joy that can hardly be called joy, that is something I could never say to Ann. . . . [The rest of the letter is about reading Audubon.]

[September 14]

Leaving summer in the town,[6] I did not look up from my book until we were in the country, and it was fall, with darkies in the fields picking cotton, and cornstalks yellow and waiting to be cut, and grasses red along the roadsides, and gums turning wine-color at the edge of the woods. I was reading *Swann's Way*. It was almost as startling to emerge from provincial France and find myself looking at cotton fields and pine woods, as to be carried so quickly from one season to another. Like going away on a boat: one minute you are on land, and the next in

---

[5] Welty story first published in 1942 in *Harper's Bazaar*.

[6] It is unclear where Elizabeth is traveling by train.

other elements; and with no transition. And I thought that the dusty September roadside could hardly be a greater contrast to the pages I had been living in, the market square of Combray, where Proust could distinguish among the tree tops the steeple of St. Hilaire. And then I thought that perhaps those woods and fields and red clay gullies and little hot towns had as much significance to me as the steeples, the two-paths and the little foot bridges across the Vivonne had for Proust.

And as I thought so, a crossroads sign flashed by. It was "Bonsal." And I thought of how every time we passed it on the train to Hamlet [North Carolina, where Mr. Lawrence and Mr. Bonsal were in business together] we said to Mother was it named for Mr. Bonsal and she said it was. And we thought how grand to have a place named for you, and just what one would expect of the Bonsals. Mr. Bonsal was from Baltimore, very tall and dark, and his elegance seemed to me to be summed up in the story Bessie told of him, that he never spoke to a servant directly. Mrs. Bonsal was from Lenox [Massachusetts]. She and the children spent only a few winter months in Hamlet, with long summers at Lenox and Newport. Bessie was her only friend in the winter, except house guests who stopped on their way to Florida. She and Bessie had tea every afternoon, and they built a little church [All Saints Episcopal], because there was none, of course, in Hamlet, and they took long drives. The Bonsals had one of the first automobiles in the early 1900s. The little Bonsals went along, but they never asked me. And I was never asked to play with them. Only at Christmas I was asked to their tree. It touched the ceiling, and had real candles that were lighted. I used to watch the little Bonsals riding by on their ponies. They had smart riding habits, and had been taught to ride as if to hounds. They were handsome children, and very large and strong—like their Yankee mother, and not at all like their father. I took great pleasure in them, as if they were children in a book. But I do not remember envying them, or ever wondering that there we were, next door, and I played alone always, and they played alone always. And we were almost the same age. But they must have been the reason that I wanted a pony more than I have ever wanted anything. So much that I asked my father to give it to me, and I do not remember ever having asked for anything else. And when I at last had the pony, and was put on his back, I found I did not ride at all like the little Bonsals. I did not know how to sit easily in the saddle, or to grip with my knees, or hold in my heels and elbows. I only knew to stick as long as I could, and try again. I was terribly mortified. So that once when I went into a country store [in Garysburg, North Carolina], and a colored man said to the men warming themselves at the stove, "See that little girl. . . . I found her lying in the road, and she said to me would I catch her pony, and do you know what she did, she got right on again and rode off" I felt guilty as if I were getting praise under false pretenses. . . .

[September 23]

I enclose my letter from Hugh,[7] I thought you would like it. I wanted to write you about Hugh, but I shall have to wait and tell you. He is like a character created by you. His vision of democracy, at once personal and abstract, is so definite and so passionate that you feel for the first time: here is one who

---

[7] One of the soldiers Bessie and Elizabeth entertained and got to know well.

knows what he is fighting for. Not that he would mention it, being British and twenty-one, but he speaks of New Zealand as a man speaks of a woman.

Every time I looked at Hugh I saw him dead. I do not mean that he is more likely to be killed than the others, but that when the war is over people like Hugh will be dead, and people without courage or imagination or passion will be living.

When I think of Hugh I think of him laughing while Bessie read Stephen Leacock.[8] I think I never saw anyone so light hearted, so merry, so responsible, so sensitive . . . and so eager.

[Hugh's letter to Elizabeth]

My dear Elizabeth,

I hope you don't mind my calling you that as it gives me someone tangible, of real flesh and blood to write to and not someone with whom it is necessary to be so awfully formal and stilted with. Having written a book you'll probably find a lot more to find fault with; you see, I've ended my last two sentences with a preposition—and now I know you'll frown on me, that is, if you're a strict grammarian as well as a now famous authority on flowers and plants etc. However to come to the point. This isn't meant to be a formal, cold letter, thanking you in well balanced and well thought out phrases for the grand time you did give me. I don't write well enough for that anyway—but my thanks are here just the same to you and your mother who really must have gone to a great deal of trouble to

---

[8] Popular Canadian humorist born in England.

put on a succession of three evenings for a pack of unregenerate rascals such as we all, our inimitable Evans included, are. I'm sorry to have missed you when I called in to say cheerio; however with any luck I may be seeing you again before I do finally leave the States so we'll leave it till then—it's a date! It was rather a comedown to have to return to this place after Raleigh, but we're bearing up. There's been plenty with hard work to get through on new machines and although I'm not a mechanic, but just a mere pilot, I've rather enjoyed covering myself with oil and grease and calling it hard work and for the last week that's been about the extent of my experiences. My world has been from hangar to sleeping quarters and believe you me the last named has been tenanted early every night. However today saw the ultimate end in sight and once we have everything ship shape—I hope the Lord will provide—and it had better be good. Well, I think that's the extent of my news this time. Let's hope next letter will be telling you how to knock an enemy out of the sky. I'll finish up by telling you a secret—I'm supposed to know all about that but I don't. Let's hope it will be fun finding out.

Best wishes to you,

Hugh

[September 29]
Monday Night

We went to the WRAL studio tonight with Mrs. [M. C.] Crowson to see how the pipes sound over the radio, and took

turns playing for each other, and they were perfectly lovely.
Very different and not at all what you would expect, but clear
and cool. I asked about the [Little Theatre] membership drive
(I meant to check up for you, but we seldom see our tenant)
and Mrs. C. says they now have 425 adults and 200 students and
haven't yet got the members from Peace, Meredith and State college. She said she was overcome by having a call from Mr. Tucker
this morning saying there would be 145 from St. Mary's. It seems
Mrs. Cruikshank said the girls could not go, and Mr. Leager[9]
went to her and talked to her, and she said, well they could. I
imagine her saying they couldn't is what made so many want
to. He said that they would stick to the advertised list this year,
which they should do (quote) and she said, Oh it was *not* the
play she objected to, all she objected to was Ada Morris's saying
"that little French Bitch."

I asked about the cast for *Arsenic and Old Lace* and she said
it was to be decided tonight. . . . Irma said Mrs. Johnson was
magnificent. She had to be helped up on the stage every time
she read, and Irma was afraid she would lose her wig. It is red.
She is here with her daughter and granddaughter and her son-
in-law Colonel Fuller who is at Camp Butner. They all swept
into St. Saviour's the night we were having our anniversary celebration. Afterward they came down to have punch in the basement. Some one told her Irma and I had made the Madonna,
and she kept coming up to first one and then the other saying,
"A perfect della Robbia, my dear, a perfect della Robbia." She
said they were delighted with St. Saviour's. Such a friendly little
church, and just what they were looking for. My heart sank. I

---

[9] Albert W. Tucker was the secretary and business manager of St. Mary's
School. Margaret Jones Cruikshank was the school's president from 1932 to
1946. Sam Leager was an actor and the business manager of the Raleigh Little
Theatre.

told Irma not to give her any encouragement or let Mr. Wulf give her any. She lived many years in India and had written an article for the *News & Observer* explaining the position of the British. But the Daniels were so anti-British they would not publish it. Afterward I heard they (the Johnsons and Tuckers, not the Daniels!) were going to [the Episcopal Church of the] Good Shepherd—to my great relief. I hope Good Shepherd and the Little Theatre take up all of her time. The daughter turned up at the Filter Center and is very nice. She and I have long talks about the granddaughter (a great awkward girl—I feel sorry for her in the South. I am afraid it will not be like India), who goes to St. Mary's and is having trouble with her Latin. . . .

Many garden club friends have raised the money for the lecture [in Asheville].

We are freezing. And Bessie will not have any furnace in case coal should "give out" later on.

[October 1]

I had been wanting to tell you—but the times when you are in the mood to be told and I in the mood to tell are so rare, and when they come it is better not to say anything—that I now owe you something more: an understanding with my sister.

I hope you have been able to do what you want to do with your play. I think about it with excitement.

This is in haste. I don't know why leaving home made me feel I have to do all the things I have left undone, but I always begin frantically to plant seeds, return things I borrowed months ago, read what I haven't read, take notes on old magazines.

Besides I have promised to talk to a book club Monday night on Modern Art, which I have lost the notes on it is so long ago, and have to look up dates, and how much Degas went in for Impressionism and how much he didn't go in for it, and to get in my radio talk which they have got to be very strict about and have to have ahead and do a plan that I promised to do and didn't. In Asheville I will be with my cousin Mrs. McLeod Patton. . . .

[October 11, Asheville]

When we started off this morning the car would not start. My cousins have two cars—one starts some times, the other only when pushed. The three of us pushed this one down the hill, it almost started, but not quite. Thus it had to be pushed up before there was more down. The three of us pushed again, Cousin Isabel and Cousin McLeod pushing with all the determination of people whose lives have been made only by supplying the momentum with their frail bodies. Just as I saw that we were not going to be able to get up the hill, a slender woman came along. "I can push a pound," she called cheerfully as if pushing cars were the accepted way of starting them. With her aid we went a few more feet, and when I could see that we would get no farther, an old, old man came along leaning on a stick. He could barely walk, but he added his weight, and the car rocked right up the hill, and over the brow. . . .

Thursday night—To New York

I got home at midnight to find out Mr. Bracelen [Ellen Flood's father] is dead. I called Ellen and caught a train at 1:30 A.M. Ellen says she is all right—I feel that it cannot but be a blessing as he suffered so much.

[October 27]
Sunday

The only thing I have learned in thirty-eight years is that the days grow shorter each year of your life, and if you live long enough it should be very easy to die, as there would be practically nothing left of them. I have been spending every day and all of it in the garden, dashing in to dress for dinner and go on to something else. Two evenings were spent with the Wulfs. Father Lambert was here. He is simply radiant. You would not know him, he looks so well. One evening he played the melody on the soprano pipes. It was great fun, as he plays with spirit and humor. A combination that I find irresistible. The nights have been spent on *Darkness at Noon* [Arthur Koestler novel]. Reading and re-reading. You know how every now and then you meet with a book that makes you start at the beginning and think through again all of your hard-won ideas. Though it has nothing to do with religion, you find *Darkness at Noon* making you apply its theory to the history of religion as well as the history of human thought. Besides I tried to take in as much of it as I could factually, as Hal[10] says it is a very accurate

---

[10] Hal Denny, American journalist reporting in Russia and husband of Elizabeth's Barnard classmate Jean Lowry.

account of the Moscow Trials and I have come to feel that they are the turning point of world affairs in the twentieth century. This sounds very dull, and not at all what I mean to say, or the way I mean to say it.

Sometime I shall take a day off, and write you a letter before midnight. I got up at six this morning to give one of the soldiers breakfast and get him off on an early bus. The other was so sad I could not resist asking him to stay to lunch, after which I just had time to fix the tea tray before the pipers came. Before they left Wylie[11] and Caroline [Long] came and I fixed highballs for them, and before they left Miss Daisy and Miss Lillian [Thompson] arrived to Sunday night supper, which was still to be gotten.

The Aldens came to play with us this afternoon and in all your life you have never seen anything so darling. Really I have never seen anything so darling as Mr. Alden. If we had been finished musicians he could not have played with us any more eagerly or taken any more interest in our problems. . . . Of course he played beautifully, and liked my pipe best, which pleased me because I do too. . . .

Emily has gotten piles of books and pamphlets and is planning to study systematically for the civil service (or whatever they are) exams. She says she is determined to get a very high mark. She says since she has been at home she has found demands on her time every minute, and now she will have to shut her door while she studies and say that no one is to speak to her short of fire. She says she now understands your difficulties.

And while I am on the subject of you. Please, will you not

---

[11] Willie Jones Long's first name was also spelled Wilie or Wylie to emphasize the proper pronunciation of the long *i*. Even the family used different spellings.

go back to the Filter Center when you come home (though it will kill our group all of whom ask for you every time and seem to hold me personally responsible for you being still away)? I never could bear for you to spend your energy on it, and I can bear it even less now. The chances of bombs in this section— always remote—are getting less every day, and the lieutenant now in charge says positively that our filter center will not be activated until there is a probability of bombing which means that we will go on with canned messages and that every one is worse and worse. It would drive you mad aside from all else. Margie—who always gets the low-down—says there is talk of abandoning all inland filter centers. Which I think is a good idea. Ours is certainly no real contribution to the war effort.

I wrote so many letters for Ellen while I was in New York that I got in a state, very rare with me, of not being able to bear the sight of pen and paper. So I never got around to writing you about Mr. Bracelen's sister Margaret and his brother Henry. Aunt Margaret is like a character out of Willa Cather. In a day when it was almost unheard of for a girl to go to college at all, she worked her way through the University of Nebraska. She has the gift, that seems common in Ellen's family, of raising any moment above the ordinary level: as when she looked up from a volume of [English Renaissance poet Thomas] Campion, and smiled at Ellen and read:

> On you the affection of your father's friends
> With his inheritance, by right descends.

Uncle Henry is quiet and gentle and recedes so far into himself that he is almost invisible, but when you speak to him his response is as complete as the attention that a person who loves to read gives to a book. I had supposed that two septuagenarians from the provinces, obviously heartbroken (they adored Mr. Bracelen), exhausted with the long and hurried trip, confused by the city, would be very much on our hands. Instead they had the perfect composure of people who live quiet and dignified lives, and far from being shocked by Ellen and me, joined in with our ways. Uncle Henry took very readily to a Scotch and soda with our cocktails, and Aunt Margaret said she did not see why she should dress for breakfast when Ellen and I came in our bathrobes. And the day before they left Aunt Margaret said that if Ellen did not think it unseemly they would like to see something in the city, as Henry had never been to New York before, and was especially anxious to see the waterfront. So they made a day of it, and ended by going in the evening to Radio City Music Hall. And when they left there was such a stillness as Ellen did not think possible from the departure of two almost entirely silent people. . . .

[November 10]
Wednesday night

The cool is creeping up gradually instead of coming with a snap as it usually does. I hope you will be able to get what you want done. I had been hoping for a "fairer summer and a later fall than in these parts a man is apt to see" [Edna St. Vincent Millay sonnet XLVI]. The leaves are fading early. I think they will fall before they turn. We have had frost in the country but not in town. The garden is still brilliant. On the first of November (All Saints Day) I went out to look for a crocus that was in bud, and instead of the ordinary lilac crocus *zoatus* I found in bloom the most beautiful little white flower that I have ever seen. It is milk white and of a texture thin to transparency, but firm and cool, and the inside is veined with hair lines of pure violet, and the throat has a scalloped design in chrome yellow. Every day for four days I went out and sat and looked at it. It is like some rare thing in a museum, but even more beautiful because any day it may be gone. I can hardly bear to go away tomorrow and leave it behind.

Irma, Father Lambert and I are going on the early train to Richmond to pipe. . . .

[December 4]

When the pattern of thought becomes apparent you see that, as the children of Israel wandered in the desert until they were ready for the promised land, the mind circles around an idea until it is ripe for it.

For a long time I pushed back all that has to do with rock plants, and then the time came to concentrate upon them. The same with Russia. I am now concentrating on rock plants and Russia. And when you are ready to embrace a subject you find the unrelated facts in the back of your mind fitting themselves together. And when you are ready to embrace the subject the material is always at hand. Not that this is remarkable in the case of Russia which is foremost in everyone's mind at present, but it is remarkable that when the time comes it all fits together. . . .

[December 14]

I walked to Irma's in a warm wet mist that reminded me of fall on Riverside Drive [near Barnard College in New York City] with the street lights blurred and the trees black and slick and shining; and of feeling of sadness without knowing what it is to be sad.

Do certain seasons and sorts of weather remind you of certain years? Every spring reminds me of being ten in Garysburg if it is sudden and warm, and of being sixteen at St. Mary's if it is rainy and cool. And a long fall full of sun reminds me of the first year Nana was in Raleigh. And midsummer reminds me of Parkersburg when I was very little and woke up to find it already hot, and heard the whistle of Aunt Teedie's parrot across the street.

And a scene can come to mean a time of day. Early morning will always remind me of something Elizabeth Thompson told me. She looked from her hospital window on to Morningside Drive [in New York City], when it was beginning to be light, and saw a group of women with shawls over their heads waiting in front of the little French church [the Church of Notre Dame]. And as she watched the sky grew light, and a priest flung open the doors, and a flock of pigeons flew from the eaves and sailed out over Morningside Park. . . .

[Monday afternoon]

Whenever I write to you it turns out to be about the war, and I tear it up. I do not mean to write to you about the war, and I did not realize I was doing it. I suppose the soldiers are more on my mind than I knew, and I cannot even get a letter from one of my unknown friends without crying. Mrs. Henry, writing me about the *Hymenocallis* from Louisiana that she grows in Pennsylvania without winter protection, writes more of her two sons in the Army. . . .

I have tried long and seriously to think about the war, and I have come to the conclusion that it is a subject for the military mind alone. All others should do what they find at hand to do, and not think. And all who can should be doing what you are doing: creating what war cannot destroy. Thought should be concentrating on peace. War is an incident. Peace is forever.

I am so excited about what you are writing. I wake up in the night and think about you in the way you think about people who are going to have a baby. It is a new feeling to me to be tense about something you have not even talked to me about. It is the cumulative effect of writing that has a fullness of meaning that includes not only the thing itself but what has gone before and will come after. I guess this is what you mean by "writing." . . .

Monday night

The work shop meeting and play were delightful—I keep thinking that the Little Theatre will suffer from the war, but instead it seems to thrive. There were many new people in the audience and on the stage, and in spite of that the essential something of work shop meetings is there and unchanged. Mr. Leager came and stood by Mrs. B. [Bridgers] to give his spot and said it was a good report but he could take no credit. "You are too modest" Mrs. B. murmured. And "not at all, it is true" Mrs. Leager answered her in an undertone.

My friend Mrs. Johnson in her red wig told Emily and me she was furious because they had given her to understand she had a part in *Arsenic and Old Lace*, and then never mentioned it again. She said "I suppose they thought I was a damn-Yankee, but I was born in India—ha! The Little Theatre would do well to use more middle-aged women." She went on (she is seventy if a day) "and I was glad to see that the two middle-aged women in the play tonight were the best actors in it."

All of which (if you follow me—I am not sure I follow myself) brings me to the conclusion that what takes the form of democracy in one country may take the form of dictatorship in another. Just as they used to say that the sort of person who was a Democrat in the South would be a Republican in the North.

Not that I could ever be in sympathy with Russians. I know from their literature that it is very Europeanized Russians [like] Chekhov, Tolstoy, and Turgenev that mean anything to me. I cannot understand a writer like Dostoevsky. But there is always a time when a person or a nation comes closer to your understanding than at any other time (even if that is not very close) and now is the time when Russia and America touch for the last and first time, like two tangents in a mathematical formula. Now, for the first time, we can see for ourselves exactly what the Russians are, and we do not have to depend for our information on the conflicting reports of ignorant, over formidable and over prejudiced observers.

Every time I get to the point where I think I cannot go on with soldiers every weekend I get a letter like the one enclosed. And I know I am in it for the duration. The letter is from Jack Fisher. He means it when he says he wants to get across. He is as passionately fond of big guns as some men are of horses. He says fighting at long range is like a chess game. You do not think of killing. You do not see the enemy. He is one of the men I want to tell you about. . . .

[Jack Fisher's letter to Elizabeth]

Miss Eliz.

Well I have passed the motors and the material part of my course and am now deep in gunnery. I sure like it in spite of the enormous amount of work and study we have to do. The discipline is very strict and the pace is terrific. Many have fallen by the wayside and I am working with all my might to stay out in front as if you fall behind on one point it's like falling off of a boat—you're gone. I would write you a much longer letter if I had the time. I will let you know of the final disposition they make of me. Hope to get across in Feb.

Give my regards to your mother.

A Grateful Soldier

[December]

The middle of the day was very mild and I almost thawed as I walked over to St. Mary's to give Mrs. Alden a message and some doughnuts Bessie made for her. . . . Mrs. Alden looked at me the way some (few) people do when they know what you are thinking, and said: "Isn't Miss Bridgers coming home for Christmas?" And I said, "No, she likes the cold, and she is very happy to be where she can work." And she didn't say anything more, but smiled into my eyes, a smile like the sudden warmth of the day.

. . . And when I turned away there was a group of colored people who work in the laundry waiting to be paid off, and I said, seeing so many: "is this a convention or a baptism?" and they all laughed and said, "Convention, lady." And I thought if you said that to a group of white people they would have stood and stared.

. . . We have entirely abandoned the Filter Board and are applying our time to a course in Air Plane identification, which a disagreeable young woman is making as dull and confusing as a simple and fascinating subject can be. In spite of doing nothing when we get there, we are expected to come as usual on Christmas Day.

[December]

I went to St. Saviour's Sunday to the late celebration and was overwhelmed with surprise to find, instead of the usual six or seven, a congregation of between thirty and forty. And this [growth] in a year. You will never see anything more darling than Irma and her vested choir of eight little girls, Mr. Wulf in the chancel, and John Cole at the organ going valiantly through the difficult plain-song and chants of the Holy Communion. John and Mr. Wulf who were at Sewanee [Episcopal School of Theology] together have an equal passion for church music, and they spare Irma and the little girls nothing, not even the "Parsifal Amen" Mr. Wulf intones. . . .

[December 24]

When Bessie and I got to St. Saviour's tonight for the Christmas tree we found a shabby old woman standing in the door with a paper bag full of little packages. She was Peggy's grandmother who had come all the way from the tracks on her old legs to bring Peggy's presents because Peggy (aged nine) had been borne off to the hospital this afternoon with a broken arm, and her chief concern was that the children should get their presents. Peggy is one of the poorest, thinnest, and cutest of the regulars. She had been down town this morning, and herself purchased a present for every child in her class. Her grandmother said that Peggy's mother had wrapped the presents when she got home from work, and please to excuse it if they were not wrapped very good.

Instead of the Christmas story as a pageant, we borrowed a lantern from Christ Church and had it in pictures: Six or eight slides beginning with Fra Angelico's *Annunciation* and ending with the Sistine Madonna. At the last Martha Ann whispered, "Oh, Miss Lawrence, look at the little angels, doesn't the one leaning on his elbow look just like Dinky." And he does. Mr. Wulf read the Bible while Irma worked the slides, and for each picture the congregation, sitting in the dark, sang very softly a verse of a Christmas hymn. Then we went down stairs to the tree, and if you think all joy has gone from the world you should see a St. Saviour's Christmas party. . . .

I never seem to say what I mean, which comes of writing when you are tired, but there are no other times. I certainly didn't mean that any one could ignore the war.

It is just that every now and then it comes over everyone and when it comes over me, I do not mean to take it out on you. Bessie came out in the garden weeping one day, and my heart stood still thinking nothing less than a tragedy to Ann could have occurred. She said that one of the little boys in our apartment (whom she did not know by sight) was going to war. I said: "But Bessie, they go every day." And she said: "I know, but this one is so young, and he came to tell me goodbye."

We stopped at the Thompsons after St. Saviour's for the annual Christmas tree trimming, at which I mount to the top of a tall step-ladder and Miss Lillian, Miss Daisy, Clanie [unidentified], Bessie, and Elizabeth hand things up and say: "Farther over Libba." "Higher up Libba," "the other twig, Libba." "Not the red ball Libba, over here, up there, lower down," etc. But the finished product is as perfect as everything the Thompsons do.

It will not be Christmas at all without you and Warren and Ann, but it is much more important to me to know that you are happy where you are than to be with you.

1943

Ann had been sending Elizabeth drafts of her play "Possess These Shores." Elizabeth dropped everything else and sat down to read them closely, then sent back detailed critiques. Ann often worked on the same play for years. Here are two letters that represent the give-and-take that went on between the two concerning Ann's work.

Tuesday morning

Dear Ann,

It was very late in the night when I finished reading "Possess These Shores," and I wanted to try to communicate my emotion and inner excitement, but the play left me inarticulate. I lay for a long time in the darkness without thinking or feeling, the way you do when you have listened to music that goes beneath thought and emotion to something that is deeper and rarely touched. Then I slept and woke again with the sensation undissipated, and lay wrapped in it still until the noises of the day became too strong.

Dear Ann. I wonder if you know how much more of yourself you have put into this play than you have allowed (except indirectly) to creep into any other. Your understanding and tenderness and vision. And I wonder if, in the travail of creation, you can see as I do your development as an artist.

"Possess These Shores" is more a symphony than a play, the intense suspense that you so skillfully build up, a counterpoint to the melody. The theme is more inherent in the rhythm of speech than in the beautiful words even, and the title is like a statement of it. It is all that a title should be: provocative, beautiful to say, and adequate to carry the full implication of all that is to follow. . . .

I thought the start was slow, but it may be, that all of the explanation and preparation [about Filter Center operations] for what is to come is necessary. . . . Once the real play gets started it is beautifully swift and inevitable.

You must have had a hearty laugh over my being so upset over your wasting your time at the Filter Center. . . .

[Ann to Elizabeth, a few weeks later]

Elizabeth dear,

My emotions on reading your good opinion of "Possess These Shores" undoubtedly equaled [niece] Elizabeth's award for the high school contest in poetry from the Federation of Women's Clubs of South Carolina. Certainly I was "flabbergasted" (as she put it) that at my age and years of effort I could be so overjoyed. The play cost me tremendous labor, and long before it was finished seemed so puny an achievement. But your letter made me think that perhaps I had builded better than I thought. One thing I accomplished through writing it—I am forever free of the shackles of realism. The play about Myrtle was the first faltering—very faltering—and unsuccessful effort to break away. In this play I made a step or two. But from now on I can fly away. . . .

I agree with you that the start is slow. But Emily insisted that I give a clear account of the procedure at the Filter Center in the beginning, and I know she is right. . . . Any criticism you make cannot upset me now. It is in the beginnings that I get upset—before I know what I am about. Emily has been noble in this instance, refraining from criticism or even suggestion. I have many times been very angry with her when I needed help and thought it was just laziness—or worse still—that perhaps she thought as little of this play as of others I have written. I wanted so much to send you my groping and call "Help!" But I sternly put that temptation aside, for I wanted your final reaction to this play—having used up Emily's from the beginning. . . .

Love, Ann

Playwright

Miss Ann Preston Bridgers of Raleigh, whose play, "Coquette," is one of the most popular of the theatrical world, again this winter will write her views and reviews of New York dramas for this newspaper. Her first column on The Theatre will concern "The Bill of Divorcement" which the Raleigh Little Theatre is presenting in Pullen Hall December 9. Following, she will report on the current New York plays. Miss Bridgers plans to be in New York for the next three weeks, returning to Raleigh for the Christmas holidays.

Left: *Ann Preston Bridgers, circa 1922*
BY PERMISSION OF NORTH CAROLINA
COLLECTION, UNIVERSITY OF NORTH
CAROLINA LIBRARY AT CHAPEL HILL

Right: *Newspaper clipping
(unidentified) announcing
Ann Preston Bridgers's reviews of plays
in Raleigh and New York in 1938*
BY PERMISSION OF THE RARE BOOK, MANUSCRIPT, AND SPECIAL
COLLECTIONS LIBRARY, DUKE UNIVERSITY

Unfortunately, "Possess These Shores" did not get the kind of recognition that Ann and Elizabeth hoped. From 1940 to 1943, Ann submitted it to various offices connected with the Federal Theatre project, but each time it was rejected. Although one reader's report to the National Theatre Conference found it "serious and impassioned writing on a serious theme . . . the place of the individual in a world-wide democracy," the play was rejected.

Ann had seemingly boundless determination and continued to work on new plays, as well as a novel.

[Saturday, January 23]

I heard Miss [Robertine] McClendon [a Little Theatre board member] upstairs, and ran up to ask her how *The Eve of St. Mark* went. She said in her burbling way: "Oh, it was so exciting to see three hundred people and not one automobile." The audience was St. Mary's girls and State College boys, and very warm, and did much applauding, which Miss McC. likes. . . . She said Mr. [John] Rembert [the director] cut the play at the end and thereby improved it greatly, because the end was government propaganda. And that a soldier in the audience had a fit over the camp scenes in the play.

We have two sailors with us tonight. They are attached to the Marines as [part of a] construction battalion. Both are twenty-one and both from Chicago, and both the gentlest and the gayest. They think the Navy is wonderful, their officers the best in the Navy, their chances of getting over quickly excellent, their camp the finest in the country, and war a great lark. One of them said that there was nothing like living in barracks for having a good time. You can't help having fun, he said, when you have a hundred and fifty men sleeping in one room. For sociability, barracks can't be beat. He has a younger brother who joined the Navy when he was seventeen, and an older brother who was just drafted. The other boy is an only child.

Sunday

We went again to pipe for the USO Club this afternoon. After everything was over, and the sandwiches circulating, a commonplace looking young man came over to me and asked to see the pipes. He said, "Did you really make them? How amazing! Gee, you must have fun. Gee, you don't know what a kick I got out of hearing you play. I play a violin."

I had not realized how much the Catholics are like the Baptists. There are so many of them and they are so hearty. I could see what our sailor meant by the fun they had, when five smart young men with wings on their sleeves called for the accompanist to play "The Old Gray Mare," and got up and sang:

> We don't have to walk with the infantry,
> > ride with the cavalry,
> > shoot with the artillery,
> We don't have to fly over Germany,
> We're in the finance corps!

But there was one boy with a strange and lovely face that will haunt me for some time. I am sure he can think of more delightful things than sleeping with 149 others.

Monday

I sat down this morning for the first time in many weeks—what with no cook and a new cook and doing over the apartment and renting it, and chauffeuring, and doing over Bessie's room and any number of other things—and had just gotten lost in Amaryllids[12] (the way you do in dreams or music) when

---

[12] The American Amaryllis Society awarded Elizabeth the Herbert Medal in 1943 for her work on amaryllids described in *A Southern Garden*. A few months later, she wrote a special essay about amaryllids for *Herbertia*, the society's publication. She returned to the subject in books and newspaper columns over the next twenty-plus years.

These photographs show the "pipers" in the Raleigh garden. In the top photograph, Elizabeth is on the right. In the photograph below, she is seated second from the right. On a memorable trip to Richmond, Virginia, she played with a group of Presbyterian pipers.

BY PERMISSION OF WARREN WAY AND ELIZABETH WAY ROGERS

I realized it was me that Maggie was calling, not someone in another world, and I was glad when I got to the telephone and found that it was Violet, that I had forgot to tell Maggie not to call me unless the house caught fire. You remember Violet? The friend of your friend, Mary Cole, who came when Father was at Duke [Hospital], with the dyed red hair and the Queen Mary clothes? Well, you have never seen such a charming person. Her hair has come undyed and is a lovely russet and she had on a very smart russet hat, and a beautiful russet suit of English tweed and looked altogether so young and delightful that I could not squeeze her enough—and she does not mind being squeezed. She covered the horticultural world, papers, people, events, and scandals in Virginia, Massachusetts, New York, and England, and a dip into the Far West, in the few minutes she stayed and sipped sherry.

Billy Hunt is in the Army, and writes that he is in South Georgia in a section where the geological deposits are amazing, and he has never had such a wonderful field for study, but not a word about the war or drilling. [Violet] supposes he is on the seas by now, but feels sure he will find a species of fern growing out of the cranny of the ship, and a rock garden in the African desert.

I should think anyone would look forward to being seventy who could look like Violet and have that spirit. And speaking of seventy, don't you love the story of the Frenchman who was walking along the Champs Élysées on a spring morning, and caught sight of a trim ankle, and sighed, "Oh, to be seventy again!"

Tuesday

Bessie and Emily and I all liked *The Eve of St. Mark* very much indeed, and Emily and I wept. . . . Emily, on the other side of me, was wiping her eyes and saying, "The Little Theatre improves right along, doesn't it?" The play was done the way *Our Town* was done, and is something of the same sort of play. . . .

I think you would have been pleased with your work. I do not ever forget that the Little Theatre (like me) is entirely your creation. . . .

I sent you some special commons to split and butter and toast for your tea. Bessie managed to get a box of them. And the pot lifter I forgot at Christmas, and some nuts which I hope did not make it too heavy for Mr. Fobes [to carry to Ann in her mountain cabin]. I cannot bear not making you things, but after the nut breads getting spoiled, which took a week's ration of sugar, I thought it was foolish. Very little candy is to be had, and Royster's [candy company's] is not fit to eat. I keep hoping some of the stores will have peppermints again. That is all I can think of to send. Once a month they have a few bars of Hersheys at the Piggly [the Piggly Wiggly grocery store] and you can get one five-cent cake. . . .

[February 4]

. . . The bus [to the garden club in Wilmington, North Carolina] was so quiet and the morning light so lovely—and the frosty fields, I sat wishing I could go on all day, riding through the still country, and reading [the novel] *Primer for Combat*. As I followed Kay Boyle in her search for truth through the confusion of defeat in France . . . I asked myself why it should be true for me to believe that salvation can come to the world only through equality for all peoples, and untrue for [another person] to believe that it can come only through Anglo-Saxon domination. After all, neither of us can know whether the lion and the lamb will lie down together. . . . [Truth] is something you have to create for yourself. . . . This is where faith comes in. We do not know whether there is a God or not. We only know that we have need of one, and that need helps us. We do not know whether there is honor among men. We only know that we cannot live without it, and that helps us to believe in it. . . .

[February 11]

We went down to the United Church last night to play for Mrs. Alden's circle, and we were delighted with them and they with us, and Mrs. Alden was pleased, which is all that mattered. While we waited in the pastor's study Mrs. Alden said, "I think I shall just call Edgar, to see if he is still alive." Cicely [Browne] smiled and said, "he was still alive at noon, Dorothy, for I saw him on the bus." Bessie and Emily are much exercised over the possible separation of the Aldens. They think no matter who has to go to war, it should not be Mr. Alden. Bessie says, "And they will probably never come back to Raleigh, and we shall never know anyone like them again."[13] Which is certainly true, for there are not many people like the Aldens to know. . . .

---

[13] After the war, Edgar Alden returned to teaching at Meredith College, then completed graduate work at the University of North Carolina and became a distinguished member of the Music Department there. Edgar and Dorothy had a daughter named Priscilla, after Priscilla Mullins, one of the members of the love triangle involving Miles Standish and John Alden, from whom Edgar was descended.

[February 14]
Saturday night

The little Marine touched the snowflakes on the dinner table and asked shyly: "Are these May-bells?"

I thought he could not have given a better example of comparative bloom, for they must bloom in May in Northern New York. I told him I was sure that they were, but they were February-bells here, only we called them snowflakes. "Oh, snow," he said. "Our place is covered with two feet of snow now. I guess it will be May when these come out."

From all of the boys that I have seen, I find that there is forming in my mind an image of an American. It is something I have never understood before, what an American is. You can not learn it from going to State College and Columbia Extension and dancing with cowboys in New Mexico,[14] and questioning foreigners and reading everything from Mark Twain to Louis Adamic—though Louis Adamic comes closer to putting it in writing than most.[15] You can learn it only by talking to dozens and dozens of young men under your own roof.

This American, whose image is becoming clear to me, is happy and gentle. He is intelligent, but not intellectual. He is friendly and very tolerant. And he has an open mind. He is not a Southerner nor a Northerner, nor a countryman nor a New Yorker. He is a citizen. This is because his mother or his father, or both, came from Europe to this country, and he has not had time to build up prejudices. Nor reason to. He has always had

---

[14] As a teenager, Elizabeth had danced with cowboys on a Western tour before she went to college.

[15] Elizabeth probably had read a June 4, 1938, article about Adamic in *The Nation* that focused on his book *My America*.

food, good clothes, good schooling, and fun. He is not a patriot. He is too dispassionate. He takes his country for granted. But he tries to enlist when he is nineteen, only his Mother will not sign for him, so he has to wait until he is drafted, or the right age—whatever it is—I do not know why he is so eager to go to war. I do not think he knows. I guess all healthy males want to go to war when there is one. But it isn't patriotism. He is not ambitious. He thinks of the job at hand, and the fun at hand. He doesn't miss any of the present by looking to the future. If he likes the service, he expects to be an officer in due time if he does his job. But he never heard of being an officer and a gentleman. He never heard of a gentleman, and does not know that he is one. (You remember Barrie said of Peter Pan that he was "good form" because he did not know he had it, for being good form and not knowing it was the best form of all.) This American is rather like Peter Pan in other ways. Do you remember when he said "To die will be a big adventure"? Not that the American would say it. But he is gentle, considerate, can discuss without arguing and is always at ease with any person, and in any place. He is not easily embarrassed because he is not self-conscious. He is very responsive to anything you say, especially if it is humorous. (Didn't you love the story in *The New Yorker* of the duchess who rejoiced to overhear her two American guests saying to each other that the old lady was a swell guy?)

. . . Now it is after midnight. The boys sat talking by the fire until 8:30 P.M. and then I washed the dinner dishes and set the table for breakfast because Maggie [a servant] had been promised tomorrow off. And then I finished what I was writing on this afternoon. . . .

[February 17]
Sunday

Bessie cooked waffles and sausage for the Marines this morning, and I left them still eating. When I got back from Sunday school, they had just got off to church. . . . The rest of the morning we spent preparing curry for the Caseys [unidentified], who are coming tonight to eat it. We have been very fortunate this winter in seeing a great deal of the young, among them the Caseys. . . .

Monday

As the Caseys left, I went on to Irma's to spend the night, Mr. Wulf having gone to hold a mission at St. Mark's, Halifax. We sat by the fire talking, and Irma said she would like me to read Father Lambert's poems, which he had just sent to her. . . . Poetry of mystics has always fascinated me, but except for a few (for sheer beauty) of [George] Herbert's, I have never been able to feel at all in tune with the writer, perhaps because he was so long dead. Father Lambert's seemed somehow more poignant. Perhaps because so detached and dispassionate; but terribly intense. Like his chalk-white face . . . And Irma is right in saying that they are very bad. They are very good and very bad. As good writing nearly always is. In the letter he wrote with them, he said, "They are all I have." Which I guess is literally true, except for his shabby clothes and his toothbrush.

Tuesday

. . . For some strange reason that I do not understand, Father Lambert's poems put me so poignantly in mind of you that I have sat down and written you all these things that I want to tell you about anyway, but probably would have sat myself down to otherwise. I suppose it is because you get inured from childhood to beautiful things from the past, but sort of defenseless before the living person.

[February 22]

The air is soft again after that last and worst gust of winter, and the cold has gone as suddenly as it came. I guess it is really spring, for I have taken to writing poetry, which I tear up. I make it a stern rule to tear up all poetry written in early spring.

I guess I shall have to make up my mind to garden to an accompaniment of children. Yesterday there were two, today, four, and tomorrow, I suppose there will be eight. Christopher and Buddy raked and put the trash in the little wheelbarrow (which they all love) and burned it on the fire. I gave them each a nickel and milk and crackers and told them that the laborer was worthy of his hire. That is what Nana used to tell me, when I was a little girl and did chores for her. (My parents thought you should find it reward enough to be of service.) Christopher and Buddy were very surprised about the hire. They had never heard of it. But now the whole neighborhood wants to work for me. . . .

[February 28]
Saturday night

I guess spring is really here, for the silver bells are out, and the golden bells are out, and the blue bells, but you would not know it from the weather. It was below thirty when I went out to market this morning.

The coming of spring is like the coming of a person you love, you always think it will be the same and it is always different. Or maybe it is you who are different.

We have a little Nazi [sympathizer?] spending the night with us tonight. A nice little boy, too, and such a miserable wretch that I am sure that you could not but feel sorry for him. But he is crazy. . . .

Tuesday we had a blackout. Blackouts are funny things. They have moods just like seasons. When I went out on the porch to see if the firelight showed through the curtains, I could hear dogs barking nervously, and children calling to each other across the street in excited voices: "I'm not in bed, are you?" And from the college dormitories a hubbub that sounded almost ominous. I wondered what had happened to nerves since the last blackout, last spring, when you could hear soft voices and laughter through the open windows, and radios turned low, and had a feeling of security as tangible as the warm spring air. I came inside quickly, and Bessie and I sat in the firelight listening to Brahms' *Academic Festival Overture* from WQXR. We never heard the All Clear, and later found that it came only over the radio. Bessie said indignantly that it did not come over ours. I reminded her that we were listening to New York. "Well," she said, "I still think it was badly managed." . . .

I still think the war will be over before long. And I am still alone in thinking it. . . . Our little Nazi said to me, very red in the face, "I wish I could be as sure of it as you seem to be." He meant he wished he could be as sure that we wouldn't win. He says he is a pacifist and a socialist. I couldn't help thinking that he meant he was a National Socialist, and that he wouldn't mind fighting for Hitler. He said that we called ourselves a free country and that we were really no freer than Germany. He said, "We say a man can say what he thinks, but he can't. Not in the army, he can't." I said, "Well, you can say what you think here, and I will listen, even if I do not agree." . . .

[March 1]
Sunday night

. . . At the concert I understood the quality of the voices that came from the college dormitories during the blackout. Major Kuchinski got up and announced that many of the boys in the glee club had been called to the army, so that they had not been able to carry the program out as planned. Most of those who were singing would be leaving for the Army when they graduate tomorrow. I guess to the [men in the] dormitories, the blackout seemed very real. Singing "The Star Spangled Banner" seemed unbearable, especially when I looked up in the middle of "the land of the free and the home of the brave" and saw the two little Freiderich children [of a Czech family living in Raleigh] singing it, too. I should think Czechoslovakians would find those words very bitter in their mouths. . . .

Tuesday

Sunday I met a man I have long been looking for: a delightful Jew. He is perfect even to the name of Harry Feinstein. Frank Casey, who went to college with him, asked to bring him out to tea, so these were added to the pipers. . . . Saturday night Mrs. Freiderich and the children came to make their pipes. . . . They came at 7:30 P.M., and at ten the children could scarcely be persuaded to stop for a cup of cocoa. The cocoa was in rose Canton cups, and Mrs. Freiderich said that the last time she drank out of cups like those, she was drinking tea with her mother in Prague. . . . Mr. Freiderich does something about planes. I don't quite see what could be done in Raleigh, but whatever it is I imagine it is vital. They got out of Prague right after Munich. . . . The children laugh at their mother because she speaks English so haltingly. . . . I rather think they got this humorous tolerance of parents from America. It does not seem to belong to their formal manners, but it makes a charming combination. . . .

Ash Wednesday, March 10

It must really be spring this time for the wild flowers are beginning to push up, and the sky is very blue. This afternoon I went out and found an hepatica in bloom that I am sure was not there this morning. It is the first of the wild flowers, and is one that I got from the mountains last fall. It is the white form of H. *acutiloba*, and is the frailest, loveliest thing I ever saw. The flowers are many-petaled like little anemones, and their short furry stems are curled as if they could not bear to get very far from the earth on account of the cold. Tomorrow I think there will be bloodroot. . . .

Ash Wednesday is one of my favorite days in the year because of the beauty of the Penitential Office, which is one of the perfect pieces of dramatic literature, and because of the verse from Joel (ii. 12) that is read in place of the Epistle. In the morning, when Bessie and I went to the early service, I thought that this year we should be more ready than ever to "weep between the porch and the altar," and that it would be a relief to have ashes to pour on one's head. All of Lent is a drama. A tragedy that lasts six weeks. Beginning with Ash Wednesday: "Blow the trumpet in Zion/sanctify a fast" . . . and reaching a climax in Holy Week, and ending with the Angel in the tomb.

We had dinner with Irma to see Mr. Carter, who had come to preach at the evening service, and who was a friend of Nana's. I was nine the time that he came to stay with Nana, and I was there with her. It is funny. I did not think I remembered him, but when I saw him I was shocked; and then I realized that I had been thinking of a young man. I had not realized before that it is so long since I was nine. I asked if he remembered me, and he said he did. I thought he was being politic until he said that he played jack-rocks with me on the porch step. No one could make up that step. It was the most wonderful step that a house ever had. A very broad smooth piece of sandstone, just right for jack-rocks, and in the summer very cool to sit on, especially in the morning when the sun was at the back of the house, and when Nana brought you a cool delicious white grape juice made of Catawba grapes and served in little glass cups with gold leaves on them. . . .

What I was thinking last night in my sleep and when I awoke was of you. I was trying to understand why it mortifies you for me to love you so much. I think I do understand. (Or maybe it is only my saying it, but you are the one who dislikes reserve.) But it should not, for it is impersonal. I worship your creative gift, and I do not see why you should not worship it with me as you would anything else beautiful in your possession, like the drawing of the old actress and her lover in the café.

Thursday

. . . Annette [sister Ann] has got a job, and is having a baby. Do not say anything about the baby until you hear it, which you probably will as she cannot refrain though it is much too soon to tell it. I am much relieved as she was going nuts. I don't think anyone ever wanted a baby as much. The job is temporary, and with the Red Cross. She said they drafted her.

[March 22]
Sunday morning and afternoon

The Aldens came in hatless and coatless out of the warm night to bring back the recorder, and pay a last call. I always love the way completely unconventional people always pick one convention and adhere to it strictly. I do not believe any upheaval could prevent the Aldens from calling on Bessie at the proper interval, and they stood smiling at each other and at Mrs. Alden's held-out hand; and there beside her wedding ring shone the smallest, brightest, clearest diamond I ever saw. I almost said, "Oh, [you bought the diamond for Dorothy,] not the violin [for Edgar]!" but changed it quickly to "Oh, how lovely!" but even so I am afraid I didn't sound joyful. But the Aldens were too wrapped up in each other and the ring to be at all sensitive to anyone's voice or expression. They sat and ate large slices of cake, and drank tall glasses of milk, and smiled at each other and looked at us vaguely, as if we were a long way off, and looked at the ring, and looked at each other and laughed, and left still in a glow. . . .

Then last night Bessie and I were having Sunday night supper with the Caseys and Longs, and Tom [Long, Jr.] was holding forth with passion on his father's fight for socialized medicine. Dr. Tom [Thomas Williams Mason Long] was trying to get a bill through the [North Carolina] legislature for a tax of $.50 a year on every automobile license, to take care of accidents. He said $.50 per person would give as much hospitalization if administered that way as the insurance companies could give for $30 a year, but he said, in spite of all the pressure brought to bear and the cries of communism and state control, Dr. Tom would have got it through if he had lived.[16] . . .

When we came out the car was covered with snow. And Saturday I gardened all day in sandals and dirndl and we had lunch on the terrace, and tender things were showing above ground, and I had to make the rounds three times to get [record] the things in bloom, because more came out each hour.

Bessie and I do not think we are going to be able to get another servant. First we gave up getting a man, and then when our little Maggie took French leave we had to get used to the

---

[16] Dr. Thomas Williams Mason Long practiced in Roanoke Rapids, North Carolina, and served in the North Carolina Senate until his death from a heart attack in 1941. He created a health-care prepayment plan for workers in the Roanoke Rapids textile mills and was credited by the founding dean of Duke Medical School with the idea behind Blue Cross Blue Shield.

idea of none. We still answer ads, of course, but the cars are lined up in the alleys. Emily sent her wonderful Mabel, and you would not have known our house it looked so clean and shining. Then Lillian [Thompson] came and cooked dinner, for the soldiers, and we have worked out a system of giving them waffles cooked on the table for breakfast. Then the Wulfs came for Sunday lunch, and Irma and Fritz washed the dishes, Fritz arranging the silver in order on the tray and saying that I would have to get him another tray unless he let some pieces touch. I told him I could get him a job in the Thompsons' pantry any day. He is a funny little boy. And very beautiful. Irma said a whole street full of cooks moved North in a body last week.

What did you think of Mr. Churchill? I think it is a mistake, all of this world broadcast. I do not see why nations anymore than families should talk over their affairs in public. . . . And all that "We alone" business . . .

[April 18, Passion Sunday]

. . . The Johnsonians [Elizabeth and Bessie's book club] took their turn at the U.S.O. Club Saturday night. All the book clubs have a night. I would like to have seen the soldiers and the Johnsonians. Irma came to dinner and we were so mowed down by the servant problem that after we had washed the dishes we just sat without even spirit to pipe.

But I do not want you to get the impression that I blame the darkies. I think we deserve what we are getting for having paid too little and had too long hours for so long.

We said prayers for your garden today, this being Rogation Sunday, the day when the Lord's blessing is asked for the fruits of the earth. I love the Rogation hymns, especially the one that says

> The former and the latter rain,
> The summer sun and air,
> The green ear, and the golden grain,
> All thine, are ours by prayer.

I have no idea what "the former and the latter rain" means—if anything—but I think it sounds charming and seasonal. . . .

Ann and Warren are coming Wednesday, and Warren has to be in Durham on Friday [for Officer Candidate School].[17] . . .

Friday

Margie brings her Biology girls over to study the wildflowers. There are really getting to be some, and when she asked them this morning what I had that they had not (in their little garden at the school), there was a chorus of "leaf mould!" Margie says moments like that make a long life of teaching worthwhile.

One little girl detached herself from the ranks, and so shorn was she of her glamour that I did not at once recognize Little Caroline [Long]. "Libba," she said, "do you remember when we used to roll down the bank to the spring at Longview? Did we have wonderful times! But," she said sadly, "those days are gone forever."

Did I tell you that Mr. Bolton [a neighbor] has cut down everything on his side of the fence and planted a Victory Gar-

---

[17] Ann moved back home awaiting the birth of their first child.

den? The garden is adorable. Mr. Bolton looks at it four or five times a day and brings friends who discuss varieties and seasons with him. He says his peas are further along than any he has seen, and they look very pretty and pale green with their white blossoms.

[April 29]

This is to wish you a happy birthday, and I hope you get it in time for that. . . .

I finally dragged Emily out last week for a day in the garden, and we had a lovely time, only it was a little chilly, but I made her sit on a rug. After struggling with my Amaryllis article and polishing every sentence, I took it over for her criticism, and when she at last returned it, every page was marked up, and some pages obliterated. But I agreed with nearly everything she said, so now I am doing it over, but feeling very discouraged. I do not think I will ever learn to write.

We at last have a cook, but I do not know for how long. We are to pay her eight dollars and bus fare, and she is to have all Sundays off. And last night (her first) when she called us in to dinner she asked if she had to wait until we ate it. She said, "Can't I just put it on the table and go?" I told her she could not, and she said no more, but I am trying to work Bessie around to 6:30 dinner. Not that I like it anymore than she does. But it is mighty nice to have that sweet little black face and the breakfast tray appear in my door at 8:30 A.M. Especially as Miss Minnie, Sally, and Aunt Lettie are all arriving next week. And maybe Eudora [Welty]. I wrote her at once, and asked her to stop, but I haven't heard. I hope she will go back to the hotel before leaving, and will get my letter. My heart is set on having her. With cook or without.

We are activated at the Filter Center this week and it is great fun. At Cora 7 [a designated site where spotters phoned in reports to the center] there is a farm woman who says she lives on a highway and it is foggy and if she cannot see the planes she cannot tell whether it is a plane or a truck, and she feels the way may be lost and all on account of planes sounding like trucks.

I got a package off to you on Wednesday and it turned out to be heavier than I thought. I hope Robert [Ann's brother] will think it worth lugging up the mountain. There are no more of the little things to tuck into corners, so I had to fill in with tissue paper. I envy you for being away from civilization. I would like to take to the woods myself. You hear nothing but ration points and how terrible the food is at the S&W [Cafeteria] and how so-and-so bootlegs gas. It is very boring.

I met Mrs. B. in the Piggly [grocery store] this morning, and she was full of excitement because Lucy [Daniels] is here. Emily is in a great stew because she sent Mrs. B. to get cans for the rest of the ration points to send to you, and Mrs. B. came back with a glass of caviar because it was only two points!

I love you very dearly.

[May 6]
Thursday

. . . In the cool of the evening Aunt Lettie and I were left alone, and fixed our supper on the back porch and ate it while we watched the light change on the iris and on the trees. She said Sam loved the place so much, and took such good care of the trees. I tried not to laugh at the idea of Father's loving the place and taking care of the trees, for Aunt Lettie seemed so to cherish the idea. She said did I find I still missed my father, and I said "Yes," that I found that you miss people more and more instead of less and less as one is led to believe, and that I always held with Emily Dickinson on "They say that time assuages/ Time never does assuage/An actual suffering strengthens, As Sinews do, with age" (punctuation mine, haven't a complete E. D.).

After I had gone to bed and turned out the light, I thought about what she had said, and tried to make a poem of it, but very unsuccessfully, it seems so simple and is so elusive. Besides, I felt conscience-stricken to be guilty of such teleology—even in a poem and even second-hand after the fine scientific training that I had from Dr. Anderson [at North Carolina State College]. . . . He said passionately, "Miss Lawrence, you will never be happy until you take up some type of research." I thought I could understand his idea of happiness, but I knew he would never understand mine, so I said nothing, and he went off on the joys of pure science. . . .

I am afraid that Eudora went on home without returning to the hotel, as I have never heard from her. I am heart-broken because I think she would have liked to stop and rest in these days of unpleasant travel, and I wanted so much to have her. I have been looking forward to it all winter, and night after night I have gone down stairs to write to her, and been so tired and thought I would do it the next night. I had no idea that she would go so early. And by another year she will have forgotten me.

I think I am almost as excited as Emily is over seeing Elizabeth [Daniels] again. Emily says you will come for two weeks the first of June, and I am afraid Bessie and I will be gone most of that time. Warren has put in for leave the first of June to go up to Tryon to see Mrs. Way, who has been and is very ill, and to bring Ann that far on her way. Bessie and I are going to drive her here.

[May 24]

. . . Mrs. Crowson [the Little Theatre office secretary] says we took in $256 at the box office for *The Women*. She says she thinks we will come out even financially. We lost 200 unpaid memberships, but that is to be expected with people so transient.

I told [Mrs. Alden] about Ann's baby and she was very pleased. I had put off telling her because I had a feeling that she could not bear to hear of anyone else having a baby, and I was right. She said she tried to tell herself that it was better to have them later because you could be a better parent when you had learned wisdom. I said I should think with musicians it would be almost impossible to have children right away and keep up the music, too. She said that that was true, but she was sure she could [keep] up the music. But, she said passionately, "I don't want a career."

One piece of luck happened in the Army. Warren is being sent to Duke for officer training. I imagine he will only be there for two months, but it means he can come all the way with Ann and at least be near for awhile. So Bessie and I will not go to Tryon. One thing about the war suits me perfectly. Staying at home . . .

[June 10]

. . . I find that exercising Annie is going to be my chief activity this summer. She will not walk unless I go with her. Last night I persuaded her to walk out to the Little Theatre with me, and then she said she would rather walk back than wait for the bus. She said when we got home that she was not at all tired, but I was exhausted. . . . Annie and Warren are the two most darling people you ever saw. We all had such a good time together. . . .

Monday afternoon

My mind was so full of the play ["Possess These Shores"] this morning that I sat down and wrote to you, and mailed the letter when I went out to do the errands. When I came in and found your letter, I was sorry I had not waited for your questions. . . .

You ask if the women are too unperceptive to be believable.

No. Unfortunately, no one who hears that sort of talk, and you cannot help hearing it daily if you listen, could possibly think them overdrawn. But you say, "It's what I feel toward America: capable of untold vision and accomplishment for mankind, but even still careless, selfish, and blind." That is not America. That is the attitude of stupid and self-centered people everywhere. And that is not the way you feel toward America. The fighters, the bomber crew, the pilots, are all America, too, and in the end the women say

We are not separate, alone,
We are one

with each other
We are one
With all peoples everywhere
Who strive for liberty.

And it is not only the foreign-born Americans who feel this. The reason I feel so keenly about it is on account of the deep impression my talks with our weekend guests have made upon us. It has been a cross-section of America, and I have never had such a broadening experience. I have in mind two who stand out from the rest. Both from the middle west, where isolationism is supposed to be strongest, one a carpenter, and one a farmer. They are the most intelligent and responsible people I have talked to about the war and the world after the war, and the aims of decent people. Neither was unusual, except for clear thinking, in mind or person. They hadn't the intense patriotism of Mr. Petroff [in Ann's play] and that is because they have never known anything but security. But they are the America you speak of. . . .

[Elizabeth to Emily, August 9]

Dear Emily,

I had just come in from the garden with the intention of writing to you about the baby, when your letter came, written on Chip's birthday [Warren Way III, born August 4]. I think you and Ellen must really be psychic as you both must have been writing to me while I sat by myself in the hospital (Ann having put me out) waiting for Chip to be born.

Warren came yesterday, and you never saw anyone so beautiful. He has blossomed at the OCS [Officer Candidate School] and looks like a general. . . . [Warren] went down to the baby room and examined all thirty of the others with his meticulous manner, and said he thought his compared very well. . . . [Ann and I] had talked and talked about how gentle we would be with [the baby], as both of us suffered from our Victorian childhood. . . . She says he is the most self-possessed baby she ever saw, and he is certainly a healthy one. . . .

Later

Ann's darling letter to Annette came in the same mail with yours, and I took it out to the hospital, and we rejoiced that you will be here for the christening. I could not bear not to have you! We found Nana's dress, made by her grandmother, in the attic. Ann and I mended it, and washed it, and you never saw anything so darling.

I shall certainly see that you get a picture [of Elizabeth in the garden, by North Carolina photographer Bayard Wootten] if you want it, which I cannot imagine. I only sent Ann [Bridgers] one because I had promised. I hope affection has impaired your judgment. I do not think I look like that.

I took Mrs. Wootten the picture of father to make a copy for Caroline [Long]. She had forgotten it (the proofs were lost in a fire) and was delighted. She said it was very fine, and it pleased her to think that she had done so well when she knew so little. And then she showed me some of her good things and one of her own father and mother, which is her treasure. It is a delightful study of an old man playing solitaire and an old woman looking over his shoulder and telling him what to play next. An interesting woman, Mrs. Wootten . . .

The garden is full of butterflies all at once, which is always the first sign of fall. . . .

[Late summer]

I have found the perfect oil heater for $33.50, and you must get it at once, and relieve my mind. [The clerk at Montgomery Ward] said that . . . if you can't get it in Asheville you can just send [her] the certificate and she will send you the heater. I think you can put it in the kitchen in place of that little hot water heater, but if you have to put it where you sit, you will find it does not take up much room. I sent the little wheelbarrow frame this morning. The whole post office gathered to confer about it, and decided it could go as was. I hope it gets there safely. They said it would. And the clerk said, "But please, would you mind telling me what it is?" I am sorry the man riveted it so badly. It was difficult getting it done at all, and I had to try several places. But I think it will hold, and you will take better care of it than I did. I broke it by running the car over it. . . .

Catherine [Irwin, a young friend Elizabeth had sailed with to Europe in 1927] left last night. She was very sweet and we loved having her. It is too bad we could not live together forever. Catherine was laughing about the time I said, "Oh, the Herberts [tenants] are the nicest people we know, we never see them." I went with her to the Poor House to see Miss Mamie (do you remember her in Jolly's [Jewelry], a perfect love) and I went to see Miss Stone.[18] Once you get to Miss Stone's little room, it seems as remote as the desert, and you can talk for hours without being interrupted. Miss Stone is not like most talkers, like Uncle Jim and Mr. Luns. Her delightful little anecdotes are drawn-out rarely, and you feel that they will be put away and not taken out again for a long time. This afternoon we were talking about language, and Miss Stone began to tell me about the Isle of Guernsey, and how the language of the people was that of the time of Louis XVI, when the French first settled: she and her mother used sometime to go there for the summer, and they took a house across the street from Victor Hugo's sister-in-law, Mme. Chenault (at least, that is how it sounded to me), who, though she was old and very frail, and though they arrived very early in the morning, would always be up to greet them, and would have their house filled with flowers. Miss Stone said she read most of Victor Hugo while she was there, reading his own books, with his marginal notes and little drawings, and reading in the room where he wrote *Les Travailleurs de la Mer*.

. . . Last night Bessie and I went to call on Robert, but he had gone to a movie. Later, I went to mail a letter, and stopped to speak to him. He was very excited over hearing about the place, and wanted to know if you would like it.

---

[18] Florence Aldine Stone, born near Boston and educated abroad, lived in Europe for many years before and after World War I; a gifted linguist, she sometimes served as a translator for the American government. Her brother, Dr. William Stone, who died in 1928, was a beloved history teacher at St. Mary's School, where Elizabeth Lawrence was one of his students. Miss Stone, having suffered a stroke, apparently moved to Raleigh to be near her brother's family. Although many residents of the county home ("poorhouse" was a familiar term at the time) were indigents who were eventually buried in unmarked graves, Miss Stone was buried in the family plot in Boston following her death in 1947. "Miss Mamie" remains unidentified.

Staying at the Hotel Bristol on West Forty-eighth Street in New York, Ann had finished her play about the Filter Center, "Possess These Shores," and she used the occasion to respond to some of Elizabeth's earlier letters. The following letter appears to have been included in a letter to her family in Raleigh, to be passed along to Elizabeth. It is one of the few extant letters from Ann written while the Lawrences were still living in Raleigh. Perhaps Elizabeth saved it because Ann included a diagram of what she wanted in an herb garden Elizabeth was to design. That herb garden was to be at Ann's new cabin. The cabin at the end of Blackberry Inn Road had been deemed too remote, so Ann bought the second cabin closer to Weaverville on Maney Branch Road in the Beech community. A bus ran once a day, which the family and visitors used. Elizabeth's mother did not like her to drive alone—or to go more than forty miles per hour, which made the trip from Raleigh take about six hours.

In Ann's letter to Elizabeth, readers hear her voice, different from hearing it through Elizabeth. Although not as confiding, Ann reveals something more about herself than can be inferred from Elizabeth's letters alone. Of even greater interest, perhaps, are her responses to some of the people Elizabeth has been describing to her. Ann knew Elizabeth's friends in Raleigh—the Thompson sisters and the Busbees, for example—but her responses to people she did not know reveal her human understanding, which her family and friends regarded as especially deep. Although letters in the correspondence of Elizabeth and Ann about Florence Stone appear to be missing or out of sequence, it is clear they had discussed Miss Stone in some detail.

What else is to be learned about Ann Preston Bridgers? In a 1999 interview with this editor, Ann's niece, Elizabeth Daniels

Squire, said that Ann had been in love with a married playwright, although Squire did not mention anyone by name. Because Ann had a close relationship with playwright George Abbott in coauthoring Coquette, *some might wonder if he was the man in question— and the source of her happiness perhaps alluded to in the January 2, 1940, letter, in which she was said to be looking "well, and young and beautiful." At the time Ann met George Abbott, he was married to his first wife, who died in 1930. (His second marriage lasted from 1945 to 1961, ending in divorce; he married again in 1983, in his ninety-sixth year.) In his 1963 autobiography,* Mister Abbott, *he remembered Ann as "a quiet, intelligent, and attractive girl." Elizabeth Daniels Squire added this observation about why Ann had not married: "Ann said, 'I never met a man who could give me a more interesting life than I could make for myself.' "*

Elizabeth Lawrence's choice to remain single cannot be linked to anything she said about marriage. She wrote for Ann, however, a story and love poem about Peter Burnaugh, the New York journalist she met during her senior year at Barnard College, alluded to in these letters. In her fifties, Elizabeth talked about Peter to a few confidants. By then, she had turned it into a romance that had broken her heart. It remains speculative whether or not her feeling that her heart was broken by Peter was the reason she did not marry. It is more certain that Ann Bridgers and Elizabeth found comfort in talking, rather than writing, about these private matters.

[Ann to Elizabeth, November 1943]

I am not surprised that you have designed me an herb garden. For the first time since I have known you I have a place to have an herb garden. The place we have bought at Beech is about two acres, rectangular in shape, sloping up a hillside long ways. There is not a tree or shrub to shade it for two-thirds of the way up—it faces the morning sun—then there is a very beautiful immense cherry tree and a magnificent oak shading the little compact log house. Above the house is the spring, surrounded by small cool trees, which Mr. Cook's brother planted, seemingly with love and care, from the tone of voice in which Mr. Cook told me. The name of the place, for me, is The Place near the Cooks. Mr. Cook first suggested it (his brother had sold it for $500 because he could move higher up the mountains where wood was plentiful, and the Asheville woman who bought it was willing to sell). Mrs. Cook said, "You buy the place and I'll have the garden and the chickens and butter." And a load of anxiety about obtaining supplies, which had burdened me for fourteen months, fell off my back. Not having any wood on the place does not bother me, for it costs me more to get wood cut than to burn coal. And there was electricity— no bathroom. But I had begun to look upon electricity as the only essential for living. Then the day Mr. Cook took us in to Asheville we stopped by the place and he and I walked up to the top. It was mine from the moment I saw the little house, well built, with fitted screens and smooth floors and even on that hot day, coolness from the shade. . . .

The [new] place answers all the needs the [old] cabin fails in. Sun and land for growing things and a postbox at the foot of the hill and a store a quarter of a mile away and no copperheads. I shall keep the cabin and when the war is over and transportation available we can go up there whenever the weather is hot. And I can still have a garden down below with a place to spend the winter if I want to.

But to get back to the herb garden. What I want—eventually—

is to terrace the land in front of the house all the way down to the road with a dining terrace, an herb garden, a garden, and fruits. And as soon as plans can be made, I want you to design it all, and then I'll work toward it slowly. But you know my first requirement—things that do not take much work to keep up. . . . It may take me twenty years to get it done. For I have a number of plays growing in my mind.

. . . I am enchanted with your story of Miss Stone [whom Elizabeth had visited in the poorhouse]—and it comes just after seeing an exhibit of photographs of Greece, called "The Beauty of Greece," at the Metropolitan. In a light room—light walls and flooded with light from overhead, brilliant but not blinding nor casting shadows—are the photographs, lent by people who took them or own them. They, too, are flooded with light and are poignantly beautiful—would be at any time but particularly so now when we do not know whether the beautiful old Greek columns are bombed or whether the lovely women on Samos dancing over the hill are still alive. There were pictures of the Greek plays given by Mrs. Sikilianos which were described by a Greek girl I met in Switzerland and which I so longed to see. You know she revived the festivals and markets—the people came from far and wide, the Greek people, to sell their wares as of old and sit in the temple at Olympus and see a play against the grandeur of the mountains. If you see Miss Stone ask her if she saw any of the productions. I would like to know Miss Stone. . . .

You should read *Village in August* [novel by Tien Chun], a very beautiful book.

Never did I read anything more delightful than Ann's [Elizabeth's sister's] letter. I know of no one so gallant as Ann. Nor one who so surely knows what is vital for life and what only superficial. Perhaps that is the essence of being gallant—to know how to enjoy the superficial without being absorbed by it.

I am happy beyond words that you appreciate Father Lambert, for I know as no one else perhaps what it can mean to him. There was great beauty in the poems you let me read—great beauty—and the sometimes rather crass statement of his emotion did not bother me as it did you at first. I think I never discussed those poems with you. It was one of the things that we never found leisure for—but I so wanted you to help the human being who was struggling so desperately to find expression. And now you have.

So you think you are an "ascetic"?

I realized you had no conception of an audience in reading my plays. They were not theatre to you but only reading as of a poem or a novel. But whatever of emotion or characterization was there reached you so you have been a satisfactory audience of one for me. Practically no one, not even those who write plays themselves, realize what one means by the phrase "writing for an audience." They think it means for the applause after the curtain. A play is like the black notes of music until played upon the instrument of the audience. You can read the notes and hear the melody without sound, but there can be no fullness until the instrument sounds. I do not know how you react in an audience—whether with them or alone. If I react alone, the play has failed.

I would like to know what you would like done about "Possess These Shores" if you do not mind writing me. The play refuses to die in my mind though I cannot find a producer. Vassar is to give it in the spring perhaps. I adopted your suggestion about the end of "Possess These Shores" and started with "Listen—" calling it "November 8, 1942." I sent it to the Office of

War Information to be used as they saw fit, but suggesting that it would be suitable for use when we invaded the continent. I hope they see fit to use it.[19] . . .

I think Mr. Alden is a good sport and prefers teletype to fighting, which he might have been called on to do. He has been saved from the abyss. But I suffer from what you say about him. When I was younger, I was always wanting to comfort everybody, but now I realize my inadequacy. Mr. Alden made the mistake of marrying, which I never did. It is not a question of courage, but of how much of yourself you can rescue from the chaos of life.

I like the poems by the English flier. I sent Elizabeth the one about the Fortress and shall send her the ones about the Gunner. I do not think she is writing anything this year, but she may be. She is the person I know who has escaped chaos most successfully. Perhaps she will write.[20] . . .

I am also reading Jefferson's letters, which I urge you to become acquainted with in *Jefferson Himself*, by Bernard Mayo. I had meant to copy out some of the things Jefferson says about flowers and gardening but that will have to wait. You will love Jefferson even more than Calhoun. He was a fighter, too, but had a wider culture than Calhoun. He is more relaxing—because he lived in a time of promise—exciting and beautiful to him—and Calhoun saw that promise close in on himself and the country he loved with as much passion as Jefferson.

---

[19] The script was rejected, the reader citing as reasons "the many technical challenges" and the large cast of women.

[20] Elizabeth "Liz" Daniels Squire went on to fame as a nationally acclaimed detective writer and the author of nine books. She and her husband and children, after many travels, returned to live on the mountain property left to Elizabeth by the Bridgers family. She often credited Ann Bridgers with inspiring her to become a reader and writer.

My love, Elizabeth dear, and to Bessie, and to Ann and Warren when you write. And Chip.

[Signed] Ann

1944

[April 28]
Wednesday and from then on

. . . Among other things I have been writing to Mr. Belden Saur [at Rocknoll Nursery in Hillsboro, Ohio] to whom I had sent an order last October (the sixth) for twenty-four plants (all different), most of them rare things that are not listed anywhere else, and that I particularly need to complete my records. I never heard from him until a few days ago when he returned my check, and wrote that he could supply four of the twenty-four things. One of the pulmonarias, "Mrs. Moon," comes from stock (he wrote) that he raised from seed that came to him ten years ago from the Leningrad Botanical Garden.

I ordered the four, though they will probably not live, being set out this late, for fear that by fall he would not have even those. He says he has been practically forced to close since his help went to make ammunitions. This is happening in all of the nurseries, and plants that it has taken a lifetime to collect are grown to wilderness. When I wrote to the Weathered Oak for herbs, they simply returned my check, with a note to the effect that they were not taking any orders. We went to Mr. Fowler's [formerly Mr. Tong's nursery] the other day and the whole front is grown up in weeds. Even the season's pansies were just holding their heads above the grass. Or their people send the wrong plants, or none at all, and some do not return the checks. Not from dishonesty, but because they are in such confusion.

I ordered from Mr. Saur three bulbs of *Lycoris squamigera* for you for your birthday, and this is probably your birthday letter, for it will be then by the time I get it finished, I have so much to say. I have been waiting to get over a mashed finger, and to get myself unconfused before writing, but I do not think either is likely soon, and the finger does not bother the typing much.

The lycoris I have wanted you to have for years. It is called Hall's Amaryllis for Mr. Hall, who brought it from a Chinese garden. The blooms come up in July from the ground and bloom all of a sudden, and look like changeable taffeta (pink and blue). But I could not picture it at the cabin.

I hope I have pictured the new house [near the old cabin] right. I am sure that I will love it, if you do. And it is a certainty if you are happy there. But one place cannot take the place of another in my mind, any more than can a person.

Forgive me for loving you so much.

. . . The lecture in Wilmington [North Carolina] was a flop. I had looked forward to it all year, and because I knew that there were a number of women there who from having been familiar with estates like Orton had got to the point of hearing botanical names without fainting, I had for the first time prepared a lecture for gardeners, not club women. Half of the audience left after the business part of the meeting, and the other half looked at me with apathetic eyes. I am still wondering why they asked me, much less paid me, to come.

But I wished for you in Jackson [near Longview]. The people there were like those at the meeting that you and I went

Longview Plantation was the nineteenth-century home of the Mason/Long family of Northampton County, North Carolina. Sam Lawrence often visited his friend Willie Jones there before marrying. In 1912, he brought Bessie, Elizabeth, and Ann to live in nearby Garysburg. The house, named for the view rather than the family, is still occupied by Long descendants.
BY PERMISSION OF JAMES BECKWITH

to so long ago in Lumberton, when I talked (so poorly) about flower arrangement. They were country people. I knew what they wanted me to say, and how to say it. And it was what I wanted to say, too. I talked to a book club. The book club is made up of all the people in the community from the school teachers and farm women and general store keepers' wives to friends of Caroline's [Caroline Moncure Long, wife of Wilie Long]. "Friends of Caroline's" was a bad expression. They are all friends of Caroline's in the real sense, and all are provincial to the same degree. We met at the school house and they had a beautiful party with an old figured punch bowl that had belonged to one of the early governors of Virginia, silver candelabra and crabapple blossoms. They had all read my book and they said they had a copy of it in the library. The war was not once mentioned, and everyone seemed occupied and happy. And yet I knew that most of them had sons in Europe. Mrs. Lewis [unidentified] had told me the night before that she had one in England and one in Italy.

I never go to Longview without vowing that I will not go again without you. But it will have to be after the war. You would never take the bus trip that Bessie and I took to get there. What worries me is that you may not see it before Miss Bettie[21] dies. I thought when Maria's little Sarah Gale [granddaughter of Dr. Tom and Minnie Long] came running up the walk and said to me "Where are my games? What have they done with them?" in the exact imperious tone of Miss Bettie, that she is the fifth generation of Longs to be my friend. There is something about a large family that has lived on one spot for many generations that is concentrated and passionate and more vital than people who have gone here and there and married strangers. As much of hatred as of love, but all of it vital . . . Willie and Caroline can talk to Bessie and me because we are of the family but not in it. Willie and Bessie talked before the dining room fire about the changes in the world and all of them for the worse, and Caroline and I talked (while Caroline got dinner) of human relationships. Caroline said how did you know when your love led you too far, beyond good and into hurt? I said you had only to ask yourself if what you were doing was what you wanted for the other person or was what he wanted for himself.

---

[21] Bettie Gray Mason Long, matriarch of the family. The Longs went to see "Gran" every Sunday afternoon at Longview, built by her grandfather, William Henry Gray.

She looked as startled as if I had said something obscene and said, "How can you know that? You can't have suffered." I knew that to Caroline this would be true. So I thought a minute, and said that it isn't what you suffer that teaches, but the capacity to suffer. And that is true.

Caroline was telling me about "Aunt Bet" [a black servant of the Longs]. Aunt Bet died this spring, and Caroline and Sally [Long Jarman, Caroline's sister-in-law] dressed her, and put flowers from the garden in her hand and asked their minister to officiate at the funeral, which was what Aunt Bet wanted. He is a gentle young man, and when he met the colored preacher at the door of the colored church, he put out his hand and said, "How are you, Brother?" and after all of the Longs and all of the colored people (there was a church full and overflowing because the word had got out that a white preacher and a colored one were to hold the funeral together) had sung and prayed together, "Uncle Sam" came up to Caroline and said it was a beautiful funeral and just what Bet would have wanted. She would have been happy, he said, to have been the means of bringing the white and the colored people together. "I knew it was not what Aunt Bet would have wanted," Caroline said (in a bitter way she has of saying true things, not that the thing she is saying is bitter, but because the truth to her so often is bitter, that the tone has become a habit). "Aunt Bet would have wanted only white people at her funeral."

Aunt Bet was like the confidants in old plays, an intimate more than a servant, and full of folk wisdom. Caroline said she could never have lived under the roof with Miss Bettie if it had not been for Aunt Bet. You would go to her cottage and sit by the fire, and Aunt Bet would cook her corn pone, and they would talk all day. Aunt Bet always understood everything. . . . I have thought, and still do, that the colored race is the most honest of all races. . . .

. . . I wrote a poem for your birthday. I hope you won't be confused by its being in the first person, and that you will like what it says. I never like to send poems that are about you. But an occasional poem is like a letter. It must be eaten hot for it is not good when it is cold. The other poem is one I wrote long ago. It is about a walk we took the first time we went to the cabin. . . .

[Emily] seems to be all right, and says she can wear her brace all day since she fixed her shoe.[22] It bothers her late in the day and not too much. She looks completely rested, too. And Mrs. B. looks young and handsome. When I told her so, she said, "Well, I don't feel well. I am as weak as a kitten," and we all laughed.

For Ann
May 1, 1944

While the light is still on the mountain top
I must come down to the hills in the valley:
I dare not wait for the light to wane,
The mountains are darker at night than the plain.

I have lived long enough in the thin air,
And I have no reason, now, to remain.
I carry the seed that is found only where

---

[22] Emily, who suffered polio as a child, was proud that she could walk with two crutches. But as she grew older (she was now fifty-one), she needed other aids, such as a brace and special shoe. Only late in life, however, was she willing to use a wheelchair.

The air is too thin for the plant to grow.
It will quicken there in the quiet hills,
It will come to fruit in the warmth below.

Ann, have you forgot the climb
To the narrow mountain ledge
That stood, unforested,
An island in the sky?

Regrets

Ann, do you recall
The ants that crossed the edge
Of barren rock
The while we talked—but not at all
Of what we came to say,
And went away
And left it still unsaid?

[August 30]

My darling Ann, I came from you [at the mountain cabin],
as I always do, feeling much ashamed of myself and full of reso-
lutions for putting an end to my dallyings, and tossing off large
quantities of work. And, instead, I have spent half of the quiet
rainy morning trying to tease into a metrical pattern a translation of a "flute song" that Uncle Jim made for me last night

from the *Oxford Book of Greek Verse*. . . . Uncle Jim made the
translation with the aid of your Greek lexicon, which he had
found on the shelves before and had made me a speech about.
He said he had used it as the subject for a sermon on the art
of living. . . which he says is to devote one's self passionately to
one's chosen work. . . .

[Tuesday, September 15, at the beach]

Annette has taken Lillian [the babysitter] and Bessie crabbing at the Inlet, and I am left with the fire and Chip and
George [the dog]. An arrangement that suits me perfectly. The
crabbing excursions are a delight to everyone but me. Saturday
morning we found the jam [Ann had sent] in our mail box, and
we had it for Sunday breakfast, and in the afternoon for tea. It
is not only the best jam we have had in some time, but the only
jam we have had in some time. If Elizabeth does not appreciate
"Tom O'Bedlam" now, she will. The important thing is to have
a chance to. I count myself fortunate that Nana read me so
much Dickens and very unfortunate that she also saturated me
in [William Cullen] Bryant's *Library of Poetry and Song* and Kipling's *Barrack-Room Ballads* (which are really very little above
"The Spell of the Yukon" [by Robert Service]). And at school
I had years of exposure to Victor Hugo and de Vigny (I can
remember how I used to weep over "*Moise, puissant et solitaire*"
["Moses, powerful and solitary"]. I suppose it reminded me of
Nana's favorite "By Nebo's lonely mountain/On this side of Jor-
dan's wave . . ." [Cecil Frances Alexander's "Burial of Moses"]
without ever having heard the name of Verlaine mentioned).
One day when we were having tea in Donia's room [at Barnard

College] I picked up a little book, and it opened to [Verlaine's] "*Il pleure dans mon coeur comme il pleut sur la ville*" ["It weeps in my heart as it rains in the city"]. And not only years after I labored through a course in nineteenth century poets did I come upon [from William Morris's "Rapunzel"] "Is it not true that every day/She climbeth up the same strange way/Her scarlet cloak spread broad and gay/Over my golden hair?"

[October 29]

I have been sitting on the garden steps waiting for the moon to rise above the pine trees, but it never did, though I could see a glow above the horizon. Have you ever noticed that the waning moon rises very, very slowly, while the waxing moon leaps into the sky? Or perhaps it only seems that way. But I have noticed it over and over. Tonight is one of those warm soft nights that seem more like May than October. There is a thin coating of rippled clouds over the sky, like the rippled sand after the wind has blown the waves. And a few stars shining through. The air is light, but so full of scents that it is weighted. I could feel George, leaning against my knee, quivering with ecstasy. I always envy dogs, the way the air is like an open book to them. . . .

Every time it gets cold I picture you hauling wood and coal, and have a fit. Just bringing in enough to keep my studio fire gets me down. . . .

I have had more correspondence from my friend Mr. [Carl] Krippendorf, and he says he is sending me a hundred Anemone De Caen. These are the big florist anemones, and I am not sure they will be hardy here, or with you, but I shall send you half a dozen for fun. I am sick over not having been able to send spring crocus for you. I meant to send you some of mine when they showed their first tips, but I am afraid I have lost them all in doing over the rock garden. . . . I had a long letter from Mr. Starker [an Oregon gardener] telling me the story of his family, and saying that he hoped you planted the crocus at once. His youngest daughter is nineteen and works at riveting. She weighs ninety-five pounds and the rivet is heavier than she is. She gets up at 5:00 A.M. or something and commutes. She is delighted with it and says that the factory hands are not rough as her father had feared. . . .

[October]

I can't remember whether I started this two or three weeks ago, but I have been trying to finish it ever since, and have not been able to, or even write my Uncle Donald [Lawrence] to tell him that I am going to stop to spend a night with him [in Marietta, Georgia] on the way home from Louisiana. Some sort of a club in Shreveport asked me to come to lecture to them, and it seems a little silly to take a week in the middle of the season to go for one lecture, but I am eager to meet one of my most interesting correspondents, Mrs. Dormon, who has a place outside of Shreveport, and another fascinating character [Mrs. S. F. Kline] who writes a column called "Lady with a Hoe," and to see as much of the gardens as I can see the first of November, and most of all to see Eudora in her native heath (or on it?). Mrs. Welty [Eudora Welty's mother], who has gotten to be a great friend of mine by letter and plant exchange, asked me to stop, so I am going to arrive at midnight one night, and leave at midnight the next, which sounds like one of Eudora's stories, don't you think? Eudora herself is just back from New York at last. This gave me about three weeks to make all arrangements, order, catalogue, get, and set out my year's experiments, and as we have had the usual coming and going and the delightful new maid turned out to be on sick leave most of the time, I have been in the department of utter confusion.

The garden has been so lovely, I have never known it to be so lovely. And entirely by accident. I got a lot of chrysanthemums last spring that were not my choice, but the only Koreans Mr. Fowler [Amos Fowler, who in 1933 purchased George Tong's Raleigh nursery] had left. I planted them in the bed in the back, and early in October they opened in cascades over the terrace wall; and as the firethorn against the fence, which has got to be truly magnificent, turned slowly from dull orange to scarlet, the chrysanthemums turned from amber to russet. Behind them were the lacquered tithonias, and some rich maroon calliopsis sprang up of their own accord and began to bloom beside them. And then by the summer house I had masses of a new annual from Texas called the Butterfly Daisy, a brassy yellow with a border of maroon and orange marigolds. And we have had so many golden days to enjoy it in.

Miss Stone came to spend one of them with us. She has gotten very much weaker and can use her paralyzed side less and less, but she is as strong as ever in spirit and determined to go back to Greece, and as soon as the war is over to study Russian and go to Russia. It irks her daily not to know Russian and she admires the Russian people so much that she wants to know them from living among them. She wanted to see the Stathacoses so I took her there, and Mr. Stathacos and Mrs. Stathacos wept, and Miss Stone wept, and I wept.

They all talked in Greek, which flowed along like a river, as they mentioned one by one the liberated towns and cities; but we all wept in the same language. I wish you could have seen that little foreign woman, in her ugly American clothes (she had just come in from the street) and her beautiful soft brown eyes looking suddenly [like] a European peasant, and Mr. Stathacos, who is so noble looking and so gentle. They remind me of

> The mountains look on Marathon
> And Marathon looks on the sea.
> And dreaming there an hour alone,
> I dreamed that Greece might still be free.

[Lord Byron, "The Isles of Greece"]

Do you suppose that always Greece will be liberated and overthrown and liberated and overthrown, and always the symbol of freedom?

I have never been able to get hold of Dorothy Alden since she got back and she is so busy that every time she promised to come to a meal she called and said something had turned up. She promised to bring some of Mr. Alden's letters to us to read. He has been flown to Assam, which is near Burma, and in the foothills of the Himalayas, and he is carried away with the beauty of the country. I am so delighted, I think that is just the sort of experience that will do him good. . . .

Another Thursday Night

. . . I have just come in from mailing letters and taking George for a short run in the little lane that runs by the Cruzes'.

It is the most delightful little lane full of the song of katydids and full of country smells. In the half-moonlight it seems as quiet and remote as any little village, Garysburg, for instance, and makes you feel as if you were walking in space without time. And now I must stop and get at one of the articles that hasn't been started, and has to be finished before I leave here Monday night.

Thank you for the apples. I loved them and so did the soldiers. I brought home from the Information Booth a delightful young officer for whom I could not find a hotel room and who said he wanted a quiet place to sleep. He and Warren Lovelace (who has taken up with us permanently and comes every weekend as soon as he gets off on Saturday, and stays until the last bus to Camp Butner on Sunday night, and eats everything Bessie and I can scrape together) slept until twelve on Sunday, and when they woke at last we took our breakfast-lunch out in the garden and ate it on the back terrace. Soft corn bread and your apples, and sausage. We had your Jugtown plates and cooking dishes and the Lt. (from Detroit) was delighted with them. He has never seen native pottery. Warren is nineteen. Sunday is his birthday, and Bessie is going to make a cake for him. I have a feeling it will be his last weekend in these parts. He is an engineer with a light pontoon outfit, and they have been on the verge of going since August. . . .

[November 1, on the train to Shreveport, Louisiana]
All Saints Day

This morning I came out of my dressing room just as we were crossing a river. I looked at it with dreadful misgiving—the way you look at the Seine, the first time you are in Paris—and said to the nearest person, "It isn't the Mississippi! . . . It couldn't be. It's so little!" [And someone said,] "Well, it's wider at New Orleans; besides, you can see it's low now."

But I had thought it would be like the Ohio [in Parkersburg, West Virginia], only wider and deeper. I always compare all rivers to the Ohio, and I am always disappointed. I suppose because all of my life I have thought of it as the River. Nothing can compare, ever. I suppose the Amazon would also look like a creek. The green fields come right down to the water's edge [of the Ohio River], and the leaves of the water willows drip in the river. It is so wide and so peaceful, lying between the hills, and at the same time sinister. And always vital, as if all that fertile land drew life from it, but without sapping at the river's strength.

I suppose all children must be in love with someone, and I think when I was a child I must have been in love with the river. I can remember how I used to lean over the sides of the little launch when we went to the Island [Blennerhassett, near Parkersburg], to dip my hands in the water; and how it felt different from any other water, softer and more caressing, and how I used to cherish the delicate pink angel-wing shells that we gathered on the beach, not because they were delicate and pink, but because they belonged to the river.

I got up this morning feeling relaxed and refreshed after being wakeful and restless all night. I have often wondered about this, and about the way you feel listless sometimes and sleeping soundly. I think when you sleep soundly you must have dreams that disturb you, only you can't remember them in the morning because in your deep sleep you retreated so far into the subconscious.

Yesterday as we came through Alabama and today as we came through Mississippi and Louisiana, I have been trying to analyze what it is about a part of the country that you have never seen before, that makes it look different to you when it is really only a variation of what you already know. While the train stopped outside of Atlanta, waiting to get into the station, I looked into a little wood, and thought that you would not know if you did not know that you were not outside of Raleigh. But you would not think that coming into Birmingham or Monroe [Louisiana] all the way there are the same such pines and fields of broom sedge, the same oaks and sweet gums, the same macadam roads and concrete bridges, and even the same billboard advertisements. But when you wake up and look out of the window, you feel as definitely that it is a place you have never seen before as when you woke up in New Mexico or Spain. . . .

[November 4, Shreveport, at night]

The terrifying thing about insomnia is that the less you sleep the less you are able to sleep. I think it must be a form of madness.

Tonight I cannot get the face of Mrs. [Ruth] Dormon out of my mind.

I have been writing to her for two years, and getting delightful and valuable letters from her, and buying her native plants. She opened up a whole new field to me, and one particularly untouched in garden literature (though known to botanists). . . . I had a note just before I left, saying "of course I am making plans to see you. I hope you will stay long enough for us to have a good long talk, and I am bring-ing Caroline Dormon [Ruth Dormon's sister-in-law and a fine Louisiana gardener] up to meet you." I read it carefully, many times. It didn't say, "I want you to come to see me," but I was sure it implied that, so I wrote that I wanted to see her garden, and asked her to call Mrs. A., my hostess, and arrange for a time. The day I left I had a telegram from Mrs. A. saying that Mrs. Dormon's husband was desperately ill, and she would be able to see me only at a luncheon to which we both were in-vited. I thought, "Poor Mr. Dormon must have met with some accident," so the first thing when I arrived I inquired anxiously for his health. "Oh," said Mrs. A. "He has been desperately ill for two years."

Mrs. Dormon's letters are extremely well-written, vigorous, spirited, and full of distinction. I pictured her as another Vio-let Walker [a Virginia gardener], volatile, erratic, and assured. What I found was a little, worn, country woman, so darling that I could hardly keep from putting my arms around her, instead of holding out my hands.

I had brought a plant list to ask her about and I said, "Do you know a Mr. Riggs?" "That man!" Mrs. C. shrieked from across the room. "He ought to be exposed! He's a Negro! Of course," she added, "his list is Botanically corrected. He is backed by a man from Connecticut who teaches at the university."

"What is there to expose?" I said to Mrs. Dormon. "I can't see why a Negro can't sell plants, can you?" "No," she said, and smiled, "No, I can't."

And that was all I saw of her.

But I finally wore Mrs. A. down. "Mrs. Dormon has had reverses," she said. "They are desperately poor, and her place has run down. She was afraid you would expect her to have a show garden. I told her I knew from your letters that you were not the kind of person who would care about that. But she is very sensitive."

As I talked to her friends, who worship her, I easily saw how Mrs. Dormon got to be sensitive. "No use for you to go out to Ruth's place," one of them said. "Just a wilderness; of course, it's pretty in the spring, with all her native iris flowering."

So here I am, taking a train tomorrow after three days in Shreveport looking at gardens of the rich, landscaped by a contractor who calls himself a landscape architect, and creates an effect much like an expensive cemetery. And I left my work and took this long and tiresome trip, primarily to see Mrs. Dormon.

I asked one of her friends if Mrs. Dormon had my book. "Oh, I don't think so!" she said. Then added, "But she may have it. You never can tell what the poor will spend money on. Ruth managed to find five dollars for one bulb of that white *Lycoris radiata* that she wanted so much."[23]

[A few days later]
On the train to Atlanta, Sunday morning

. . . It was two in the morning when I got to the Weltys. I wanted to sit right down to discuss art and literature, but they seemed to take it for granted that we would go to bed. They did, and I took a bath and read Chekhov's letters so that left only the day and evening to talk, and most of that was spent

---

[23] On September 14, 1944, the local garden columnist reported that "the great event of the week was the flowering *Lycoris radiata alba* in Ruth Dormon's woodsy garden on Mooringsport Road . . . the mecca of all rare bulb fans."

with Mrs. Welty, who is a real gardener, and with the president of the Garden Club, and a next door neighbor—looking at camellias not yet in bloom and wondering what they would be like when they did bloom. And with Mrs. Lyell [Frank Lyell's mother], who looks just like Frank, and smiles like him and talks like him, and has his sweet and affectionate nature.

. . . In the odd snatches of conversation I had with Eudora I gathered that she is very restless and at loose ends, and I imagine that's why she stayed in New York this summer. She wants to write a story about the Mississippi Delta, and says if she does she will have to go there, and if she goes she will have to see people and do things, and then she can't write. She got the idea from John [Robinson]. John is in Italy now, but he went to high school with Eudora. She did not know him much then, because he was older—and later she knew him well, and he told her about the Delta people. [The Delta people] love one another and are very rich, and then very poor, but they go on just the same in a carefree, happy existence. It sounds like a novel of the Old South, but I am sure it would be very different as written by Eudora. When we were interrupted she was just telling me how John, when he went home from a late party across the Mississippi, would take off his clothes and swim the river.

I told Eudora about a woman [Cammie Henry] near Shreveport, who had cabins for writers on her plantation [Melrose]. She goes all over the countryside hunting little slave cabins and having them moved to her artist's colony and put up just as they were. There is an author to a cabin. Eudora said that was just like the place [Yaddo] at Saratoga Springs [New York], where she stayed with Katherine Anne Porter. She said it made everyone so self-conscious that you couldn't possibly write. On her studio door was a sign that said (just like the little signs at Putnam's) "Quiet: author at work."

[November 28, back home in Raleigh]
Thanksgiving

I was raking leaves in the garden late this afternoon when I looked up and found Warren Lovelace [a soldier the Lawrences often had as a house guest] standing before me. He had come over from Camp Butner, and brought a friend—a nice shy, low-voiced boy, who, Warren assured me, and I could see for myself, is "tops." Before we came in to supper we burned the leaves in the driveway. It was almost dark, and getting chilly. The nights are cold now, but the frost has come so gradually that the garden still has the fresh green look of summer, and the marigolds are still spilling brightly over the paths, and there are roses and ageratum and crotalaria, and the alyssum is as clean and crisp as linen fresh from Miss Carrie [the laundress].

I can't remember what I told you about Warren Lovelace. He is over six feet and looks like a pleasantly homely little boy, with round eyes behind thick glasses, and upturned nose and unruly hair. Sunday was his twentieth birthday, and when Bessie brought in the cake with the lighted candles he was very near tears. He came a couple of times last summer, and then was sent on maneuvers, but he turned up again in the fall, and has been here every weekend since. Sometimes he brings a friend, and sometimes I pick up another boy at the information center, but mostly he comes alone—usually arriving Saturday afternoon and staying until Sunday night. He is very hard to fill up, but getting several extra quarts of milk helps. He likes to lie on the floor by the fire when he gets back from the dances at midnight, and drink milk and eat bread and butter and tell me about his family and his girl. . . . He says he has read a lot of books about [marriage] and from what he reads wonders if he and Jeanette have enough in common. They both like to read and to walk in the woods and they both know what they want out of life. Bessie assured him that was plenty. He looked very relieved. . . .

The other day in church I thought that some time you must go with me to communion at St. Saviour's if you have never been to a communion service. When I say "you must go with me" I don't mean for spiritual gain, I would consider that presumptuous on my part, for I know that you are much more religious than I am. I mean as an artist.

1945

[January 17]

In a letter to Mrs. Dormon last fall I complained that I had been working on it [the rock garden book?] for so long and had been interrupted so many times that it was impossible to tell what I had meant to say. She wrote back, "And I thought I was the only one who got interrupted! Sometimes when I am called out of the garden, I have forgotten where the tools are by the time I get back." I laughed to read in extracts from Washington's diary [from February 1785] some accounts of his difficulties at Mount Vernon: "Laid off part of the Serpentine Road on the south side of the grass plat, today. Prevented going on with it, first by the coming in of Mr. Michael Stone about

10 o'clock (who went away before noon)—then by the arrival of Colo. Hooe, Mr. Chas. Alexander, and Mr. Chs. Lee before dinner and Mr. Crawford, his Bride, and sister after it. The same cause prevented my transplanting trees in my Shrubberies, and obliged me to cover the roots of many which had been dug up (Dogwood, Maple, Poplar, and Mulberry) the ground not being ready for their reception." This would be a perfect description of any of my mornings in the garden, only I never supposed that G. Washington ever dug anything up before he had the place to plant it ready.

The *Yale Review* came from Mrs. Sammel [an old family friend in Parkersburg, West Virginia] today, and I opened it to a review of a book about [Woodrow] Wilson, and a sentence which said, "His treatment of Wilson himself . . . is highly critical. Those of his readers who find satisfaction in the sentimentality of a recently produced moving picture, which portrays Wilson as its hero, will doubtless be shocked by what they will regard as harsh handling of the President." And he goes on to say that the author's criticism is without rancor, and yet I am sure that I would not like his picture of Wilson any better than I did the movie hero.[24] I thought about this as I walked through the starry night to St. Saviour's, and realized for the first time what it means for a creative writer to present an historical character. I thought after you went home the other night that it must be very annoying to you every time we are working on Calhoun to have me going off on tangents. . . .

Bessie was delighted to get the [ration] points and we will get pineapple juice to make the glace for the tarts by your receipt. Only I am afraid we got them on false pretenses. The

[24] In Darryl F. Zanuck's production of *Wilson*, a 1944 Oscar nominee for Best Picture.

soldiers have all been sent out to replace those lost in the last few months. Bessie and I spent Saturday afternoon cooking for the two invited, and none came. At dinner time Miss Flora [a volunteer] called to tell me not to come to the information booth because there were so few in town.

[January 20]

. . . I can't imagine anything worse than a square of dogwoods back of the house. I thought your idea was that you wanted to clear that all out (except for the service berry, which is to one side) so you could look out of the kitchen window and up the mountain side instead of being hemmed in? If you want to put dogwoods there, I would suggest putting them to the left side (as you look up the mountainside) in a group near the fence. And not so as to hide the prettiest view of the woods, to frame it if possible. If you keep the apple tree you might have a seat under it. . . .

I don't know what you mean by spider lilies, but I am sure that you won't hurt whatever they are if you take a big ball of earth and do not disturb the roots. The point is not to break them when they are growing. I feel sure that white pines will be the best and quickest screen for the pigsty. . . . If you order any, be sure to have your holes all dug before they come. Dig three feet deep and four in diameter, and fill in with woods mould, and put a good mulch of leaves over it, and if you have it where you can water, I think every one would grow soon and make a screen. Be sure to write to me before you do anything drastic. . . .

[January 23]

We had thin toast and your wild strawberry jam for tea this afternoon by the fire in my studio. . . .

I have been thinking all afternoon of what it is that is so arresting in a priest. I mean a real priest, like Uncle Jim, Mr. Wulf, and Father Lambert, who has chosen the priesthood for its own sake, not a Chamber of Commerce minister who considers the priesthood a profession like any other, and takes time out for golf. And I decided that it is because he is like a creative artist in his relation to his calling. . . .

Mr. [William] Lea, our new rector [at Christ Church], brought Father Lucemore to lunch with us today. Father Lucemore is a monk in the Church of Canada. Like a Roman Catholic monk, he has taken final vows, and like a Roman Catholic he is celibate. Otherwise, he is very Protestant. There are eleven in the monastery, nine priests and two lay brothers. They are a missionary order, going to the mill people, the lumberjacks, and the farmers of Canada, and if they are all like Father Lucemore they must burn themselves out while very young. But he is very gentle in his manner, with a quiet voice and a slow smile. . . . You would find him very much after your own heart, I think, in his humanity and his religion. And I know you would love his stories of his teachings and of the mill people who come to him and the Canadian farm women.

Bessie and I took a salad and a pan of rolls and went to have supper with your family last night. Mrs. B. insisted upon adding both ham and chicken. We had [Ann's mountain friend] Blanche's walnuts for dessert. And Robert and I made Cleopatras, not so good, somehow, as the ones at Christmas. Emily is very happy in her work [in state government], and full of all sorts of stories about the people in her office.

I must put the puppy to bed before he chews up all the files of *Gardening Illustrated*.

[February 12]

After seeing Bessie off on the bus to Wilmington at 10:30 [to see Ann and Warren] and promising to have tea with Irma and Lydia at Mrs. Penick's, there was so little left of the day, I decided to call off work and write letters: to a friend on a plantation in Louisiana who wants to swap *Amaryllis macropodastrum* for *A. advena*, and from Mrs. Knock in Crooks, South Dakota, who saw in *Herbertia* that I wanted *Vallota purpurea* and wants to know if I would like her to send me one in exchange for "some bulb I do not have, such as *A. advena*, or *A. rutulum*, or something unusual." . . . You can see how long overdue the answer is, and I am afraid she will think I did not care to answer. These letters are the hardest and most important part of my work. You get all of the things that cannot be got for money. And advice that cannot be got for anything. . . .

I never did write you or tell you about Miss [Katherine] Hawes and Miss [Rebecca] McKillip nor about that fantastic visit we paid them [in Richmond, Virginia], Father Lambert, Irma, and I. Miss Hawes is one of the most magnificent people I have ever looked at. She is like a mountain or a lake or the Grand Canyon . . . and I really love her. In order to understand her you have to know that she is a Scotch Presbyterian. You always think me a snob because I have to place people, but it is the only way to understand them. It is like any other system or any other art, and is my one heritage from my mother, my grandmother, and my great-grandmother (and on back, I am sure, but I did not know any more ancestors personally). . . . I have a suspicion that she is no less than seventy, and I know that she is far from well, but she walks and talks and acts with vigor. She is so scathing in all her remarks that people always recoil. I was so charmed with this fine-looking, white-haired, ruddy-faced woman playing on a fragile reed and without the least self-consciousness, and was so impressed by the way she could draw real music out of amateurs and homemade instruments that I didn't care what she said to me. She would say things like this: Miss Mc was fidgeting with a pipe Irma had made for me, trying to get it in perfect tune, and the cork so that the tone would be clear and pure, and Miss H said, "What are you taking so much time and trouble for, Kippy? It is already far better than anything that child will ever come up to." (I agreed with her.) . . . Miss McKillip is small and pretty and shy and very gentle and eager to have everyone happy. She was very poor and worked for a living (when women didn't if they needn't) and had a mother who suppressed her. Miss Hawes rescued her and brought her to live with her, and they have lived happily ever since. Miss McKillip directs the household, gets out the linen and china for tea, orders the meals. But as if it were her own house. I could never detect the slightest hint of the paid companion, and I am sure Miss Hawes would never allow one, though she speaks to Miss Mc as if she were a small child or not very bright. Miss Mc comes from Philadelphia and is the kind of Yankee who is much more of a Southerner in feeling and manner. While Miss Hawes would be perfectly at home in New England. They live in a large but unpretentious house with very large grounds. The house is about the period of ours, but much larger and with endless enormous rooms, and enormous furniture and expensive and ugly things. When we were there they had a man-servant who had been with Miss Hawes for years, and a darling maid who cooked and did everything in that big house. And the meals were served in courses on expensive china. That was about the time that Bessie and I were beginning our struggles, and I could not get over the peace and order of that smooth-running household. . . .

[February 14]

. . . It is spring at last. When I came home from the concert [by the Philadelphia Symphony] last night, I went out to sit on the garden steps while Mr. Cayce [the family's young dog] took the air, and I could hear the frogs down by the railroad tracks. After you grow up some things get less exciting, but the signs of spring never do. We have been having lovely summer days and today a real spring rain. Bessie discovered that Mrs. Carl works in gardens and we waylaid her in the five-and-ten one day. She was sitting at the counter drinking coffee and smoking a cigarette with a little aura around her as if she were sitting on a terrace on the Riviera. She said she would come, and would appear and disappear and I would find little piles of raked-up leaves. Yesterday I heard a great rustling and there she was again. I had just come out from under the house where I had been clearing out the ash pit, and I was covered with dust from head to heel, and wearing a ragged red sweater and a torn skirt, and Mrs. Carl looked at me approvingly and said, "You look almost as bad as I do." Which was not true, as she looked enchanting with her bright pink hair and her chalk-white face, and her one gleaming eye, and a beautiful long leafgreen sweater of soft wool.

. . . I have been typing since early this morning and have been writing to Warren Lovelace and Mr. Krippendorf. We had our first letter from Warren. He is in France and frozen and starved. He says he dreams about food from home, but he did not ask for it specifically, and I am afraid the postmaster will not let me send it. They are very strict. You have to show the letter. I will write more about Mrs. Carl. She reminds me of "Her sisters were the craggy hills, her brothers larchen trees/Alone with her great family, she did as she did please [John Keats's "Meg Merrilies").

A friend of Bessie's brought me fresh pine straw, the first I have had since the duration. At last I got the rock garden cleaned up and the pine straw on the paths. It looks warm and bright and smells sweet in the sun, and on the rocks along the edges, the winter aconites are like a pool of sunlight, and the columbines unfurl in all shades of purple and lavender and the first little species of crocuses are silver in the bud and mauve in the first flower.

I do not see how it got so late, and my fire has gone completely out without my knowing it. Mr. Cayce kept inching up in his sleep until his nose was in the ashes. He has lost his baby look and is all legs like a colt. When he came he was round and soft. Emily is getting attached to him, and thinks maybe she will like him as well as George after all.

. . . I hate to end a letter, the way you hate to finish a book. . . .

[April 6]

I was thinking that letters are the best practice and training that you could possibly have for writing, for they are like translations in being very exacting. First, they are for one person, and are limited by that person's reactions. Then they are limited by facts. If you are trying to tell a person what really happened, there is no use making up or leaving out things, while if you are writing a story and find something hard to express, you can just change the situation to something easy to express.

I could hardly enjoy Mr. Alden for wishing for you. You would be delighted with him. The Army has done for him all that I had hoped. Besides, it is very amusing to hear him talking about the Army with the pride and affection [of] an old West Pointer. You could not believe the poise and assurance that he has acquired. I cannot wait to hear it in music. Instead of working desperately to draw him out, and having the feeling that he may stop abruptly any exciting thing he is telling you, if by a fleeting expression or shade in the tone of your voice you break the mood, all you have to do is to relax and listen, for he is eager for an audience. . . . He asked about you, and wanted to know what you were doing, and I told him about your cabin, and that you had gone to live by yourself so you could write. "And is she writing?" he asked very eagerly. (That is the sort of remark that makes me think so well of him.) And I said, "Yes." "I think that is what I am going to have to do," he said. And Dorothy caught her breath, and said, "Oh!" And he put his arm around her quickly and said, "You needn't worry. Not without you." And Dorothy said that she thought she had learned a lot since he left. She said that having taken over his work [teaching music at Meredith College], she realized what it was to do a man's work. That even though she had always worked hard, the work had been secondary, and now she knew what it was to put the work first, and not to have anything of yourself left over when you got through. Mr. Alden said that was what he meant when he said you had to be alone. "But it takes a lot of courage to do it," he said. "It must have been very hard for Ann to do. But she is right."

Later on he said that one thing he had gained in the Army was to learn that he could make a living other ways than by music, and that he even thought he might be happier making his living another way, and leaving music for his leisure. "Which," I said, "would really be putting music first," and he smiled in the charming way that he smiles, and said, "Exactly."

[April 14]

It was nice to find your letter when I got home this morning [from a trip to Parkersburg, West Virginia, and to Ohio to visit Mr. Krippendorf]. I had wondered all week about the fruit and the garden and whether you could get to work on Calhoun. Sylie was asleep in my bed, and put on her dressing gown and came down to breakfast and we spent most of the morning talking, and at last went to market and to do the errands and did not get back to lunch until very late. When I got to Emily at last I found she had been expecting me all day, having got up early and got dressed and got the house work done so she would be ready if I came by on my way back from market, as I usually do. She is all to pieces [President Franklin Roosevelt had died on April 12], and I sat and talked to her all the rest of the afternoon, and told her all of our plans for the cabin in and out, so that she would like them when you tell them, and not think it was something between you and me. . . .

[Emily] said that she had wept for three days, and Bessie had, too, and both will weep still if given an opportunity. I was on the verge of hysteria myself, but looked up to see that Mrs. Sammel had gone ahead carving the turkey, and her white maid had gone ahead serving the dinner, and both of them are the most fanatical Roosevelt followers that I know. I was so glad I was there instead of in Cincinnati [visiting Mr. Krippendorf]. But my first thought was that I could not bear for you to be alone when you heard of Mr. Roosevelt's death. Maybe you would rather. But I always forget you are not like me, and I cannot bear anything alone. Vera, that is Mrs. Sammel's maid, went on talking all the while she served the plates as Mrs. Sammel carved. She spoke in a very controlled and even voice that sounded like an oracle. She said, as if she were repeating something that was being told her, that Mr. Truman was conversant with all of Mr. Roosevelt's plans, and that he would be able to carry them out. She said Mr. Roosevelt had thought of everything, and had known he was going to die, and had left instructions down to the last detail. . . .

Today . . . I took the clothes to Miss Carrie, and she said to me, "Well, Miss Elizabeth, our President has left us. What will we do now? We will have no one to think of us. When we had that black depression, and people were starving, he found work for the poor, and put food back in our mouths. Next time, there will be no one to look after us." I thought of Vera and heard her voice again, and knew for the first time what is really meant by "the people" and what Mr. Roosevelt had been to them. . . .

I need not have worried about the Garden Club of America

[in Cincinnati]. It was largely made up of delightful old ladies who might have been any of my relatives from Georgia, several counter-parts of Mrs. Royster with dirt in their finger nails, a couple of Isabelle Hendersons, and one delightful and aged gardener who sat herself down by me with a list of questions and a handful of plants to be identified, and a list of things that she had collected from old gardens and would send me if I would like. Practically all of them came up to me to apologize for Mrs. S. and said that "they" did not know where she got the idea that they wanted daffodils, and that "they" wanted to hear about North Carolina plants. By the time I got ready to lecture I felt as much at home as if I had been at the Johnsonian Book Club, which is all there is to lecturing. It does not really matter what you say. Some of them already had my book, and some more said they were going to get it, though I kept telling them that it was meant for the South.

I was in need of every encouragement as a day with Mr. Krippendorf had got me in such a state of nerves that I could not even eat my breakfast. He was exactly like you about the frost, and I felt I could not bear to begin all over again. After we had walked over the thirty acres of daffodils, all wilted or wilting, and several miles of blackened lilacs and magnolias, he said, "You are very sweet. But you know and I know that it was not worth your coming." I said I had come to see him, and did not care about the lilacs and daffodils, which was perfectly true, but he was not listening. We went back to the house and sat down in utter dejection. I said he had better call me "Elizabeth" and he said, "Well, Elizabeth, shall we go back out again?"

We walked down the hills along about one-half mile of the most beautiful stone steps made of rock from the creek, and with little ferns and wild flowers growing in them. All he had done to the magnificent beech woods was to make those perfect steps in a long winding curve, and cut out the underbrush, and encourage the groundcover, and plant certain things for effect. At the bottom was a beautiful creek and you walked up a little green lane to the waterfall. By this time it had got cool, and the light was soft, and the grass was dotted with white violets. The hillside had a cover of ferny leaves dotted with little white dutchman's britches, and in the copses were masses of deep blue mertensia and phlox. I am sure the English woods must look that way when they are filled with bluebells.

Mr. K. is very German, though he was born in this country; and though he has not spoken German since his youth, he still has the rhythm, and says "Tink" for "think" and "How?" for "What?" He said when he was a boy he would come out to see the farmers who then owned his place, and swim in the creek, and search for the wild flowers in the woods. . . .

Before the train I asked him if he would write down the name and address (which I had lost) of his sister who had me to breakfast, and the friend who had given me the luncheon, so I could write to thank them. When he handed me the slip of paper, he asked wistfully, "Are you going to write me a thank-you letter, too?"[25]

Mrs. K. and I were soon buddies. If she had not wanted me, she got over it. They were all upset because their only and idolized granddaughter had just got married on Saturday, and her father was dead, and her brother hadn't been heard from in the South (or whatever it is) Pacific. . . .

[The Sammels] are all very sweet and affectionate and love

---

[25] For many years, Elizabeth and Mr. Krippendorf exchanged letters, which became the basis for *The Little Bulbs: A Tale of Two Gardens* (1957).

me because of Nana. I got to Parkersburg in the middle of the night (2:30 A.M.) and when I got off the train, I wished for Jake, a colored man who had a cab and used to meet us when we came on late trains, and you would go clopping through the sleeping streets, one of the most exquisite moments of childhood.

When I got in the taxi and gave the address, the driver turned and said, "Don't remember me, do you? I knew you the minute I heard your voice. I used to drive for Mrs. Sammel. Do you remember my baby that you gave the silver spoon? He is twenty now, and a six-footer, and on an aircraft carrier." Then he said, "And whatever became of the little lady that lived across the street?" I said that that was my grandmother, and she died. "I liked her," he said. "She was so soft-spoken, and had a word for everyone." . . .

Sam Lawrence and other members of his Georgia family were interested in history and kept journals and letters. Elizabeth thought that her cousin Harriet Lawrence Cann Huston had a copy of a letter written to John C. Calhoun by one of their relatives, a Georgia governor. Elizabeth hoped to get a copy for Ann, who was still working on a play about Calhoun.

[May 12]

I decided after going to the doctor in Durham, Bessie and I had better go over to [Chapel Hill] to take the letters to Dr. deRoulhac Hamilton [professor of history and founder of the Southern Historical Collection at the University of North Carolina]. Did you ever see him? I had no idea he was such a delightful character. I don't know where I got the idea that he was very cross and forbidding, and instead, he has a little round, twinkling face, and a manner of speaking as if the person he is speaking to is the one above all others that he was hoping to see at the moment. I had never laid eyes on him before, but before I could finish my sentence—"I brought these letters from my cousin [Harriet] in . . . ," he added, "Savannah. I am delighted that she has decided to let me have those papers at last. I have been after her for years." Then he went on, "and did your Uncle McDonald[26] ever look in the attic at Marietta? And did your uncle in Americus send the ones he promised me?" . . .

I thought he would be very disappointed to find that the letters of [Georgia] Governor [Charles J.] McDonald were only those to his daughters in boarding school, telling them to mind their manners and be a credit to their mother, and not the one to Calhoun. But [Dr. Hamilton] had never heard of the Calhoun letter, and didn't seem particularly interested. He said it was the family letters he wanted, and that from those alone could you reconstruct a picture of the times. "Every one of them," he said, picking them up tenderly, "is of historic value." . . .

We [went to see] Anna and Mrs. Braun [book illustrator and her mother] in the same darling little house with everything in the exact place where it was when I last saw it. And Anna looking like a Renoir. She was all dressed to see a woman who might give her a job, and she had on a very thin cheap blouse (white, with a high neck, and an exquisite and ornate gold locket of the kind people wore when they wore that kind of blouse). Her hair was fixed high in the back and with frizzled bangs exactly like the French women that Renoir painted, and

---

[26] Elizabeth's paternal grandfather married into the McDonald family.

her skin has that same creamy look. She has the same radiance, too, a glow of warmth and good health and high spirits. . . .

From there we went to the library again to find Miss Nellie Roberson [the Extension Division librarian]. She was delighted with the idea of Emily's doing an outline for her, and said she would write to her at once, only she wanted Russia in general, not just the theatre. Emily was very clever to pick Russia. I said she would do it this summer while she is with you, and that she would be excellent.[27] . . .

Well, that was today, and tomorrow I have an altar duty in the morning, which I am glad of as I like to go to communion anyway on Ascension, which is one of my favorite days, and the Little Theatre box office in the afternoon, and I am sure that there will be something on Friday, and then Saturday there is market. So that is the way I get so much work done. . . .

[June 22]

. . . I measured our herb garden this afternoon to give you some idea. It's twenty feet square, and the paths are two feet wide. I think it is a very pretty size, and you could get enough herbs in it, but I am afraid it would look small in your space. The next time I come I will lay it off. You should have the part you are going to cultivate plowed next spring if you can, and planted in a cover crop, and turned under, so the soil will be good when you are ready for it. . . .

---

[27] Emily Bridgers wrote numerous publications for the University of North Carolina's Extension Division (which ran from 1934 to 1958), including *The Arts in the Soviet Union* (1946), historical novels, and books about Africa, the sea, the West, and Southern literature.

Miss Toose's [Louise Busbee's] death makes me very sad. The Busbees are an integral part of my life.

Emily was so cute, she has been talking for weeks about fixing a picnic supper and bringing it over to have in the garden. We finally got together on it Sunday. She made a wonderful salad out of Mrs. B's dates. They were soaked in rum. We had a little difficulty in keeping the sandwiches out of the reach of Mr. Cayce.

I have been wanting to write to you all day, and now I am too tired.

In July, Emily went to join Ann at the cabin, returning in September. Elizabeth wrote long letters to Emily. Here are excerpts from several.

[Elizabeth to Emily, July]

Bessie and I finally paid the call on Lucy [Daniels]. . . . We found Lucy and Jonathan on the terrace, and had such a good time we stayed all evening. . . . Jonathan is very delightful as pater familias [in addition to Elizabeth from Jonathan's first marriage, he and Lucy had three girls—Adelaide, Mary Cleves, and Lucy—all of whom Elizabeth and Bessie met]. . . . Lucy said Adelaide had become a great Methodist, and did Bessie know anything about the Methodist church. Bessie said tartly that she knew that there should never have been any Methodist church, and that John Wesley never left the Church of England, or intended for anyone else to. I said hastily that I had gone to the Methodist Sunday School [in Garysburg] at Adelaide's age, and was devoted to it. Jonathan was going to have no glossing over, however, and said that there was no difference between the Methodist church and the Episcopal church. The Methodists, he said, got everything from the Episcopalians ("in a garbled form," Bessie muttered), just as the Episcopalians got everything from the Catholics. I felt Henry VIII near at hand, and said firmly, "The Episcopal Church *is* the Catholic Church." Elizabeth and I exchanged glances. . . .

[Elizabeth to Emily, August 17]

Mrs. B and Robert and Bessie and I celebrated the Peace together and had a delightful evening. Only we did not catch on that it was the Peace until the middle of [British prime minister Clement] Attlee's speech. But then we turned on the radio, and I was reassured that Attlee spoke so much better than he looks. Bessie thought he was Churchill. . . .

Somehow I find Peace very depressing, and Baker Wynne [Raleigh gardener and North Carolina State teacher] still a Sergeant and looking so anemic, and Frank [Lyell] still at midshipman school depressed me no end. We went to communion at 7:30 Wednesday morning, and the church was full, and the Bishop had a beautiful service as he always does everything, with drama and restraint, but I found I could not be at all thankful, and could only cry and think about the atomic bomb and if it would be Bracelen or Chip in the next war. . . .

[Elizabeth to Emily, September 3]

Dear Emily,

When we got back from Virginia, I found the proof of the outline[28] waiting for me, and Annie helped me read it, but it took us several days to do it, as we could only read when Chip was asleep or on top of us. Annie is a very fine proof reader, and is disgusted with me for reading so inaccurately and making so many mistakes. . . .

. . . Beside Chip and Cayce weaving in and out, we have turned into a sort of day nursery. I am continually dealing out crackers and grape juice and settling squabbles and drying tears, and taking to the johnny, and getting Mr. Cayce out of one place into another. If he is in the garden the children want to go out, and if he is in the house they want to come in. . . .

We still have a struggle for existence. Our only help is Savannah, who is almost, if not quite, as pregnant as Ann. We did not know, as we hired her over the telephone. . . . Fortunately, we have the Reverend Saunders, who does everything from mowing the lawn and making Chip a sand pile to covering the pool with chicken wire. . . .

Mrs. B. called tonight, and said, "We thought maybe you and Mr. Cayce would come to see us, so we went and sat on the porch for a long time."

---

[28] For Elizabeth's *Gardens of the South*, a study guide for the University of North Carolina's Extension Division.

[Elizabeth to Emily, September]

Dear Emily,

. . . I hope you are not getting these terrible rains. The garden is so sopping that I cannot get ready for fall planting. The bathroom ceiling has leaked so that the water comes in spates, and we have three buckets to catch it. The cellar is a pond. And Chip and Cayce are wild. We had to start the furnace to get the house dried out, and it has been very chilly. But you cannot have everything, and we should be very grateful for this cool summer. . . .

Warren is getting out of the Army. . . . He is going back to his work with the Farm Security, but they allow him ninety days, so he will stay here until the baby comes. . . .

There is more to be told, but I am sunk in gloom. Savannah departed today, and we have to start our struggles anew. Two [servants] have promised to come in the morning, but I doubt if either turns up.

Tell Ann that none of my Lycoris from Mr. K. bloomed. It is the season, not the situation, and not to worry. Even my old dependable clump failed me. I was bitterly disappointed. The plants [sent to the cabin] were basil. I thought you could have them in salad even though small. . . .

[Elizabeth to Emily, September]
Seventh Sunday after Trinity

Dear Emily,

The other morning I came sick and exhausted to Irma's after a morning of talking to as many of the Christ Church vestrymen as I could corner (Mr. Lea in a very underhanded manner is trying to get rid of St. Saviour's and Mr. Wulf)[29] and found Irma looking the same, and still in her housecoat. "Libba," she said. "They've been trying to get you all morning. They called me, and finally they got Bessie and she came home from the Red Cross." But this time I was weak in the knees and all but voiceless and kept saying, "Well, what is it, just tell me." "The Thompsons have got you a cook." It turned out that she was neat, willing, polite, liked Mr. Cayce, didn't mind evening dinner, and was pleased with ten dollars, and would come the next morning. And we have not seen or heard of her since. And she was going from door to door looking for work. I am defeated.

. . . I went by to get ice the other day to make the Thompsons some daiquiris before dinner, and a cheery character who waited on me said, "Ain't you the little lady that done that work with us at the Little Theatre, planting them shrubs?" I said I was, and I remembered him well (which of course I didn't, except that I remember all of those men as good workers

---

[29] The Christ Church vestry did indeed close St. Saviour's, on December 31, 1948. Elizabeth also protested at St. Saviour's when its vestry met with members from Christ Church; she surprised everyone who knew her as quiet when she stood and urged her St. Saviour's friends to speak for themselves. But it was a lost cause, and she felt it deeply.

WPTF

680 KC. 50,000 WATTS
NBC NETWORK

WPTF RADIO CO.
Raleigh, N. C.

PROGRAM SCHEDULE, WEEK OF AUGUST 19, 1945

One of WPTF's Public Services . . .
Keeping the Listening Women "In the Know"

Harriet Pressly, WPTF's Director of Public Service Programs, interviews Mrs. Sam Lawrence, Red Cross worker with 17 years experience, in a recent "We the Women" broadcast from the Red Cross sewing room at the Raleigh Woman's Club.

Mrs. Pressly will interview a "Woman of the Week" each Thursday on "We the Women" at 9:30 A. M. **WPTF** **680** on your dial

Bessie Lawrence, a longtime volunteer with the Raleigh Red Cross, organized sewing groups to make articles for American soldiers in World War II. Here, she was photographed for a broadcast over WPTF radio in Raleigh.

By permission of Warren Way and Elizabeth Way Rogers

and eager and willing) and was glad to find I had a friend so near. . . .

[Elizabeth to Emily, September]

Dear Emily,

. . . I shall let you know immediately about the sex of the baby, and all other items. But don't keep worrying. Dr. Oliver says now that Ann is doing so well he may let nature take its course. In any case he thinks it will be two more weeks. He says the baby may be either a girl or a boy. Chip was definitely a boy, even before birth there was no question. He is now what they call "a real boy" of which always beware. He has been put to bed twice today and spanked three times. . . . I got him a dark blue suit from Best's with a striped jumper, and with his beret he looks like a Frenchman. He is very merry. . . .

. . . It has poured steadily for three days, and we have had Chip and Mr. Cayce underfoot all of the time. I had them in my studio this morning, and it took me an hour to get them settled. It rains day after day and everything is moldy and we are all depressed. But no heat since you left.

[Elizabeth to Emily, September]

Dear Emily,

. . . I started a letter to you Saturday night at the information booth, but between Mr. Cayce's admirers and the soldiers' questions, I found that I could not even concentrate on *The New Yorker*. Mr. Cayce has his regulars now who never fail to look for him: the girl that says, "Kiss me, Mr. Cayce." . . . My first batch of plants came this morning, and Mr. Cayce and Chip and I put them out. . . . Whenever you have dug a nice hole and filled it with fresh dirt [Mr. Cayce] likes to lie in it. Then when you are on your knees he likes to sit on your knees and lean against you. Chip loves planting. He has got the idea that the little plants are something very choice and opens the papers they are wrapped in with a long drawn-out, "Ah!!" . . .

[Elizabeth to Emily, September 28]

Dear Emily,

Ann has a little girl, born this evening at 6:30. She is perfectly darling. Ann is fine, but the doctors nearly scared us to death again, and we have decided not to have any more children. The baby's name is Elizabeth, and we are to call her "Brady"— Mother's school name. [Instead, the baby would be nicknamed "Fuzz" because of her golden hair.] I know you and Ann [Bridgers] will have a fit. But you will love Brady. This time you must not miss the christening. We have wonderful christenings. Enclosed is an unfinished letter [mostly about Mr. Cayce and Chip] and love to you and Ann. I am so relieved.

1946

[February 5, upon returning from seeing Uncle Jim Lawrence in Georgia]

This has been a very depressing trip. I would write several Russian novels from the human material, but I could never write it. I will tell you some day "for the record," as Annie says. I am too weary now.

Uncle Jim is very much broken and he does not break easily. When he came in and told me the doctor had ordered him to give up his missions, I was as despairing as if I had not been angrily demanding it ever since I came. He will keep St. Simons, Pennington, along with his new parish, and he still hopes to get his beautiful house.[30] He has all of the materials ready, except the cypress logs, which are still in the swamp, and he has the money, only the labor is lacking, and if any one can get that he can. My only hope is that his next [heart] attack will be his last, and that he will not outlast it. Uncle Jim's story is one I cannot ever write, but I will tell it to you.

I wished for you the day we went to Pennington. The little log church is even more beautiful than I remembered it, or else time has made it more beautiful, and perhaps the quality of prayer. In the woods at one side is a small graveyard marked

---

[30] The Reverend James Lawrence raised community support to build a log church, St. James, at Pennington, Georgia, near Americus, where he had been rector of Calvary Episcopal Church for more than forty years. Uncle Jim died in July 1947, before the new home could be built next to the log church. The church was restored and moved in 1975 to Andersonville.

with large rough stones. Some of them had fresh flowers, white narcissus and the sweet-smelling yellow jonquils that grow in country dooryards. On our way we stopped at the last house. The family were all out in the yard. A little girl, two small boys and two men, and a woman with a baby. "Well, Mr. Lawrence," one of the men said. "We are proud to see you." Uncle Jim said he had three plants (two camellias and an azalea) to set out in the churchyard, and would they dig for him. The men and the children piled in eagerly. They were so like the Justices [a mountain family Ann knew] that I cannot get over it. They had the same quiet movements, the same sympathy, the same low voices, and the same courteous manners. One of the plants had been a present to Uncle Jim in the hospital. When he took it out of the pot, he took the pink gauze off and tied it around the little girl's hair. One of the little boys took the silver paper and made himself a crown. . . .

[April 17]
Holy Week

Robert is so excited over finding Eudora's picture and a review of her book on the front page of the *Times Book Review*, and Emily is so hopeful of *Delta Wedding*'s becoming a Best Seller so poor Eudora will have enough money to buy herself some clothes. I tell her in vain that money doesn't seem to be one of Eudora's problems, and that she would dress the same, and probably ride on the day coach no matter how much money she had. Emily always goes back to "poor Eudora." She feels sure that no one who could afford to dress and eat would wear such clothes or look so undernourished. . . . I keep thinking of

Eudora and wondering if John [Robinson] has returned from Italy, and what will happen.[31] . . .

You must have gotten to the mountains just at the right time. I had to go over to Chapel Hill last week, and the dogwood in the woods was as beautiful as I have ever seen it. I went to see Anna Braun, and found her about to take off again for Alabama. She and her mother are going to spend the summer in the rectory of a little town on Mobile Bay, while the rector goes to stay with his sons. . . .

Everything that I start to tell you, I think, oh, I must wait and let Emily tell Ann that. . . . She is so happy about coming to the mountains and you will be delighted to find her so well. She has not seemed so well and happy since I have known her. I shall miss her perfectly terribly, she is my one comfort. Please tell her that for me sometime for she will never let me say anything nice to her. Mrs. B and Robert are equally happy over the prospect of freedom from Emily's standards.

Warren got back from Atlanta last Friday and is starting out again on the house hunt. Chip has learned to take his comings and goings very philosophically and say, "Daddy is gone. But he will be back." . . .

[April 23]

Bill [Ann Lawrence's friend Veronica, nicknamed "Bill," from Parkersburg, West Virginia] is having another baby, and sent Ann a box of dresses. Among them a quilted satin evening

---

[31] Welty dedicated *Delta Wedding* to Robinson.

dress from Bonwit Teller that filled in Ann's need for something newer than her Macy's days; and an ivory rayon made in peasant style gathered at the waist and with faggoting across the shoulders, otherwise absolutely ungarnished. You could not find anything more perfect for the belt that you gave me.

After getting a box of Pablum for you this morning, I could not bear the thought of your eating it, and hastily gathered up some more palatable food to go with it. You may be like Chip, and require two bowls for breakfast every morning. But I doubt it. He likes it best with much sugar and milk ice cold. But I make him have hot milk in winter. I heat Mr. Cayce's morning milk, too, in cold weather.

Yesterday I went to do some work in Wilson [North Carolina]. It was a beautiful day after rain, and as I drove through the countryside almost every field was being plowed, and the latest trees were coming into leaf. . . . The people I was working for in Wilson have had plans for two years, and they hope to build next fall, but say that now they hold out no hope as to when they will be able to do so.

We had a letter from Warren Lovelace today. He is back home again and out of the Army, so that is one thing off of my mind. . . .

[Elizabeth to Emily, June]

Dear Emily [in the mountains with Ann],

Mrs. [Elsie] Hassan [a market bulletin correspondent in Alabama] sent me the information that I asked for about seedlings, but she added more about cuttings, so I had to rewrite that part. I don't think you will have any trouble [editing it]. . . . I have already changed it about a good deal, even the parts in quotation marks. I hope it doesn't sound as if I had. I always like quotations to sound as if they hadn't been tampered with, especially if they are from Wordsworth. I have them nicely abbreviated now, and if you get through what you have, will reward you by sending that section on!

The garden gets more beautiful every day, and I think it is as perfect as I can ever make it. This is such a wonderful season, so much rain, and no hot blistering wind. . . .

Baker Wynne [a Raleigh gardener and North Carolina State professor of English] called at 6:30 last night to demand that I come to see an enormous and brilliant orange daylily that was blooming for the first time. Bessie answered, and answered irately, that I certainly could not as I had not even come in from the garden to dress for dinner, and Miss Daisy and Miss Lillian were waiting for their cocktails. . . .

[July 25]
5th Sunday in Trinity

Dear Ann,

I am going to send you, as soon as they are ripe, some seeds of *Campanula americana,* which came to me from one of my delightful farm women correspondents. I asked Mr. Krippendorf if he knew it, and he said yes, it was his favorite weed. Scatter them as soon as you get them along the drive. Along the fence at the foot of the terrace, and on the other side near the tiger lilies. Then in the spring I will send (or maybe fall) some roots of the day lily Margaret Perry. It will spread all along, and bloom with the campanula and the lilies. . . . The campanula is an annual but it will self-sow, and the combination will make a mass of bloom for six weeks or more. Then I am going to send you seeds of *Cassia marilandica* ("The virtuous and beloved dead need neither cassia buds nor myrrh") to scatter lower down on the driveway. . . .

I expect that you will have more lycoris. Mine are still coming, and I dash out very quickly to stake each one before Mr. Cayce can get to it. Mr. Krippendorf wrote that his were coming out fast, but that he did not expect them to last long as he was bringing out his granddaughter's boxer to spend a week with his, and he thought the two of them would break off thousands. Mr. Krippendorf feels as I do about dogs. But Bessie does not. . . .

The summer has been so cool and green, and so many of the choice and difficult amaryllids have bloomed,

> So am I as the rich, whose blessed key
> Can bring him to his sweet up-locked treasure,
> The which he will not every hour survey,
> For blunting the fine point of seldom pleasure.

[Shakespeare sonnet 52]

[A smudge at the end of the letter bears the explanation, "Mr. Cayce—his mark."]

Bessie Lawrence was a controlling mother, but Elizabeth seems mostly to have found the balance she wanted between dependence upon Bessie's taking care of finances and running the house in return for her own freedom to garden and write (though she often complained to Ann Bridgers about the many interruptions). Ann was just the outlet she needed to discuss conflicts, some of which she mentioned obliquely in letters. Elizabeth's chronic insomnia often left her tired and anxious. After a sleepless night, it had long been especially hard getting up on a day when the furnace was out, another servant had quit, or the war news was worsening. In such a letter as this next one, written to Emily, Elizabeth expressed another recurring anxiety—that she had not pleased Ann.

[Elizabeth to Emily, August 21]
The Ninth Sunday after Trinity, and your birthday

Dear Emily,

It was I who wept. As we drove down from the mountains I grieved to think that I had done anything to upset you and Ann further, or to disturb the beautiful visit which you both had given so much forethought to, and taken so much trouble to make perfect, and which was perfect except for me. And the worst of it is that I shall do it again the next time that worry and insomnia reduce me to the same state of nerves. I can't help it.

I am very grateful to you (and Ann) for not writing to me. It was very much better to talk to you. And I take back (just this one time) about always counting on you for the truth (just this once). If Ann was ill again from our visit, do not tell me. . . .

Does it ever seem to you that time stands still for years and years, and then suddenly leaps to catch up, just the way the hand of an electric clock (that old kind in banks and railway stations) does? I had a shock like that this morning when Bessie and I went into [Christ Church], and found Al in the vestibule looking as old as Mr. Frank Heyward used to look, standing there, when I was a little girl. And then when we went into our pew and I looked across to the north transept, and there was Dr. Root suddenly (in two weeks) looking as old as his father.

Have you seen the new Liberty dimes, with Mr. Roosevelt's head, and directly under it, "In God we trust"? I hope none of his enemies get hold of them. . . .

[Later]

Dear Ann,

As we drove away, Bessie said, "Wasn't Ann wonderful to get such a delightful dinner so easily?" and I said, "Yes, Ann is wonderful." We would both rather be with you all than anywhere else in the world, but I was very much upset, and Bessie was, too, to see you looking so bad the morning that we left. I shall never forgive myself if our visit was too much for you. . . .

I wrote like mad to catch up on my garden correspondence before I left home, and when we got back all of my letters had been answered. You can see why I don't want to be better known. One letter was from Mr. [George] Lawrence [a botany professor] at Cornell. He is the one that sent me all of the ivies. The last time I heard from him he was in the Pacific, and I was sure that by now he was at the bottom of the sea. But I finally got up courage to write, and he is back and out of the Navy and at work on the manuscripts he left unfinished when he went to war. It is encouraging that somebody is going on where he left off. It makes you feel somehow a little safer. . . .

[Elizabeth to Mrs. Bridgers]
Tuesday

Dear Mrs. B.,

I had thought that the end of August was somewhere in the dim future, but I see by the calendar that it is next Tuesday, and I am much cheered to find that you will soon be home. Robert and I will be at the train to welcome you.

Bessie and I felt lonesome when we got home and were confronted by an empty playpen and an empty high chair and a quiet orderly house. . . .

With a heartful of love for all of my darling Bridgers.

Aff-Elizabeth

[Elizabeth to Emily, August 28]

Dear Emily,

You have never seen anything more delightful than Mrs. B. tripping off the train last night in the best of spirits and full of conversation. I feel awfully sorry for you and Ann and Annie and me; we have not the stamina of the last generation.

. . . I went to Chapel Hill this afternoon to see Mr. Wilson (who said he did not remember me, but finally admitted that I looked vaguely like my sister Ann).[32] As you may imagine the conversation did not follow at all the lines that you and Ann mapped out as we sat on the porch of the cabin. You remember that wonderful passage of Barrie's when Tommy returned to his native heath (having come up in the world decidedly) and says, "How we change," and Aaron Latta mutters sourly, "How we dinna change," and Barrie observes, "and Aaron's word was the truer" (one thing you can always count on Barrie for is grammar).

I was not mistaken in my man. Take a Rhodes scholar (with too much good looks and an Episcopalian) with New York publishing connections and four years as an officer in the Navy, and you cannot expect too much. But no matter how little you expect you are always disappointed. Even Bessie was so agitated that she sent me back to change my earrings, and called from the porch, "And don't forget to tell him about the lady you heard from yesterday who was going to review your book at the Williamsburg Garden Club, and where could she get another copy." But Tommy J. [Wilson] is not the kind that you tell things to, not even when coached by Ann and Bessie.

He sat behind his desk (quite as attractive as he thinks he is) and said (with a memorandum in front of him), "I believe you wanted to talk about your book."

"Yes," I said. "I never saw Mr. Couch after the book came out ('but you saw him before, I presumed,' he interpolated, and I said, 'Oh yes, before—in fact, entirely too much' and

---

[32] Thomas J. Wilson succeeded William T. Couch as director of the University of North Carolina Press. Wilson and Ann had been undergraduates together in Chapel Hill.

we couldn't help laughing) and have had no communications of any kind from the Press except biannual statements, and it seems to me that the Press owes it to its clients to say at least, 'Your book is a complete flop' or 'Nice going, old girl.' "

"Oh," Mr. Wilson said kindly. "Your book is not a complete flop," and he added reassuringly, "In fact, you have nothing to be ashamed of." "But I am certainly far from ashamed of it," I stammered, completely baffled at the turn the conversation was taking. "I only thought . . . ," and then we proceeded to figures which I made him write down on a pad which he is to send me, but I cannot remember, but I will tell you approximately, as Ann said I was to get figures. I was not sure, exactly, what figures she meant but I said to him sternly, "The figures, please, and write them down" and he did look impressed: He said that so far somewhere around 1,200 copies had been sold, leaving 800 (according to Ann, I was to trip him up here, but I couldn't remember how) and that if the sales went on at that rate the university would have its money back in three more years (including my royalties, and not including royalties in one more year: and I felt I should say, "Oh, do let me return the royalties, I have no use for them") and in five more years they would have sold out of the first printing, and made a small profit, and (if I understood) would then reprint, and before the book was dead would have a fair (or slightly unfair) profit. This did wring a cry from me. I said, "But it won't ever be dead, it is plant material for this part of the country. It will always be the same!"

Finally, I gave up on *A Southern Garden*, and said, "Would you like to hear what I am working on?" He said, politely, that he would. "A book on rock gardening." "Oh," he said, enthusiastically, "that's fine, there is a great interest in rock gardens. Of course, it would not apply solely to this section?" And then

I just gave up. I had begun by explaining to him in words of one syllable how you could write a good gardening book (that is, a useful one) only if it was for a certain geographical area (explaining the area) but I could see that his attention was wandering. He hadn't the slightest interest in anything but results, or probably results. The press will very soon, mark my words, be an adjunct (is that the word) of Broadway. Or already is.

. . . One thing I satisfactorily investigated is the personnel [at the press]. Only Porter Cowles and Miss Paine are left. Porter greeted me with tears, and promised to keep my memory green. [Elizabeth's copyeditor] went with the Red Cross to Australia and had an unfortunate affair of the heart (her love was sent to England and wired that he had married his nurse) and she is recovering in South Georgia.

So then I went up to see Mrs. [Bayard] Wootten to ask if she would come over to do pictures of the children in the garden with Mr. Cayce. Each time I see her she has aged so that I have to hastily readjust my vision. I had taken her the pictures she took of [sister] Ann and me in the garden with our fox terrier, Pit-a-pat, and she agreed they were among the best she had ever made. They must have been taken twenty years ago, she murmured. (Twenty-five or more, I added.) And she looked at me blankly and said, "And these pictures you want me to take . . . Is it of the same children?"

I really don't know how I got home.

With love to you both,

Elizabeth

[December 12]

Dear Ann,

It is fortunate that you meant for me to keep the script ["Henrietta," an opera about "a large and noble looking Negress" during the year after the Civil War] for I had no intention of parting with it! I shall read it again the first time that I can find a quiet evening, and in the meantime the emotion of the first reading fills my mind and heart.

The scene that I keep coming back to is the one between David and his father at the end of the play. You are the only person I have ever known to say or write that "the most difficult creation for man is a relationship with a fellow human being." Human relations are generally conceived as growing vigorously and naturally like a tree that can be destroyed only by deliberately cutting it down.

That the relations between races must be created in the same patient and painful way as those between individuals is an original and penetrating observation. . . . The relations of the black race and the white race are not at their beginning. The beginning has been destroyed. It can never be recaptured anymore than a relation between individuals can be reestablished once it is lost. If we are ever to have an understanding, it will have to be built on life as it is and not as it was, as you say in the play. The form it must take I think I see in the new relationship we have with Lillian [a new employee]. It is not of our making. It is hers. And the Negro must make it from now on. The former relationship was created by the plantation owners. But it is the Negro who has the genius for it. He will always be the one to teach us.

This is something that I have [mulled] over since childhood, and written about since I was seventeen. So far only sketches, but I mean some time to gather it all together, and your play makes me want to do it. Only, if I start writing the things that I want to write I shall never finish my book. (However, another of the things that I have got from you is the impression of being immortal.)

You are wrong, my darling Ann, when you tell me that it is not necessary to see a person once your relationship is established. The only static relations are those with the dead. Grown people change even more than children (childhood is comparatively all of a piece—unless that was true only of me), and the change in creative people is the greatest. You yourself have changed more in the months since I was with you in the mountains, than in the years that I have known you. By change I don't mean that you are different. You couldn't be. With every play that you write you become more yourself, but with every labor that you undergo in order to write it you become more defenseless. And this play, in spite of your saying that you wrote it more easily, was a terrific tax emotionally. I felt this, when you came home in November, even before I had read the play, and now that I have read it and your letter I can see the reason. And now that I have read the play I can understand what I felt, and I love you more deeply than ever.

The character that you have created in Miss Sally is not a Negro-hater. Only a Negro has the talent for feeding the ego as it would like to be fed, and Miss Sally loves it. She would like to be surrounded by adoring slaves, and before the War, and in a house where she herself chose the servants, she would have been. It is not because their loyalty and affection goes to the others of the group that she hates them. And it isn't that she wants to destroy the relations between the races. She would prefer smooth ones, but she cannot bear for anyone to have a relation with anyone other than herself. I think it makes the play much better for her not to hate the Negroes as a race. She is just as determined to enslave all of the white people she comes in contact with.

And I have changed, too, more in the last months than in years before. I have been changed by the things that have happened to me. It is something very disintegrating, something I never knew the meaning of before.

I have a lot of things on my mind to write you about, but they are all things that take time. Some letters are best written in a hurry, but I cannot write to you in a hurry.

Your loving Elizabeth

1947

There are no extant letters to Ann in 1947, and only this one to Emily in the mountains. A typical letter, it does not suggest any change of heart or habits; it probably suggests that letters to Ann were written and lost. When Emily was with Ann in the mountains, Elizabeth wrote to Emily rather than Ann, always conscious of not coming between the sisters.

[Elizabeth to Emily]

Dear Emily,

. . . Ann took Fuzz to the doctor for her routine check-up, and he said that she is the brightest two-year-old that he has come across in his practice (he is a very young pediatrician) and that he had never known any child to respond and cooperate as she does when she is being examined.

I had a wonderful time at Tarboro [in eastern North Carolina], and could write several novels from the situations that arose overnight. It seems sometimes as if time is as elastic as in dreams, and you have really lived several lives in a few hours. And real life is better than novels, as in the novels you do not

Bessie, Elizabeth, and Elizabeth's namesake and niece, Elizabeth "Fuzz" Way, looking into the garden at 115 Park Avenue circa 1945.
BY PERMISSION OF ROBERT DE TREVILLE LAWRENCE

know anything that happened before or after, but in actuality you pick up people you saw twenty years ago, and go on with the story. Tarboro is all of a piece. The houses are all so spacious and calm, the furniture all from ancestors and none from stores, no interior decoration. The gardens all dark and cool with more green than color. No urns and no birdbaths. And all so English that when I went to bed with Trollope's *Small House in Allington* it was as if I had only turned to the next village. Margaret [Long, who had married John Tyler] came for Bessie and took her back to Roxobel [North Carolina] for the night, and I went for her the next day. Bessie is so pleased with Margaret, who has turned out to be a very fine person, and Bessie is very proud of her. Ridley [Margaret's daughter] is now five and an engaging little girl. She is adorable looking with Jack's gentle manner, and the Long temperament not far beneath. . . .

Love to you and Ann. I hope you are coming home soon. Elizabeth and Miss Lillian [Thompson] are back in Blowing Rock having their house done over.

Aff-Elizabeth

1948

In 1948, Elizabeth struggled with myriad challenges: older friends and family members had died (Uncle Jim in 1947), the neighborhood was changing, the old house was difficult to keep in repair, tenants and servants came and went, St. Saviour's was closing. The heavily planted garden had grown to be more than she could handle, along with everything else. Ann and the two young children, who often had lived in the Park Avenue house while Warren was in the service, were moving to Charlotte, where Warren returned to civilian life as an employee of the Internal Revenue Service. Ann Bridgers was often in New York or at the cabin, still writing new material but discouraged by failures to find publishers or producers. More important, Ann's family increasingly needed her; her mother was in her eighties, and the effects of polio hampered Emily more dramatically.

For these reasons, and perhaps for others unknown, there is only one extant letter for 1948. It seems likely that Elizabeth did write, because she had always written. Perhaps Ann had reason not to save letters from a discouraging time. And it is possible that she lost some of Elizabeth's letters as she moved from one place to another. But the intense correspondence had served its purpose for Elizabeth; a period of personal awakening was over. Elizabeth thought more now about how she could help her mother and her sister and the children. Bessie was still capable of handling their finances, and her careful management freed Elizabeth to make plans for what they must do next. The two families—Elizabeth and Bessie, Ann and Warren and the children—worked in tandem in an impressive display of family solidarity admired by everyone who knew them. Elizabeth continued to seek Emily's and Ann's help revising manuscripts, and she critiqued Ann's latest work. It was a sad and confusing time, but there was no rupture in the friendship between Elizabeth and Ann, only a necessary loosening of the bonds. Elizabeth had grown up under Ann's tutelage, and she was now prepared to make more decisions for herself.

Apparently, Ann was using names of plants native to Wilmington, North Carolina, in the setting of a play she was writing. Elizabeth began the following letter with a long discussion of botanical nomenclature.

[June 14]

. . . I have been thinking that maybe you will get more out of Dr. Wells[33] than anyone else if it is native things you need. He is B. W. Wells, Park Drive. I think if you tell him you want what would be seen on a trip up the Cape Fear, and give him data, he would be delighted to tell you. You can look in his book, but I have done that, and the dates are not exact enough. Just spring or summer. I think Cape jasmine could be in bloom in Fayetteville in May, if they had them then.

No, my dissatisfaction with the introduction to my book [on rock gardens] was not due to distraction, though perhaps the trouble with it was. I did it all over and then took it to Emily who said it was still incomprehensible. She pointed out the difficulties, and we worked on it with the scissors, and I came home and rewrote again, and she seemed pleased with the revision and took it off to the mountains to type. I am sure you would agree with all changes, as Emily is severe but consistent. The trouble was I had not straightened out all of the point of view that I am trying to present. Also Emily said she could not make sense out of the construction of the garden by Page [an employee of the Lawrences]. This is because she has never walked around the rock garden beyond the hedge (which is why you did not see any fault with it, because you had in mind the picture that I have, and didn't need a fuller explanation). I drew her a plan, and then she showed me where I had failed in description, and I did that over. The book will have a plan of the rock garden. I think Emily likes it in spite of her criticism (all of which was excellent) but I could not tell, as I was feeling

[33] Elizabeth's teacher at North Carolina State College and the author of *Natural Gardens of North Carolina*.

The Lawrences lived at 115 Park Avenue from 1918 to 1948. Tenants sometimes inhabited the two basement apartments. In 1968, the home was purchased as a chapter house for the FarmHouse Fraternity of North Carolina State University. In 2004, after failed efforts by Preservation North Carolina to find someone willing to move the home, the fraternity took it down to make way for a new chapter house.
BY PERMISSION OF THE FARMHOUSE FRATERNITY, NCSU

so discouraged myself that I gave her the impression that I was not worth the effort. Emily is very impressionable.

. . . It is very warming to have your family described to you by Mrs. Bridgers. Ann does not look at all well, and is very worn . . . and [Chip has] that combination of animal glow and shell-like delicacy in his skin and coloring that seems irresistible to the ladies of all ages. But Fuzz really is enchanting. She is so cool and self contained, with even her temper like a small storm that is soon over, that it took me more than two years to learn the intensity beneath. She hates to be read to, and always takes the book and says, "No, Aunt, I read to you," and improvises long stories. . . . She is so sophisticated that it is hard to believe she is only two. She said "Chip, talk if you want to, but lower your voice, and do not shout."

Bessie and I have bought a lot with Ann and Warren in Charlotte, and we are both going to build as soon as Bessie and I can sell this house. Do not mention it to your family until they do to you (and then be surprised) as I had not the heart to tell Emily before she went away. I thought she would not be likely to hear it up there [at the cabin], though every one here knows it now. Even our tenants. I am afraid not to try to sell the house at once, if we can do so to advantage, as the neighborhood is fast going down for residence, and also the market for old houses. The Boltons [neighbors] have built a duplex on the garden, which has ruined it to live in. Of course, the idea of going to Charlotte was mine, but Ann, Bessie and Warren, and, needless to say, the children, are all enthusiastic. I hope I have done the wise thing. Bessie has not been well all year, and I could not face another depression—and this old house and a sick parent and no servants. Also, I hope I am not fooling myself, but I think that I can do more work if we are not always either going to Charlotte or the Ways coming here. I never feel settled, and the children still have hysterics at every parting. I do not know what I will do without Emily, whom I see so little but depend upon so much, but otherwise it is a very sad commentary on my character, but true, that there is no one else I will be unhappy without. As to friends in general we have as many in Charlotte as in Raleigh, and the same is true of most any place we could go. Bessie and I are going to have a small but roomy house all on one floor, so Emily can come to stay with us comfortably. The living room will open onto a terrace and the garden will be a long narrow one with flowers around a series of little courts, and shrubs beyond. No grass. Between us and Ann

I am going to build a low double stone wall with dirt between the stones for rock plants.

I hope I have done a wise thing. And that we will all live in harmony. I am sure that the children will be happier, and that is the most important thing.

Your loving Elizabeth

P.S. Ask Emily to send the manuscript when typed if you want to read it again.

Elizabeth entered another happy phase of gardening after she and her mother moved to Charlotte in 1948 to live next door to Ann and her family. Elizabeth loved to walk with friends and newcomers through her garden, where she tried to have something in bloom every season of the year.

PART THREE: 1951–1966

A House of One's Own
The Charlotte Years

"I have found to my delight that a house
is a companion."

ELIZABETH TO ANN

*Elizabeth and Bessie moved to Charlotte in 1948 and rented a
small house while they were building their own. The next year, they
moved into their new house on the edge of the stately Myers Park
neighborhood at 348 Ridgewood Avenue, next door to Ann and her
family. Elizabeth still kept in close touch with the Bridgers family,
most often by telephone and occasional visits, both in Raleigh
and at the mountain cabin. Elizabeth's way of life was now well
established, and she had only to follow the pattern set down in the
last thirty years or so in Raleigh, though she was busier than ever.
Hannah Withers, Elizabeth's contemporary and new good friend
in Charlotte, observed that Elizabeth always looked "so refreshed"*

when she came back from visits to the Bridgers family—which Elizabeth called "those peaceful hours," a description family and friends often used for their own visits.

After the labor of building and moving into a new house and designing and putting in a new garden, Elizabeth still wanted to entertain Ann (and Emily, now more often a part of the correspondence).

In the following letter about a Colonial Dames reception for immigrants newly arrived in Charlotte, Elizabeth exhibits the powers of close observation and candor that had enlivened so many of her earlier letters.

[November 19, 1951]

Dear Ann,

I was glad to find out from Emily where you are [the Hotel Wolcott on Thirty-first Street in New York] as I have been wanting for weeks to ease my mind of its burden. I don't know why I have to do it to you.

The Colonial Dames gave a Christmas party to displaced people newly arrived in Charlotte, to which I went as chauffeur. The Mint [Museum] is so beautiful with its large and perfectly proportioned rooms. I wish I could really describe the guests. There were a number of thin, worn and beautiful old men, maybe not so old, really, who looked like Toscanini, but I think were all Hungarian.

The Dames all murmured together, and the Guests all murmured together, and in equally modulated tones. Only I crossed the dividing line and got into conversation with a young Hungarian and her little child, and her name was Eve. A nickname, they said, and were not as amazed as I that it is pronounced as Evelyn Way pronounces hers (and as Adam's wife) and not as the British mispronounce it. She said she wanted coffee, and her mother said "No." I am sure that two months, maybe one month ago, Eve would have subsided, but she had been for three months in the Eastover School [in Charlotte], and has learned that in America "No" has no meaning. She continued to tease, and in fifteen minutes had the coffee, and of course did not touch it.

One of the things that interested me most is that while most of the Dames present were the ones who work hardest for the Museum, only the foreigners were interested in the pictures. All [pictures] were of the lowest order, but nonetheless each guest seemed to feel that he must look at each carefully, and critically and with understanding. Little Eve drew me over to a seascape (or maybe it was a landscape) and said, "What means this picture to say?"

. . . One [Greek] was vivacious and responsive and the quickest to understand; he translated for the others. Not that he knew what I was saying, but he caught on to my way of thinking. The other was small, dark, and gloomy. "Uncle," the bright one said, laughing, and pointed to himself, "nephew. I two years older." This pleased them so that I called them "Uncle" and "Nephew" the rest of the evening, and the laughter never flagged. I learned these things from Uncle Jim when we were in Spain.

I started on the Church and having found that they belonged to the Greek Church, I gave them a brief history of the Christian Church, to which they all listened gravely, nodding and pursing their lips. "Three in one," I said, holding up fingers, "Greek, English, Roman." And suddenly wondering why no one has ever given this explanation of the Trinity, at least not in my reading or hearing. Sometimes I think I am the only Catholic. It was the word "Rome" that baffled them. Finally, the gloomy one said (he works in a Greek restaurant and goes to school), "Ah, Catholic!" They never did understand about the English Church, but they took my word for it, and when I told them I went to St. Peter's, they believed me, having heard at least of St. Peter's. . . . And I explained where it is and told them to be sure to go as we have inter-communion with the Greek Church. They were very eager about this, and just when I thought they had understood nothing, the policeman of Athens suddenly named the seven early churches, all in Greek, but I could understand what he said, as the names of the cities, like Alexandria, are all the same. But we had to go back nearly 2,000 years to get together. When we exhausted [the conversation] I called Bessie over and introduced her, and the policeman beamed and said, "seventy-five?" Bessie said, "yes," and he said, "My Mother, Athens, seventy-five." It seemed to make him very happy.

Bessie launched into a long and complicated story about a family in Virginia in which the uncle was younger than the nephew, making no effort to speak slowly or clearly. They all looked blank, but at the end of the recital, the right one turned to the other, and I could see by his gestures that by some strange alchemy he had understood every word, and was repeating it, translating verbatim. They were all delighted. Bessie's idea being that the way to make conversation in any language is to find friends in common, she said, "We have a little Greek friend, Hari Venizelos, I am sure you know her grandfather who was Prime Minister"; and they shook their heads and said, firmly,

"No, no, Sophoklis (or whatever his name) Prime Minister."[1]

[P.S., handwritten] I wrote this ages ago, and saved it to add to, but I can see I never shall so I shall send it on. With love, Elizabeth.

Before completing the manuscript for The Little Bulbs, *Elizabeth sent it to Ann in the mountains, and Ann took time to read it and write a long response.*

[Ann to Elizabeth, 1955?]

Elizabeth, dear,

I don't think my reflections on your book are worth anything, but since you want to know my opinion, here it is.

As I read the first chapter my feeling was one of disappointment—oh, dear, this book is not for me. A feeling that I had never had before when reading your articles on gardening. When I reached the third chapter in which you tell specifically of each flower, I realized the reason for my disappointment at the beginning. As I read descriptions of the flowers, my old excitement over your writing returned. Imaginatively I was enjoying your garden again.

It seems to me that your book is written for specialists this time, people like Mr. Krippendorf and Violet Walker and the others you

---

[1] Sophoklis Venizelos served three times as prime minister of Greece; his last (and longest) term was from August 1950 to November 1951.

Bessie and Elizabeth in the new Charlotte garden circa 1950. Ann and Warren Way's house, next door at 348 Ridgewood Avenue, is in the background. Elizabeth's signature rock-lined gravel path is in the foreground.
By permission of Warren Way and Elizabeth Way Rogers

quote, and not for the general amateur gardener—who is also lazy, as well as ignorant. It occurred to me that Mrs. Walker and the others (who, as you once remarked, tell only a small, very small, part of what they know in an article) were holding back, not just to have something for the next article—but in consideration of the ignoramuses who must read the article. You realize, of course, this is not a criticism of your book, but it is an explanation of why a publisher, who must make his money out of the amateur, hesitates to publish it. Nobody, amateur or professional, could fail to realize the quality of the writing and the voice of authority and knowledge which informs it. But making money from the book's publication is another matter.

I agree with Mrs. Woodward [an editor] that Mr. Krippendorf should be made more realistic. Couldn't you tell something about him in the introduction, a description of his looks, how he happened to go in for planting on so large a scale? It is intensely interesting to me that he was a most successful business man who devotes his last years to gardening with so much passion. I have a very clear picture of Mr. Krippendorf in my mind, compounded of many little things you have told me (whether the picture is right or wrong doesn't matter) and I kept it severely banished as I read the ms. For I agree with you that Mr. Krippendorf must seem real from the first page of the introduction—the first paragraph. No self-made man is ashamed of his beginnings. And this too would make him seem real. Nothing is so appealing to the American as the story of the poor boy whose dream comes true. This would give added charm to his acres of bulbs. In other words, the story of Mr. Krippendorf's garden would make the man who loves it so materialize. It is a fairy tale you do not take advantage of.

I would certainly try some of the small publishers before doing anything to the ms.[2] Surely there is a publisher for it— even if they ask you to cut it. Katherine Barnard [a Smith College classmate and publicist at W. W. Norton] said to me once, "Don't get discouraged—there are forty publishers"—about my novel. And more, counting universities.

Have you thought of offering this to some of the garden magazines—to be published in continued form? It is impossible for me to imagine a gardening publishing world refusing

---

[2] *The Little Bulbs* was published by Criterion Books in 1957.

Elizabeth continued to amass thousands of plant records, including more than two decades of bloom dates for Helleborus, *a favorite.*
BY PERMISSION OF WING HAVEN GARDENS & BIRD SANCTUARY

to make your book available to gardeners. Even I, sick with flu . . . feel an energizing impulse to make a rock garden at Beech, write for catalogues, and get a trowel in hand.

. . . The cheese biscuits arrived in immaculate wholeness. I marveled. Tell Ann I wrapped her delicious raisin cake in foil and kept it in the refrigerator. I had the last piece with a cup of tea yesterday. And I'll write her how grateful I felt very soon. And I'm still harboring those delectable cheese biscuits, indulging in one or two at the time—which can't increase the flu and stretches out my pleasure in them. I shared them with a few, then hoarded the rest. And I treasure my visit.

[Signed] Ann

[Ann to Elizabeth, summer 1958, Raleigh]

Elizabeth, dear,

. . . Emily read your column before I did. She said, "Mrs. French's garden [in Gastonia, North Carolina] sounds perfectly delightful. Hurry up and read this and tell me if Elizabeth exaggerated." I read it and said, "No." Just the same it *was* written with great communicativeness of a happy day spent. I decided I hadn't ruined yesterday with too many interpolations. I do remember it—our day—with the greatest of pleasure. I am still living the satisfaction of those days with you.

. . . I now have your letters out of my trunk—there are an awful lot of them—absolutely delightful letters. When I told Emily you would use parts of them, she said, "But I thought they'd make a book," such disappointment in her voice. But we'll get them in order[3] and you can do as you like with them after you finish your "Winter Gardens." I do pray you are getting on with it.

[Ann to Elizabeth, 1959?]
Hotel Wolcott, New York

Elizabeth dear,

Emily finally sent me your manuscript [of *Gardens in Winter*]. I found it when I came in tired and I thought, shall I read it now or wait until tomorrow morning when I have something

---

[3] Ann did not return the letters and in fact saved the new ones written from Charlotte.

to give to it? But I didn't need anything to give to it. It is all so clear, so beautifully written, so easy in its presentation, it is like a flower unfolding. I had thought you could not improve your style, but certainly you have perfected it. You had a certain willfulness before which I rather enjoyed than not, but now your style is disciplined and so beautiful that I was filled with the pleasure of response to balanced and controlled prose which yet frees the imagination.

I am so delighted that this is true. I can see now it is what you have been working for. I was afraid the struggle for time and thought would affect your work, leaving it ragged. But I think the struggle has been to say perfectly what you had to say perfectly and this takes more than time.

I must get at my novel. I am very happy.

[Signed] Ann

[P.S.] Have you written any more and is Chip all right?

[Ann to Elizabeth, 1961, Raleigh]

Elizabeth, dear, I can't bear it not to come, but I added up the reasons why I shouldn't and they weighted down the scales to no. For one thing, Emily seems to be able to bear the contemplation of my seven weeks absence in England, but not one day more for anywhere else. For another thing, Miss Smith has ordered me two books I am very anxious to see from Duke and I have to take notes on them and return them quickly. They are due here tomorrow I guess. I am working on the play I wanted to do about Elizabeth I—really getting it outlined and some sort of structure taking shape. I hesitate to interrupt this process. Then finally, I would no sooner get there than your own work would be demanding your attention and you'd wish I had not come. Not really. *I'd* wish I had not come. To interrupt your work.

. . . Your book [*Gardens in Winter*] is beautiful from the first instant it comes into one's hands—the color and the photograph of the flower in the snow, and then on opening the drawing above "Other Books" by you—the index [table of contents] which stirs the imagination and then the beginning of the prose which is poetry, with the lovely flower drawings [by Caroline Dormon] scattered as if to be come upon with joy to match the response to the prose. I am sorry the getting of the book published couldn't have been pure joy to you. I am so overwhelmed with pleasure in the result that I miss nothing.

Tell Lucille [unidentified] God meant for her to be your friend—and nothing could endear her to me more.

I'll mail this so you and Ann won't be buying me any delicious food. Tell her I can't bear not to come, but another time.

[Signed] Ann

[April 14, 1963]
Good Friday

Dear Ann,

I have just discovered that it is not next Thursday but the Thursday afterward that I go to Connecticut [to see Ellen Flood], and so I have a whole extra week, and can write your birthday letter without worrying about whether there is time to get my watch fixed, Bessie's bills paid, and my column written up until I get back.

I wish I had had this extra week last Tuesday. I would have gone to Davidson [College] with Hannah [Withers] to hear Eudora read "The Worn Path." I thought I couldn't afford time for both, so I saved the time to have her here. I met her at the bus at eight, and put her on the Durham bus at noon. We had breakfast by the door, and walked in the garden, and had sherry by the fire, and forgot about time until Eudora said, "Mercy!" and I went to get a clock and put it in front of her.

Marie [unidentified] says some people always make you see how shabby your things look, and others make them even more beautiful than you thought. I thought the garden had never been more beautiful than when I walked around it with Eudora. It was still early and the shadows were cool, and there was dew on the white tulips and the snowflakes, and more of the banksia was out than I had thought. Eudora stood still in the path, and said, "I am thinking how to tell my mother."

"I can't make the doctors believe," she said (when I told her that Be[4] said I suffer more than Bessie does, and I know he doesn't know what he is talking about), "that it is grief for the death of my younger brother, and not her ailments, that is killing my mother."

Eudora was baffled when I asked her about her troubles with editors. She said she never had any, never heard of anyone who did, never had a word or comma questioned. "But it may be different now," she said. "It has been a long time since I dealt with editors, and Diarmuid [Russell, Welty's longtime literary

---

[4] "Be" was Dr. Walter B. Mayer, the Lawrences' Charlotte doctor, close friend, and fellow gardener.

*This now-iconic photograph of Elizabeth Lawrence welcoming
visitors into her back garden at 348 Ridgewood Avenue in Charlotte
accompanied her first column for the* Charlotte Observer *on August 11,
1957, "The Garden Gate Is Open: Enter a World of Beauty."*
BY PERMISSION OF THE *CHARLOTTE OBSERVER*

agent] tells me the publishers are nothing but book factories. He hates them all, and says the personnel changes so steadily that he never deals with the same editor twice." . . .

Later

I had to go to the dentist, and when I came back I worked in the garden and thought about Eudora. It came to me that Mr. Russell must edit her, and then wrestle with the editor. Eudora has always thought I should deal with him. She said, "You need somebody like Diarmuid to do for you what you can't do for yourself." . . .

Love to you and to Lula,[5] Elizabeth

October 9, 1964

Dear Ann:

I was so entranced with the Elizabethan songs that I dropped Mr. [B. Y.] Morrison's *Back Acres Azaleas* in the middle of a paragraph, and got out the songbook. I love that book. I will work on some of the songs with the pipe, to see if I can give

---

[5] Lula Glaze Flinn van der Voort had been a close friend to Ann Bridgers since their Smith College days (class of 1915) and a fellow traveler in Italy in 1932; following that trip, Ann had joined her family while Lula went to Zurich to attend Dr. Carl Jung's seminars in psychology. Lula, who was twice divorced, later moved to Tryon, North Carolina, and sometimes visited Ann at the cabin. In one or two early letters, Elizabeth alluded to Lula's being with Ann, but this closing is the first indication that Elizabeth and Lula were friends.

you any idea of them, but I feel sure that it will be impossible to find any old tunes to fit your words. All Elizabethan songs are so irregular. "Come over the Bourne, Bessie" went through my head as music at once, so I hastily got out a pipe and tried to put it on paper. . . .

I finally got back to the azaleas, and finished them. They are a dozen new ones that Mr. Morrison has developed since he retired [as director of the United States National Arboretum in Washington, D.C.], so it is very exciting (that is, if they are as beautiful as he says) that they are now on the market. That delightful character, Mr. Caldwell, whose passion in life is Mr. Morrison's azaleas (and whom Mr. Morrison considers a worthy soul but not one to interest him, and who considers Mr. Morrison a pistol) phoned at once to say that he had got them all, so I will have a chance to see for myself. I am going to send you a copy of the *American Horticulture Magazine* with Mr. Morrison's picture in it, but I am waiting for the next issue to send with it, as it has a long piece by me. The first time I have done a long one for them. It won't interest you, but I thought you would like to see it. Don't return either. They send extra copies if you have something in it (as they do not pay) and I never know what to do with them. I could spend my time happily writing for such (and always feel guilty when I don't) but that is not the same as writing a book. And you know I can't stop. I enclose a piece on St. Luke out of Ann's paper for you, and please return the others as I haven't extras. Some I may have sent before. They seem to be all mixed up. All those about the saints and the church I mean to gather into a book when I have done enough. There is a charming English book called *The Saints and Their Flowers*, but it is out of print. Hannah

After living in a large, old house near downtown Raleigh, Elizabeth designed a small home near Myers Park, one of Charlotte's finest neighborhoods. The house was all on one floor, with two bedrooms, a kitchen on the front, a large living room in the middle looking out through a window and a curtain of bamboo, and a study off the back. The second story was added by a subsequent owner, Lindie Wilson, who maintained the property until 2009, when she sold it to the Wing Haven Foundation, which has partnered with the Garden Conservancy to preserve the house and garden.
BY PERMISSION OF LINDIE WILSON

[Withers] thinks the Seabury Press would publish mine. But that is in the far future.

I am anxious to hear again from Mr. Morrison, as Pass Christian [Mississippi] is very near New Orleans, and he wrote last Friday that he would be in the path of the winds.[6] There he was sitting serenely among the blooming camellias and azaleas in his shady garden with the grass all freshly mown. It seems incredible.

Amorite [a housekeeper] finally got the floors beautifully polished; Alza Lee [another housekeeper] has everything else shining, and for the first time in my life I have everything in its place—the place *I* want it. But I would rather have someone to annoy me. Nevertheless, I have found to my delight that a house is a companion. . . .

May 27 1965

Dear Ann:

I don't mean to worry you by begging you to do anything that will interfere with your work, because I go to pieces when anyone begs me, but would it really matter if you stopped over for at least a night with us. There is no telling when you will ever see us all together again, and all so happy. The Navy will have Chip in its clutches by the end of August, and Fuzz goes off to a summer job in Maine—I'm not quite sure when. I am sorry I gave you the impression that I was doing something

---

[6] Pass Christian, on the Gulf Coast, was spared the deadly effects of Hurricane Hilda in October 1964. It was not so lucky in the summer of 2005, when it was almost totally destroyed by Hurricane Katrina.

against the grain in order to please Mr. Brimer [editor at Macmillan who was reading Elizabeth's early draft of *Gardening for Love*, a manuscript the publisher ultimately rejected]. On the contrary, his criticism was both fair and constructive, and I am not only willing but eager to carry it out as far as I can. What upset me was his saying I was to get it all done before the seventh of May, and send it back, and he would then let me know definitely about taking it. I told him that that was impossible to begin with, and that I was not willing to do such a considerable amount of work until he let me know whether he intended to publish the book. I said that if he is not going to take it I would rather put the work on something he will take. I said I would redo the first section, and send it on, and we'd go on from there, and if that were agreeable he needn't bother to write again. I said the last, as he has been in great trouble. His mother fell down the steps, and he had to go to Denver to put her in a nursing home, and was to go back the seventh of May to close her house. He did write, however, a long and reassuring letter. He said he could not offer me a contract until the manuscript was accepted by the Editor-in-chief, but felt sure it would be accepted if he urged it strongly, which he meant to do. He said, "Don't fret."

A contract, of course, is the last thing I want. I can never sign one until I am sure we are in agreement.

In the meantime I have about got the first section done over, in spite of having the kitchen done over. In order to get the dishwasher in, I had to have the sink and disposal taken out, and new ones put in, and a new cabinet. What precipitated it all was the floor. It began to peel, and I was afraid I'd trip. Now it is all done, and the painter will be out by afternoon, and on Monday Alza Lee can get things back on the shelves.

And Mr. Brimer says that this is not a book to hurry, and that it is better not to set a publication date yet. It is certainly better for me. I told him I do everything I can, but I'm really not equal to work under pressure, and I had already made two lecture dates for fall, and have to finish a garden I've been working on for several years.

I have every intention, no matter what, of coming to the mountains if you are equal to having me. In addition to editing, and writing books himself, Mr. Brimer takes tours in Europe, and he had already arranged one for the summer when he took on the job at Macmillan's. So I doubt if we move forward very fast before fall. So you see I am just sitting here doing nothing, and wishing for you.

With love to all, Elizabeth

P.S. Post card enclosed, in hopes.

July 20 1966

Dear Ann:

Your dates will do very well. They will give me time to get washed up and off to Washington on the fourteenth of August, if I am able to go. I am planning to go to the International Horticultural Congress with Be [Dr. Walter B. Mayer] and Dr. [Herbert] Hechenbleikner [botanist at the University of North Carolina at Charlotte], but I feel very uncertain whether I shall be up to five days with those two, especially in the heat. Dr. Hechenbleikner is a mountain climber. He has climbed both Popocatapetal (however you spell it [Popocate-petl]) and that other one. Both of them are tireless . . . but it is a wonderful chance to go to the National Arboretum with two such congenial companions. I don't care about the meeting, but these are wonderful trips. Those, too, are grueling.

. . . I was so upset, as Ellen is really going to sell her house, and there isn't room for me in the apt. now that Bracelen is there. Did I tell you that Bracelen's book[7] is done, and will be out in about a year. Ellen and Mary Ellen think it is his best. They are all happy about it. You ask how I am. I don't know. My surgeon is pleased with the x-ray, says the calcium is all gone, and that he took off just the right amount of bone, but he is mad with me because my shoulder still hurts.[8] . . .

I enclose a carbon I made for you from Chip's letter [from Vietnam, where he was a naval engineer]. It was the first time we had a clear idea of what he is doing. He kept writing how safe he is. . . . He is working on the construction of the recreation center. Chip must be all Way and Smith, as they were all generals in all wars back to the Spanish. In our family there was only one Patriot, Captain James Neal, who fought with Washington at Valley Forge. No Lawrence ever got near a gun (even to kill a squirrel) if he could help it.

---

[7] Ellen's son, Charles Bracelen Flood, became a novelist and historian. Her daughter, Mary Ellen Flood Reece, also was a writer.

[8] In the spring of 1966, Elizabeth had an operation on her shoulder, apparently to remove a calcium deposit. The operation enabled her to use her arm, but it did not, she explained in a letter to Katharine White, "do away with the pain in the back of my head. Darvon has helped a lot." Elizabeth and Katharine White often exchanged reports about their health. Since Emily had been crippled since childhood and never complained about her inability to get around, and since Ann was also a stoic, Elizabeth was less likely to tell them much about her ills.

Well, must quit, and go to Fifteenth and Alexander Streets to see if I can find two old colored ladies and a Mulberry mock orange tree that has flowers that are purple balls with orange petals.

Did I tell you that I am about to retire to my new car for the summer? It is air conditioned and has a radio (which I didn't want but I bought it because it gives Fuzz so much pleasure. All I need is a bar).

With love to Elizabeth, and tell her I can't imagine anything nicer than coming upon the heels of her visit and hearing all about it. . . .

Elizabeth

[Elizabeth to Emily, summer]

Dear Emily,

. . . Thank you for all you do for me. I am sure you have no idea how much. It is impossible for anyone to write without a reader, and it is impossible for me to write without a sympathetic reader. I am sure that without your support I would never have arisen from the blow by Mr. [John] Macrae [editor at Harper who rejected *Gardening for Love*]. Which reminds me. I think I forgot to tell you that Eudora said Mr. Russell said there were no publishers anymore, only book factories. I think I also forgot to say that I gather that Mr. Russell does for Eudora what you and Ann do for me, supply the technical (if that's what you call it) part. She says all his clients form a sort of society or club, and they all worry about how he can possibly make a living. I always thought if I had to have an agent he would be the one, but he refused to take me, and if he would, I certainly couldn't add another impecunious author to his list. . . .

Epilogue

"I want you to know how much I have loved life and how necessary it was just the way I played it."

ELIZABETH TO HER FAMILY

Having learned to live the life she wanted in Raleigh, Elizabeth was determined to have it her way in Charlotte. For the most part, she did. In her forty-fifth year, she started over, designing a small contemporary cottage, creating a new garden, and writing more books. Nothing gave her greater pleasure than her Charlotte Observer *garden column, which she frequently discussed with Ann and Emily. By now, she carried on such a voluminous correspondence with gardeners everywhere that her letters to Ann and Emily were more hurried and often about work. And she had long arguments with editors about changes they proposed to her manuscripts, both those that were accepted and those that were rejected. She kept Ann and Emily abreast of all these frustrations.*

Living next door to Ann and Warren and Chip and Fuzz (who preferred to be called Warren and Elizabeth as they grew older) gave Elizabeth all the pleasures she hoped for, and "Aunt" was much beloved by the children. They grew up in both houses, spending time in Elizabeth's garden pool, having meals with her, reading together, and often spending the night. When they went away to prep schools—Chip to his father's school, Virginia Episcopal, and Fuzz to her mother's and aunt's, St. Mary's—Elizabeth looked forward to their holidays at home as much as did their parents.

On several occasions, Ann Bridgers came to visit Elizabeth in Charlotte; their times together refreshed Ann as well. On such occasions now, Ann was the one to write to say how much it meant to be able to talk to Elizabeth. Increasingly, Emily Bridgers was less mobile and more willing to use a wheelchair and a ramp, but her mind, many thought, was still the liveliest in the room. She and Ann spent hours helping Elizabeth get manuscripts ready to send off to publishers. But it was Ann who was unable to place manuscripts—plays, an opera, a novel, a proposal for a movie script. She tried everything, but agents did not think her manuscripts, largely on Southern themes, were meant for Broadway or Hollywood. Ann relied upon her own reserve and kept writing.

Following the death of Mrs. Bridgers in 1958, Ann, Emily, and Robert stayed even closer, often entertaining Jonathan's family, their niece Elizabeth, who had married journalist C. B. Squire, and the Squires' three sons. Ann and Emily also got to know Fuzz when she was a student at St. Mary's and Chip when he was a student at North Carolina State. On one occasion, they entertained Bracelen Flood in Raleigh after he had graduated from college and published his first novel.

After Mary Ellen Flood married and had a family of her own, she continued to stay in contact with Elizabeth, visiting her in

Charlotte. Elizabeth was anxious to introduce her old friends to her new Charlotte friends—Hannah Withers, Eddie and Elizabeth Clarkson (whose beautiful house and garden down the street later opened as Wing Haven Gardens & Bird Sanctuary), Be and Helen Mayer, and so many others. Elizabeth and Bessie and the Ways joined St. Peter's Episcopal Church in downtown Charlotte. The life Elizabeth had lived in Raleigh was being replicated.

Elizabeth's reputation as a writer was bolstered by the publication of Gardens in Winter *in 1961 and by the popularity of her garden column. She was inundated with letters from gardeners near and far, which delighted her. She tried to answer every one.*

As Bessie's health began to fail dramatically in 1957 with the first of a series of strokes, Elizabeth and her sister shared responsibilities for their mother's care. Elizabeth had sitters with Bessie around the clock, often taking the night shift herself. Ann brought over meals and had lunch, which Elizabeth found a saving grace. After one of Bessie's strokes, Ann Bridgers wrote, "A heartful of love to all of you and take care of yourself as best you can, dear Elizabeth. You take perfect care of Bessie, but you are important, too." By 1960, Bessie's health had declined to the point that Elizabeth felt as if she were living alone. In frequent letters to Caroline Dormon, Ruth Dormon's sister-in-law and a great gardener (whom Elizabeth visited at Briarwood, near Saline, Louisiana), Elizabeth alluded to the difficulty of caring for her mother, at the same time confessing that she did not know how she could live without her.

After Bessie's death in 1964, Elizabeth was blessed to have the company of a young friend she had known for many years—Caroline Long Tillett, now married and living in Charlotte. Caroline was the daughter of Willie and Caroline Long, friends Elizabeth had known at Longview and later, when young Caroline was a student at St. Mary's. After Caroline lost her mother in 1965, she and

Elizabeth drew closer to one another in Charlotte, having lunch every week and going to church together (though both were discouraged by changes in the Episcopal Church). Willie Long suffered so after his wife died that Caroline went to Longview, brought him to Charlotte for a visit, and dropped him off at Elizabeth's. When she returned, she discovered that her father and Elizabeth had fallen silent. Willie had asked Elizabeth to marry him, and she had refused, saying she loved him too much to ever try and fail at being mistress of Longview.

Fuzz married Walton Rogers in 1967; their children, Blair and Ann, like their mother, played in Elizabeth's garden pool. In 1972, Chip married Fran Heisler. They enlarged the family circle with their two children, Evelyn (named for Evelyn Way) and Bobby.

In 1967, following a year of battling cancer, Ann Bridgers died a day after her seventy-fifth birthday. Elizabeth went to the graveside burial in the Bridgers family plot in Wilmington, North Carolina. Elizabeth and Emily continued an occasional correspondence, especially when Elizabeth had something she thought would entertain Emily. And they talked on the phone. Elizabeth found it a comfort to hear Emily's voice.

In May 1968, Elizabeth and Hannah Withers went on the first of two trips to England, visiting two of Elizabeth's favorite gardens, Sissinghurst and what was left of Gertrude Jekyll's estate; seeing "the hut" gave Elizabeth much pleasure. The following year, Emily Bridgers succumbed to cancer, like Ann at age seventy-five. Elizabeth wrote to Katharine White, with whom she enjoyed a correspondence during this period, "Ann and her sister Emily are the friends who have most encouraged me in writing, in fact who started me out in writing about gardens when I had never done anything but poetry. . . . As they were much older than I, I knew

I would be likely to outlive them, but I don't yet see how I can do it."

Elizabeth did outlive Ann and Emily Bridgers, by some sixteen years, during which letters (as gardening became increasingly difficult) were her most constant source of information and contact. She grieved over never finishing the project of a lifetime—a book based on letters from "farm ladies" who advertised in the state market bulletins—but she had the satisfaction of turning her materials over to Joanne Ferguson, editor at Duke University Press, who saw to the posthumous publication of Gardening for Love: The Market Bulletins, for which Elizabeth was credited as author and Allen Lacy as editor. From time to time, Elizabeth was visited at home by well-known gardeners wanting to meet her, among them John Jamison, Bill Neal, J. C. Raulston, Edith Eddleman, and Pamela Harper, with whom she exchanged letters. In 1977, she started a long correspondence with Carl Wells, a librarian at Northwestern State University of Louisiana, who in cataloging the papers of Caroline Dormon had alertly contacted Elizabeth for her letters from Caroline. That led to Elizabeth's sending her papers to Louisiana and began a lively correspondence—which Elizabeth loved—about history, books, family, and travels.

Two more losses were inestimable—Ellen Flood in 1978 and Elizabeth's sister, Ann, in 1980, from cancer. The death of her younger sister was something Elizabeth had never considered, and she struggled to live alone. Finally, it was too much for her. In 1984, she moved to Annapolis, Maryland, to be near her niece, Elizabeth ("Fuzz"). Though losing physical and mental strength, she remained responsive to people around her. She died June 11, 1985, and as she wished was buried in the churchyard at St. James' Episcopal Church near Lothian, Maryland, a beautiful country church she loved.

Perhaps Elizabeth's letters to Ann Bridgers, more than anything else she wrote, best tell her story and deepen the meaning of what she said to her family near the end of her life: "I want you to know how much I have loved life and how necessary it was just the way I played it."

Editor's Note

More than a decade ago, when I began writing about Elizabeth Lawrence, I discovered several hundred of her letters in the Ann Preston Bridgers Papers at Duke University's Perkins Library. They were the kind of unexpected discovery that keeps writers working, and I used them more than any other source in *No One Gardens Alone: A Life of Elizabeth Lawrence*.

But I always hoped I might find an audience for the letters themselves, because I think they are some of the most charming I have read. Moreover, they represent the last hurrah of an age of letters we are not likely to see again. I am grateful to Carolyn Sakowski and the staff of John F. Blair, Publisher, for believing also in them. Steve Kirk has been an exceptional editor and a perceptive reader.

This is a book for readers who enjoy letters, rather than a text for scholars. Readers and scholars interested in facsimile copies can read the letters for themselves at Duke. A small number of the letters are in the private collection of Elizabeth's family members Fran and Warren W. Way III and Elizabeth Way Rogers.

I am grateful to the Rare Book, Manuscript, and Special Collections Library at Duke for permission to publish excerpts from the Ann Preston Bridgers Papers and to Jonathan Hart Squire, executor of the Bridgers estate, for his support of this project. For permission to publish the letters of Elizabeth Lawrence, I once again acknowledge with deep gratitude the permission of Elizabeth Way Rogers and Warren W. Way III. Over many years, Warren's wife, Fran, has helped answer questions about their beloved "Aunt."

I especially thank the incomparable and generous Susan Faust, who has made this book possible in so many ways, not the least of which was to transcribe many of the letters. Archivists at St. Mary's School, Smith College, Mary Baldwin College, Duke University, the University of North Carolina at Greensboro, the University of North Carolina at Chapel Hill, and the North Carolina State Archives answered my persistent questions with unfailing courtesy and helpful information. A reporter for the Raleigh *News & Observer* was especially alert in helping me identify Miss Florence Stone. The Raleigh Little Theatre staff provided information and photographs. Bobby J. Ward once more provided expert advice about plant names and saved me from other kinds of errors. Among those who knew Elizabeth Lawrence, I am especially grateful to Ruth Long Williams; for Long family genealogy, I thank her nephew, James Beckwith.

Elizabeth's letters presented a few problems: she was a poor speller, she seldom dated letters, and her handwritten letters were sometimes difficult to read. Duke archivists cataloging the collection provided most of the bracketed dates, usually taken from postmarks. Other dates are approximations by year only. I have added information in brackets within the line and in footnotes (as well as in the "Cast of Characters") because today's readers are used to having their questions quickly answered; Google is our friend. I have also provided other kinds of information that might be helpful to readers' understanding, such as occasional English translations. But I have done so sheepishly, knowing that Elizabeth Lawrence's own choice was to liberally sprinkle throughout everything she published (with no explanation) first names of people and snippets of verses, confounding her editors (as she often told her friends). Elizabeth expected her readers—like her friends—to know everyone and everything she did. Alas, alas.

Those caveats aside, I transcribed the letters with faithfulness to the originals while correcting misspellings, standardizing punctuation when necessary for clarity, using *and* instead of the ampersand, omitting occasional ellipses for pauses, and otherwise retaining the informality of Elizabeth's letters, in which her mind moved quickly from one subject to another and back again. Since this is a book of personal letters and not a botanical or horticultural manuscript, I have not made corrections to plant names that are no longer in use. I have left them just as Elizabeth Lawrence knew their botanical names. Because the letters are long and sometimes repetitive, I deleted probably a dozen or so of them (mostly having to do with the Raleigh Little Theatre and Elizabeth's critiques of Ann's plays) and portions of others; in these cases, I indicate the omissions by means of ellipses. I have only on a few occasions omitted someone's name.

In the early 1960s, Ann wrote Elizabeth that she and her sister, Emily Bridgers, intended to get Elizabeth's "delightful" letters together and return them, hoping she could use them for another book. I believe that Ann's and Emily's illnesses and deaths—within a year of one another—make it clear why they never got around to their files. In 1974, their brother, Robert Bridgers, who needed to move out of the house he had shared with his mother and sisters, sold the Ann Preston Bridgers Papers to the Perkins Library at Duke. After discovering the cache of letters from Elizabeth Lawrence, I received permission from both estates to use them for a Lawrence biography (*No One Gardens Alone*) and the present collection of letters.

About two-thirds of the letters were typed. Many began without a salutation. Most closed with "Your loving Elizabeth" and some of the remainder "With love" to other members of the family. Some were written over several days or more.

As for Ann's letters to Elizabeth, most are missing. I suspect that Ann told Elizabeth things in confidence and that Elizabeth, knowing Ann was a well-known public figure at the time, did not want to keep those letters. About a dozen letters to Elizabeth from Ann are part of the Lawrence family papers. I have included some of these to suggest the quality and tone of Ann's letters.

Finally, because this is a reader's book not intended primarily for scholars, I wish to acknowledge the important work of the latter group—past, present, and future—and to say that I will contribute my research papers on this and my other Lawrence books to the Elizabeth Lawrence House and Garden in Charlotte, North Carolina. Those persons with research interests can seek permission to use them from the directors of the Lawrence House and Garden and Wing Haven Gardens & Bird Sanctuary.